PRAY FOR BROTHER ALEXANDER

Fig. 1. Hieronymus Bosch, *Ship of Fools* (1490–1500)

Rugați-vă pentru fratele Alexandru © 1990 by Constantin Noica
Originally published by Editura Humanitas, Bucharest

Translation published in 2018 by punctum books, Earth, Milky Way.
https://punctumbooks.com

ISBN-13: 978-1-947447-52-3 (print)
ISBN-13: 978-1-947447-53-0 (ePDF)

LCCN: 2018936900
Library of Congress Cataloging Data is available from the Library of Congress

Book design: Vincent W.J. van Gerven Oei
Proofreading: Joyce King
Cover image: Annett Müller, *Fort 13, Prison of Jilava* (2015)

HIC SVNT MONSTRA

Constantin Noica

Pray for Brother Alexander

Translated by Octavian Gabor

CONTENTS

TRANSLATOR'S NOTE

After the end of World War II, the Communist Party took over power in Romania. The social and political changes transformed the life of philosopher Constantin Noica as well. Considered an "anti-revolutionary" thinker (the files of his trial reveal that his writings on Hegel's *Phenomenology of the Spirit* were considered anti-revolutionary*), Noica was placed under house arrest in Câmpulung-Muscel between 1949 and 1958. In 1958, he was sentenced to 25 years in prison. He was freed after 6 years; *Pray for Brother Alexander* covers his experiences during this time. For more on his life and philosophy, see my article, "Constantin Noica's Becoming within Being and Meno's Paradox."†

This is the third volume by Noica published in English. The previous two were both published in 2009, both translated by Alistair Ian Blyth: *Becoming within Being* (Marquette University Press) and *Six Maladies of the Contemporary Spirit* (University of Plymouth Press).

For this edition, all footnotes belong to me, unless otherwise noted. At times, I have chosen to keep Romanian terms, explaining their meaning in a footnote. The register of Noica's writing varies throughout the book. At times, it reads as a diary, while at other times as a philosophical treatise.

I remain indebted to Dana Munteanu for her continual support during the translation of this volume and for reading and

---

*   See *Prigoana: Documente ale procesului C. Noica, C. Pillat, S. Lăzărescu, A. Acterian, Vl. Streinu, Al. Paleologu, N. Steinhardt, T. Enescu, S. Al-George, Al. O. Teodoreanu și alții* (Bucharest: Vremea, 2010).

†   In Zara Martirosova Torlone, Dana Lacourse Munteanu, and Dorota Deutsch (eds.), *A Handbook to Classical Reception in Eastern and Central Europe* (Chichester: Wiley-Blackwell, 2017), 300–311.

offering helpful suggestions. My wife, Elena, and my son, Andrei, have often suggested the right word whenever I could not find it. For this and for sharing their lives with me, I am forever grateful.

ROMANIAN PUBLISHER'S NOTE

This book was written by Noica after his release from political prison, in 1964, but it remained unpublished until 1990. Its chapters were sent to England starting in 1971, as letters addressed by the author to his first wife, Wendy Muston, with the idea that Wendy would translate them and publish them abroad. One version of the manuscript was kept in the author's archive; this version was at the basis of the edition published by Humanitas in 1990. As will be seen, that version was incomplete.

The present volume contains four new chapters compared to the 1990 and 2008 editions: XIII, which was present in the previous versions in the form of a summary written by the author (we maintained this summary within brackets), XVI, XVII, and XVIII.

These texts were found in the archives of the former Securitate,* and were returned to Mariana Noica, the widow of the author, by Virgil Măgureanu, the chief of the Romanian Intelligence Service, in 1994. Marin Diaconu published them in *Viața românească,*† year LXXXIX, November–December 1994, nos. 11–12, and we have took them from there. We thank Marin Diaconu for his help and kindness.

---

* The secret police during communism.
† Romanian literary journal.

PREFACE

Toward the end of World War II, a nunnary from Moldova* was occupied by the conquering Soviet troops. The nuns left and looked for refuge in other places. When they returned, they found a note on the altar: "The commander of the troops that occupied the monastery declares that he left it untouched and asks you to pray for his soul." Beginning with that moment, the name of Alexander is mentioned at every religious service.

Pray for brother Alexander! You too, reader, pray, because this name does not concern only the commander of the victorious troops (But what have you done, brother Alexander, in the meantime? Have you spent your days in prison or have you become a conformist? Have you slaved on the fields like the others, or have you written books and sent them abroad?†), but it also concerns all the other brothers Alexander, the insecure victors. Pray for brother Alexander from China, but do not forget brother Alexander in the United States; pray for the strong everywhere, for those who *know*, physicists, mathematicians, and super-technicians, but who no longer know well what they know and what they do, for all those who possess and give orders, together with their economists; pray for the triumphant wanderers through life without culture, but also for the wander-

---

* Moldova was a province of Romania. Since the monastery was occupied by the Soviet troops, Noica probably refers to the part of Moldova which was annexed by the Soviet Union first in 1940 and then also of the end of WWII: Bessarabia, the current Republic of Moldova.

† Due to censorship during Communism, writers from the Eastern bloc sent their manuscripts to the West with the help of acquaintances. Aleksandr Solzhenitsyn's *The Gulag Archipelago,* for example, was first published in the West.

ers within culture; for the European man who triumphed over material needs, for the modern man who triumphed over nature and over the good God. Pray for brother Alexander!

Pray for Brother Alexander

I

When a victor asks you to pray for him, it means that he offers you his victory. "Can you do anything with this victory?" he seems to say. It is true, not anyone can triumph over his own victory and feel as deep as brother Alexander that he has nothing to do with it. At his own level, however, a common man offers various victories on the market, victories that he cannot always use, so that today's world seems to be one in which victories are suspended, are for sale. At every step, there is a victory of the modern world, having no master, being certain of itself.

Being certain of their deed, some say, "Take, eat, this is my victory, which spills over the world for you and your happiness."* Others, more uncertain about what they have to do, say, "Here is my victory; see what can come out of it." A few get angry: "Don't you see what I accomplished?" As good mercenaries, the scientists, the politicians, the technicians, all of them won the battle, receiving their money and glory. The rest of the people are, with or without their will, for sale.

But don't we find a human miracle and a blessing even in this situation? The conditions for a deeper solidarity among the people of today have been created through it; a solidarity between unequal people. It would have been such a spiritual disaster if victory remained in the hands of victors, if the physicists, the biologists, the sociologists, and the politicians knew what to do until the end, or if the super-technicians became better manag-

---

* During the Orthodox Liturgy, at the moment of the Eucharist, the priest intones the words of institution at the moment of the consecration of the Eucharist: "Take, eat, this is my body, which is broken for you for the remission of sins." See also Matthew 26:26.

ers! It would have been such a disaster if brother Alexander had the conscience of a victor when he entered the monastery! The world would have been separated between human subjects and human objects or, rather, between privileged humans, the victors, and the sub-humans. The human miracle is that victory can be shared.

And it is shared even on a political level, where the victor thinks that he maintains victory with power. The one who has lived attentively and especially serenely during communism realizes that an apparently odd result is reached: this revolution is, after all, for the benefit of the rich, not of the poor; the poor people's wealth now comes from the rich, which is no big deal; but the poor is given *the ideal* of enrichment. But a man frustrated by the ideal — and at this level this means "meaning of life" — is in a way destroyed. In the meantime, anyone who possessed something and was alienated by possession can at times feel that he is reinvested as human, reestablished. Some people from the upper classes, who no longer knew their human measure because of their easy lives, discovered when they were dispossessed of their goods and privileges that they *knew* something and that they *could do* something; they even discovered that they *wanted* something and that they *could do* something, and even that they *wanted* something with all their hearts. In a sense, they discovered their own necessity. Today, they no longer aspire to regain liberties, in plural, but only that liberty which fulfills their interior necessity.

After all, it should not be surprising; if someone was alienated by his possession, this was the possessor; instead, the man who lived *under* the level of possession was in sub-humanity. The revolution just raised the latter to the condition of a human being. Doesn't he risk his humanity only beginning from here? The victory of communism in a large part of the world is not for *him* at the end. Who can do something with this victory? The true surprise could be that one day we would see that those who defend the menaced revolutions are not their supposed beneficiaries — just like in the chapter from Hegel's *Phenomenology,* where the generosity of the one who wants to help the oppressed encounters the opposition of their solidarity with their oppressors.

If, however, communism, which wanted strongly to obtain a certain thing, has a chance to obtain *something else,* then capitalism, which does not want almost anything, has even more chances to obtain something completely different. There is something else beyond the two worlds opposed today. It's not the two of them which are still interesting, but rather a subtler thing, a third human condition different from these two. A child is a *third* starting from a certain moment: it is no longer important what the parents want from him and what they invest in him. It is not important what the tree bringing forth the seed wants. From a certain moment, it is no longer important what the states and the governments want regarding a *person,* whom they fostered directly or indirectly; this person entered another growing process, under another law. From a certain moment, it is no longer important what happens *to* us externally. Very serious things can happen to us, but they no longer mean anything, in a sense…

II

"It is of no importance," I tell him.

He is 22 years old. We are both imprisoned in a cell for two people, with a shower and the water closet under the shower. When he takes a shower in the morning, I can see how well built he is, with long muscles. Sometimes, when the guard does not watch through the peephole in the door, my young man jumps and touches the ceiling. He used to be in the national volley-ball team. They played in East Berlin, and a girl asked him if he wanted to see the other Berlin. He did not like it so much in the West because the authorities bored him with various interrogations. When he came back to East Berlin, he was well received at the beginning. Then, as he was returning back home… Now we are both under investigation.

"It is of no importance," I tell him.

"For you, perhaps," he bursts out. "You are over 50. But for me it is! You see that 'this thing' puts you in prison. And then you say that it is of no importance?"

"It is very serious, but of no importance."

"Look, you kind of bore me, sir! According to you…"

The door's latch is moving.

"Take this and come," the guard tells me while entering.

He gives me opaque glasses, made out of metal; we must put them on any time we come out of the cell. The bloke takes you by the arm and, at times, seeing that you wobble, makes fun of you: "Careful, don't step into water." You hesitate to put your foot down, and he laughs. But what a gentle thing to walk like that, *guided* in the unknown! It is like in a ritual of initiation or like in a dream…

I return after two hours. The guard takes off my opaque glasses and closes the door loudly, locking it up. For a moment, I remain confused in the middle of the cell. I feel my cheeks slightly swollen, and my young man must have seen something as well, since he asks me, "They have beaten you, haven't they?"

"Yes," I finally consent after a hesitation, "but…"

"But it is of no importance, I know," he completes the sentence. "Nevertheless, why did they beat you?"

"That's what I wanted to say: they beat me without a reason."

"How so, without a reason? That's what they do?"

My young man is worried. The idea of being hit without being able to react probably offended his pride of a sportsman. Or perhaps he would react… I have to better explain to him the non-sense of everything that happens in our situation.

"I was beaten because I did not want to take a cigarette."

"Are you mocking me?"

"But I assure you it was because of this. The guy who was interrogating me started by asking to whom I gave a book that I had received from abroad. I replied that the work had nothing problematic for the regime. 'Scoundrel,' he said, 'you will see how things are with this book. Now tell me to *whom* you gave it.' 'I am not obligated to tell you,' I said, 'since this cannot be a criminal charge.'"

The young man interrupted my story: "This is the moment when he hit you."

"No," I answer, "the guy was more skillful. He took from his pocket the list with the names of the five or six friends who really had the book in their hands (the informant I feared had done his work fairly well). Then all of a sudden I had the idea that I could save my friends by paralyzing my interrogators with a cloud of names. 'Ah,' I said, 'you were referring to these people? But there are tens of other people to whom *I could* have lent the book, or to whom I actually lent it.' I was reckoning that they could not arrest eighty or one hundred people who had a perfectly innocent book in their hands. So I say,* 'You have taken my agenda with addresses and phone numbers. Give it back to me for a moment, please, so that I could remember.'

"They give me the agenda and I read absolutely all names from it. From time to time, the interrogator stops and says with satisfaction the first name of the person who is mentioned; at other times, he asks me who that person is. I follow how he puts down on paper name after name methodically, for around 45 minutes (They have a good stomach, I tell myself; they can handle any quantities). At the end, he offers me a cigarette.

"At that moment I realized[†] what an idiot I had been, perhaps even criminal, for I had put under his eyes so many names from which he could have chosen whomever he wanted. I refused the cigarette. 'Take it,' he said. 'No,' I replied. 'Take the cigarette!' he shouted. 'I won't.' 'Take it or I'll dislocate your jaw!' he yelled, as if peeved.

"I was afraid, of course, but a kind of 'no' came out from my lips. The next moment, I was surprised by a strong blow on the neck, with the side of the right palm (I had not known of such special blows), and then some slaps that shook my head quite seriously. I felt how my left eye was trying to come out of its socket. I thought of two things at the same time. First: so there is a concrete meaning for the expression 'he hit him so hard that his eyes popped out.' The second thought was totally different in kind: he hits me — I told myself — in order to check my strength in resisting. He probably wants to be sure that he can obtain from me whatever he wants, and in any case that I am not able to hide anything from him. The pretext with the cigarette is as good as any other; or, precisely because he has no other occasion to verify from the beginning my capacity to hide something, he uses this one. It is a simple question of technical skill or virtuosity — on my part or his part. What if I *gave up,*

---

*   The switch from past tense to present tense takes place in the original here, and I decided to maintain this change.

†   At this moment, the author changes back to past tense.

all of a sudden? It would be the best assurance for him that he dominates me totally, while for me it would be a chance to hide something from him another time…

"'Take the cigarette,' he shouts after he hits me.

"I took it."

"Oh," my young cellmate sighs.

"You see," I try to explain to him or to justify myself, "it can be a tactic to show that you are weak…"

"But I would have *never* done this," he exclaims disapprovingly. "After he hit me? Never…"

He looks at me. I probably have an uneasy air, in my incapacity to clarify the subtleties of my game; after all I am not certain about it either. His indignation stops all of a sudden, and the young man turns things around, changing his tone. He does not want to offend me, at least not entirely, in the conditions in which we find ourselves.

"You know why you took the cigarette?" he asks me.

"Why?"

"Because you felt like smoking," he said.

My young sportsman is not stupid at all. In a way, he was right. The slaps I got had brought me to reality: nothing made any sense in that moment. I could smoke a cigarette.

III

I wake up the second day before the sound of the prison's bell, and I see Alec sleeping calmly, his hands outside, according to the rules here, on his back, under the light that must be on all night.* (My young cellmate is named Alec, from Alexander. He could be a brother Alexander as well, a victor for whom you must pray. But aren't all young people this way?) He has already learned to sleep according to the rules in prison, and he's been here only for four days. Poor young man... I am more and more overtaken by a feeling of responsibility for him. Could I do anything good at all for him?

But I realize all of a sudden how ridiculous this pedagogical temptation is. On the contrary, I run the risk of irritating him and of making him reluctant, as it happens with those who are very close to you or those who make it a point to make others happy. After all, perhaps they, these communists, also want our good — perhaps the improvement of our human condition, the overcoming of alienation, welfare for all, or at least welfare without the feeling that you are privileged if you have it — but they create such resistance in us! Nothing from what they offer has taste, and the world is so ungrateful for their trouble to make us happy that I wonder at times if we are not a little unfair to them. But they came too close to people; they installed themselves in the people's storerooms, in their shelters, in their drawers, and, as much as possible, in their consciences ("say this," "make your

---

* According to the testimony of many who suffered in communist political prisons, this was one method of torture: to force the inmates to sleep in one position only for the entire night, and always with the hands in sight, above the covers.

own critique"). They make you uncomfortable just by using their simple voice, just with their newspaper or *speaker*.*

In fact, they are too demonstrative. They have no discretion. Imagine that someone would take, or would imagine that he takes, the responsibility of food digestion and would speak in this way: "Now the food comes into your mouth. The teeth should do their duty and crush it; the salivary glands should attack it from all sides. Behold, new juices are waiting in the esophagus, well prepared, to hurry its decomposition, and the stomach must be ready not only with its acids, but also with its ferments and especially its pepsins. But where is the trypsin? The trypsin should not be late! I tell you food passes well by the duodenum at this very moment, where the pancreas and the liver send their subtle juices to accomplish the work. In a moment, the intestine with its complex organization, concentrated economically in a small place, will absorb the water, the salts, the sugars, the fats, and the proteins, and even some vitamins from the food in order to nourish the all-nourishing blood. The plan has been accomplished!"

I should not be like them with Alec. Life is a problem of digestion. I have to let him digest alone everything that happens to him. Everyone has his own stomach. Do I know what the good is? Perhaps he does not know it himself. I want for him the *better*— how to pass through this event more easily— but not necessarily the good. And perhaps if I say it this way, I do not fall into platitude, *le mieux est l'ennemi du bien*.† I think I want to say, *le mieux est l'ignorance du bien*.‡

After all, this is how all politicians, of one kind or another, behave with us: they want our "better" and think that they want our good. In large part, the dirtiness of our modern political life is a grammatical problem: people confuse the comparative with the positive, and they even no longer think of the positive. (The Americans no longer consider even the comparative, but direct-

---

* "Speaker," in English in the original.
† "The better is the enemy of the good," in French in the original.
‡ "The better is the ignorance of the good," in French in the original.

ly the superlative: "the best"). The politicians come and tell us, "Wouldn't it be better if you all have an apartment each?" "Yes," we answer in a choir, "it would be better." "Wouldn't it be better to have longer vacations?" "Yes, it would be much better." "You see," they say then, "we want your good and you have to vote for us, to fight with us. And if you are not aware of your interest, we have to take the responsibility to fulfill it for you, running the risk to encounter your misunderstanding, your inertia, even at times your evil disposition."

I actually indisposed Alec a little. I only realized it yesterday morning, when I was doing my two gymnastics movements, precisely for digestion. He told me, "I have been here for three days, and I see you doing the same two movements. Don't you know any other one? Let me teach you." I also got angry a little myself, and I did not ask him to teach me a third movement. I am as childish as he is.

"How did the fellow from yesterday look like, the guy who got on you about the cigarette?" he asks me after he stands up.

"To be honest, I did not really look at him," I answer. "We do not have to register and remember all things. I decided to not remember their names, so I would not recognize them on the street when I will be free one day. They do not matter. They are not themselves."

Alec looked at me with pity.

"Perhaps your eyes darkened because he slapped you."

"No, my dear, honestly, I am not interested in how he looked. They are not *themselves,* I repeat; there is something else or someone else behind them."

He shakes his head at what he takes to be my platitude.

"You mean the Russians…"

I wait for him to wash, and we sit on the blankets, waiting for the poor substitute for morning coffee to come. I then try to explain.

"After all, it is not about the Russians; I think there is something else in place, which transforms all of them into objects."

"Ah, the system!"

"If it were only this! But our entire Time, time with a capital T, pushes them to do what they do."

"But you, is it still the time with a capital T that threw you in here?"

"Of course, and also those who must guard us. In fact, our time has already been described almost to the letter. Goethe did it, in the second part of *Faust*. If I told you the story, you would see…"

"Well, culture! You explain everything with it perfectly, even when you do not know anything. If you were so clear with *Faust II* about time, then how come did you get here?"

"Such things cannot be avoided; you cannot evade your own time. They* are victims as well, just like us."

"What, isn't it going well for them?"

"I could not say that it is going so well for them.. Consider these guards: they have to look at us through the peephole every five minutes, to see whether we are not plotting something or trying to take our own lives. If they have five cells to oversee, this means that they look through a peephole every minute. Is this a human job? They are like the dogs, running from door to door."

"I see you pity them. Perhaps you pity the investigators as well…"

I sense how he is about to boil. I try to avoid being too categorical and provocative in my judgments, and I tell him:

"My dear, regardless of the situation in which one finds oneself, it is good to ponder on the situation that may follow."

"Should I have pity on them because they run the risk to be judged one day?"

"This does not even cross my mind. I pity them (if I can talk this way in our situation) because I see that they are not placed in the condition of being humans, beings who do something and find out something from life. There are so many things they could learn about man from this entire gallery of human specimens that go before them! But how could they learn? They must

---

*   "They" could refer here to the investigators or more generally to the communists.

reach a pre-established result; they have to make people recognize what they want. They do not want to learn even new words or new ways to speak. You will see that they do not allow you to write your declaration alone, but they write it, in their terms and with their clichés, and you are only to sign it, if you cannot refuse and resist. I often thought that it would be interesting to investigate an investigator, that is to cross-examine him about the human types he has encountered. But in fact, he is trained to precisely destroy different human types and even man as moral being. They do not realize that, with people, if you destroy the other, you annul yourself. What will they do in life when this story is finished?"

He listened to me until the end, but when I raise my eyes toward him I see that he is suffocated by revolt. Coffee came in the meantime. After he drinks it, Alec recovers a little. It feels as if a demon makes him to continue to put traps for me.

"And those in power, the bigwigs, are they also not doing well?"

I breathe deeply. What can I do but tell him my thought, even if I really attenuate it?

"There was a French writer, Montherlant," I answer, "who had the courage to write in a book published during the German occupation: *'pitié pour les forts!'** I let aside the fact that the communists, after they dreamed, fought, and crushed all adversity, they have to do simple work of administration. This is the misery of any political delirium. But what's the curse that makes them, the materialists, who spume of anger against idealism, to practice the worse idealism, the type that deforms reality by their idea instead of forming it by the idea taken from reality? Everything is disfigured, starting with them, the materialists, just like in *Faust II*. Someone told me that the most painful thing is to watch one of their parties: they are afraid to drop an

---

*   "Mercy on the strong!" in French in the original.

inappropriate word, they or their wives.* They can't even party anymore! They are not interesting…"

"As if it were about this?" Alec bursts out. "About this? You don't believe yourself an iota of what you say! They hold us in their claws, don't you see? They hold us in their claws. It is as if you would say that the lion that caught you is not really interesting because its manes are too short or its eyes too yellow!"

I watch how he stood up. He is furious, and I truly feel like I am in a cage with him. There is a feeling of animality coming from him. I would deserve to be crushed since I provoked him like this. If something took place… Anything…

Then the miracle comes. The door opens widely, and the guard brings a bucket with dirty water and two large rags. "Wash the floor," he commands. I jump to take one of the rags and I begin to feverishly scrub the concrete. Alec became calm all of a sudden. The idea that he has something to do restores him to order. He recovers even the strength to be ironical: "This too is in *Faust II,* isn't it?"

---

* Noica probably refers to the fear one would experience during a communist regime. People avoided to express any opinions that may be construed as opposing the regime because such opinions could send you straight to prison. The Securitate, the secret police, had informants among all people, especially among the Communists themselves, and one could never know how his or her conversations would be reported.

IU

I do not say anything and I ponder while I continue scrubbing the floor: where does this scene or a similar one appear in *Faust*? It should be somewhere in Goethe's work, for this is about something profoundly human: the work of a slave…

However, to wash the floor of your own cell does not seem to really be the work of a slave. This is work as well, and it has something good in it, regenerating. In the lack of meaning in which they threw us (and in which they threw *themselves,* because of the excessive power that they assumed), any useful work is a blessing. Alec fully feels it too, and he gets more and more on my half of the floor, until he decides to take the bucket with water to him, not allowing me to do anything else. Perhaps he wants to spare me. He does not realize that *I* take pleasure as well in washing the floor.

"I was afraid that you would not have cleaned the floor well," he tells me so as to give an explanation. "For you, all things seem without importance, while for me the cleanliness of the cell is important."

"This is more important than the great historical events," I answer.

He sits on the bed. He is content that he did good work, but after one moment he remembers my previous reflection and he revolts again.

"How can you make such cheap paradoxes?"

I am afraid to say the littlest thing. In fact, I don't even think that he would find a meaning in what I am tempted to say now. He is too young to know of the *vacuum* of many of the so-called "historical" events. I remember some events from the more recent past that seemed historic to their contemporaries and to the media. "The historic meeting in Bermuda."* Who remembers this? Churchill met there with some American president, and some president of a French council could not come because he had a cold. How historic would the meeting have been if the latter had not had a cold... Making order and cleaning around you have a positive meaning for both you and the society, while some great events can be a simple stammer of history.

In fact, if it could be said about nature that it stammers, then this can be said even more about history, since it is done the way it is done by this approximate being, the human. Perhaps we live now during a stammer of history, an organized one — this is what I would like to tell Alec. It is terrible or it is stupid, however you want to take it. It is like in the English proverb: the dog barks, but it barks up the wrong tree (where the cat is not).

You often have the impression that the people of public life bark up the wrong tree, even if you do not know which tree the cat is in, either. (The unbelievable thing is that these people, the communists, ask you to bark like them, up their tree. "If you don't bark, I will bite you." And they really bite.)

Alec cannot know that two generations, those before him, were troubled by two world wars generated — at least on the continent — by something incredible today: the French–German conflict. It is as if the left hand would fight the right. In all of Europe, people were divided in public life but also in private life on this theme: are you with the French or with the Germans? Parents were fighting their children. I do not want to say that we can delete these wars from history, started by Teutonic blindness, or the communist revolution that came between them. How could they be deleted, since they had so many consequences? But anyone can see today that the Europeans barked up the wrong tree. Three great nations in Europe were fighting one another so that two other greater nations from the margins of Europe, the Americans and the Russians, could take the foreground faster than even they could desire it. And even behind

---

* Noica probably refers to the 1953 meeting between Churchill and US President Eisenhower.

these two and their unnatural and forced antagonism there was something else: the fact that Europe, together with the Americans and the Russians, was destined to wake up Asia from its sleep and Africa from its animality. By its civilization — historically the first one that was established on exclusively rational values and perfectly transmissible to any human mind — Europe, this peninsula of Asia, was about to wake up the whole globe to life. It almost did it in a different fashion, through colonialism, but this was more abusive and too slow. It quickened, and now things happen too fast. But it is *this* waking up to life of the globe that is important, or something of this kind (the demographic explosion, the indirect and direct pressure of the Third World), and not the barks of the first half of the 20th century. Someone said, "the stupid 19th century." You could rather say, "the stupid first half of the 20th century." At least some art was done during it. Otherwise, it would have been a perfect stupidity of history.

"Tell me something. Tell me about a movie," says Alec.

He cannot stand this prolonged silence, even though he would stand my rattle about history even less. I have to do what he asks of me. But I do not like movies too much, or I don't like those with a "subject." The absurdity of the movie with a subject is that it wants to fixate the imagination of the spectator with a few images. But it should, I do not know how, *free* it. Perhaps giving the same scene two or three times, in different fashions. But, behold, I act like someone wise when I do not know to narrate a simple movie.

"You see," I tell him, "I do not think I could describe one as you would like, with details, especially an action movie."

"How so? You are telling me that you can narrate entire books, and you are not able to tell me a movie? Then tell me something else, a story.

"Yes," I say, "yes, of course."

I try hard to remember a story.

"You won't say that you don't know a story?"

"No… yes… of course yes; who doesn't know any story?"

I feel worse than under investigation, and I try to invent something. I begin, "Once upon a time… there was… there was a village which had only one well, and that well did not have a lot of water either. (It's an idea, I'm telling myself; it's an idea). The women had to come very, very early to find the water accumulated during the night. One morning (*now* I have to invent something, now is the moment), one morning when they came to get water, the woman found at the well... an outlaw with his saber in his hand, an outlaw who told them, 'Nobody gets water unless I allow her.' (I breathe, relieved: now I have a subject, one with a possible conflict). The women began crying, saying that children are waiting at home; one even said that her child was sick, but the outlaw did not have pity. The elders of the village came to implore the outlaw, even promising anything to him, just so that he would go. But the outlaw enjoyed showing how powerful he was and, as any other earthly powerful man, he began to believe that he was also wise. He took out a bucket with water, placed it on the edge of the well, rather to provoke them, and began to give them advice: 'Just look: do you call this water? You should dig a well there, in the valley, a deeper one, so that you could find better and more water. I'll teach you.' Saying this, he really enjoyed seeing how they listened to him obediently. 'You are right, and we thank you,' one of the elders said, 'but, for now, let people take from this water too.' At that moment, a blackbird descended from the air to the bucket, dipped its beak into the water twice, and flew away. 'You see, not even the birds like your water,' the outlaw said. 'Actually, I suspect that you do not have good order, and some people take more water, others less. I am certain that the *chiaburi** of the village come and take water by the barrel. We must do things right, as I will teach you.' And time passed this way, with well pondered words, as taken from a book, until evening, when the outlaw took pity on some more troubled women, but he left all of the others thirsty...

"Next day early morning, the entire village was lined nicely around the well, men on one side and women on the other, waiting obediently for the decisions of the outlaw. 'This is how I like

---

*   The *chiaburi* were wealthy peasants who owned land. In Russia, they were called *kulaks,* which is the term that is also often used in English.

it,' he said. 'Now we can work well.' He gave to some the right to take water, but not to all, but all of them thanked him and praised him, so that they would not upset him for future days. And the outlaw did the same thing for a few days, proving his power and right judgment, until he thought that the only thing he got out of it was the empty rule over people. He then said to them, 'If you continue doing as I told you to do and if you give me what I need as payment for the good I did to you, I will leave. But know well that I can return anytime.' People rushed to give him even more than he requested, vowed submission even in his absence, and accompanied him to the forest.

"The outlaw went into the forest, being content with the work he had done, and he went on until he became thirsty. He was loaded with goods, and it was warm. He headed toward the spring that he knew was there, but the spring was no more. He went toward the creek in the middle of the forest, but the creek had drained. An uncertain fear took hold of him, as if nature and the forest were punishing him for the power that he had assumed over the people. Exhausted, he sat down on the bed of the creek. At that moment, a child came close to him. He had been sent by the people in the village to make sure that the outlaw had indeed left. 'I'm thirsty,' the outlaw said. 'Bring me a pail of water.' The child went back to the village in a hurry to bring the news. Some said, 'We should not give him water.' The woman who had a sick child said, 'Give him water.' And the young man* went back, carrying the pail on his head. When he went down to the bed of the creek, where the outlaw was waiting, he stumbled, the pail broke, and the dry bed engulfed all the water. The child was terrified, thinking that the outlaw would kill him; but the outlaw had understood that it was not the child's fault. As he was staying there…"

I stop, happy that I succeeded in inventing at least those things.

---

* The change between "child" and "young man" takes place in the original. It was a story invented on the spot, so we should not be surprised by the lack of accuracy.

"As he was staying there…," Alec continues.

"Yes," I say to him, "we can continue the story together."

For a moment, Alec is caught in the fairytale:

"As he was staying there, the blackbird who had drunk from the bucket comes to him and places two drops of water on his lips. Then, the outlaw…"

But he stops abruptly.

"What did you mean with this story?"

"How so, what I meant? I just told you a story…"

"Is this story not *true*? I mean, a story that others tell?," he asks in a harsh voice

"I no longer know. It just came to my mind. Perhaps I invented it."

He looks at me with a sharp look. One of the veins at his temple swells, and he shouts:

"*I know* what you wanted to say. You wanted to say *the same* thing, the lesson you have been giving me; you wanted to say that those who cut off the springs of people cut off their own springs; that if somebody takes away the life-giving water, he takes it away from himself; that these people who torture us, the communists, should not be hated, but rather pitied, pitied. Aren't you ashamed to repeat yourself that much?"

"I swear, Alec," I say, "that I didn't think of anything when I began…"

But a wave of shame takes hold of me indeed. How didn't I realize what I was saying? And how did things get so connected to end up in a homily? He, the young man, wanted to dream; he needed air, gratuity…

"You are… you are just an educator," he shouts. "*Educator!*" he thunders again and turns his head from me. (He says it as a true insult, as if he said, "Demagogue! Mystagogue!")

The guard shows his face at the peephole: "Where do you think you are that you yell that loudly? Stand for an hour facing the wall in the back!"

I look at Alec, who doesn't even wink. He would not talk to me for two days.

U

We both stood for an hour, facing the wall in the back, without exchanging looks or words. No one is in harmony with anyone else any longer, and the relations between people are no longer natural in these socialist regimes. I do not know how these regimes move everything out of place, dislocating even people's souls. You would think that only the public life is changed and that you can take refuge in your private life; for a moment you are even delighted that you no longer have public responsibilities and that you are restituted to your personal life. But even here everything is vitiated. You no longer get along with your wife ("you no longer bring home enough money and you are not worth anything in society"); you no longer get along with your child ("your truths are no longer in agreement with those of the school"); with your friends, it is even worse: if you complain, you risk being politically inappropriate or even dangerous; if you do not complain, you offend them.

Something does not "click" any longer. The relationships among people, just as the relations humans have with objects, have in general something of the complexity of a mechanism which, once established, must "click" and begin functioning. In this socialist world, the ultimate adjustment of things disappeared. Everything moves forward, I don't exactly know how, but without making the "click."

It is like this in *Faust,* at least in Goethe's version. Faust, the hero, no longer "clicks" with anything. This is what he says to the devil when he declares that the devil cannot make him exclaim, "just a moment, stay a while": he tells him that he will not make him feel the "click." He is *der Unbehauste,* as he calls himself, the man without dwelling, without being in agreement with anyone and anything. In fact, he no longer wants anything after he wanted everything at once, thoughtlessly, and so he allows himself to be dragged by the devil here and there. In the scene with the drinkers from Auerbach's tavern, where Mephistopheles has terrible fun at the expense of the others, Faust says only one thing: "Let us leave!" (This would be the first "Faustian" work, according to interpreters.) In the love story with Gretchen, all poetry is poisoned by falsity, by the crookedness of the situation. It is true, Gretchen falls in love with her whole heart with the "sage of the four Universities," who was artificially rejuvenated by the devil and the sorcerers. She dreams of bringing everything to a final "click," which would have been the religious wedding; but she feels, with her feminine intuition, that Faust cannot do things properly with her because he is not properly in order with himself (he does not have the right faith, he does not "click" with the good God). She, who is the victim in all things, will have to have mercy on him sometime.

What a typical brother Alexander is this Faust: a conqueror for whom you need to have mercy! However, he is a complete victor. He has overcome ignorance, he has overcome human weakness and helplessness, and, after all, he has conquered any religious sentimentalism or illusionism, allying himself with the devil absolutely and without any fear. He is in the situation of being able to do anything, due to the means and allies that are at his disposal, but *he does not know what to do.* You must pray not only for his soul, as Gretchen does at the end, but for his deeds as well, for the risk he runs to do things that are not to be done, like modern man. How could one claim that Faust is representative of modern man due to his *aspiration* or his "creativity" and that our world is Faustian because it wants and it knows what it wants? Our world is Faustian because it *doesn't* know what it wants, just like Goethe's hero; because it has prepared its means and victories with which it has nothing to do.

However, when you do not know what to do with the means you have at your disposal, they begin working by themselves. This is why, just like in *Faust,* the possible has precedence over the real in our world. This is what I wanted to tell Alec, in my conviction that I was helping him understand what is happening to him, that is that we live in a world in which the possible, from the possibility of technology to that of politics, has precedence over any reality. But he is confused when faced with his own time, just like Gretchen with Faust.

This girl — just like my young man — embodies the world of the real, while Faust brings with himself the world of the possible. His youth is "possible," not real, and even this being with whom he fell in love is, for him, "a possible Helen" (just like the devil had prepared him to feel, when they were in Hexenbüche and he made him see beauty in a mirror). Something crooked has appeared in the world, substituting the real, and now it takes being, with its false sound. Everything is a question of sound, after all. There is something that Gretchen does not like, just as the story that I improvised did not sound well to Alec. He felt that it was a possible story, not a real one.

The devil interfered between us, just as he interfered between Faust and Gretchen. After all, what does the devil mean? It means the unending possibility, but a *bare* possibility. In itself, the world of possibilities represents something good and human, just as the technology of the modern world is something good and human in principle. Due to technology, our world has moved from the harsh or indifferent real into the kindness of the possible, and we no longer live among realities, but among the admirable realized possibilities. An automobile is a realized possibility and is something good. But when science or technology comes to make, as it has tried, some sort of insect to correspond to the idea of "chimera" from Antiquity, then it is about an empty possibility and it is no longer something good. Or when an ideologist comes to make a state...

When we go directly from the possible to the real, with a deeper necessity, and when, for example, we make up states that do not match the souls or we want to make (just like "engineers," in this tender matter) souls that do not match people, then it means that the devil somehow interfered. The entire *Faust II* is — at times it is even acknowledged to be so — a fit of the devil, reprised over five acts. But the strange thing is that everything that takes place there also happens in our time. And this time of ours is no longer always the work of the devil, or *it is possible* for it not to be so.

I would have told Alec that *Faust II* is, act after act, the realization of the empty possible, of the possible deprived of any necessity. After all, the empty possible reigned in the first part of *Faust* as well, beginning with the devil entering the play; but the emptiness of the devil is not seen there because there were still real people in play. In the second part, though, there are almost no people. You look for them with a candle and you only find specters. There is no real human in Act I, and even less so in Act II, the act of the homunculus. Only in Act III does the face of a real man, Lynceus, the guardian of the Faustian city gate, appear timidly. He remains mute with admiration when the beautiful Helen appears in the city and brings to him, later, his gifts of a poor man. Then again, there is no human during the entire Act IV, the act of the diabolic war, but, in Act V, we finally find two poor real men, the old Philemon and Baucis, who resist against forced agricultural collectivization, just like now. Other than that, only specters, specters…

In such a spectral world, the empty possible is, of course, at home. I would have liked to tell Alec how, in Act I, Goethe unleashes over the real world of some state the empty possible of *money* without coverage, the banknote, when Mephistopheles suggests to issue banknotes on the basis of possible treasures buried under ground; then, in Act II, how a small man comes out of the tube — again as empty possibility, unrequired by any need — so how a technical-scientific revolution is made and what science-fictional consequences (the return in time) it can have. After these typical Mephistophelic exploits, you have in Act III the empty possible in terms of culture: the marriage of Faust with the beautiful Helen, the marriage of the modern spirit with the Greek one, as a true anticipated movie, directed by Mephistopheles. No commentary is needed any longer for Act IV, the act of the war led with devilish means, as today. The last act brings into play the *political* possible, which is the unleashing of ordering and planning reason, and Alec and I find ourselves now under its hysteria.

However, it would be worth saying now, when faced with our time, that you can no longer exclaim as you did about the happenings in Goethe's work: this is the work of the devil! Even Goethe's work no longer appears like this today, since the 20th century made it true, so it came on man's account, in a way. In any case, things may be different with us. For us, the issue of banknotes is not an empty game of financial magic; science is not the projection of a singular genius or a form of exasperation, like for Faust, but rather a slow accumulation, often anonymous, for centuries; the myth of the beautiful Helen has been democratized, with her image (or the image of her sisters, the stars*) multiplied on our screens, leaving us free for another encounter with the Greek spirit; war has become so devilish that the god Ares must be really expelled from the skies and from the earth, if man still has judgment; and the political delirium, which comes into our world as well, like in Act v, to colonize a new humanity on a new and renewed earth, to the level of suffocating it, the political delirium, then, is hit steadfastly not only by some old people like Philemon and Baucis, but also by a strange challenging young generation.

Are we, the moderns, distorted or not? Goethe anticipated us with some repulsion. But the problem is whether we are or not in order, even us, who got thrown into prisons. Is there something deprived of necessity, perfectly arbitrary, and, after all, without importance, as I think and say, in everything that is done above our heads, as from the surplus of the possible over the real? Would this be an organized stammering, something fabricated and revocable, just as these communist parties continue to return to their orientation, making their self-critique periodically, like in a chess match in which they would take back their moves? Or is the good and human possible at stake, which comes into the world in whatever way and by whomever it can? If Napoleon could tell Goethe that, from him onward, *le destin*

---

*   Noica refers to today's stars, the stars of cinema, music, or television.

*c'est la politique** and that the destiny of the ancients is done for, it was not only about the self and about his politics. But about *which* politics? The politics of the poor electoral agents from one part of the world? Or the politics of the poor "central committees" from the other part?[†]

As I stay in prison with this young man, taken out of the reality of life or perhaps separated from a frieze of its temple, as we both stay like this, innocent with a *possible* guilt, I feel the full primacy of the possible over the real and I think that I also understand why we are here and why they[‡] will have to take us out. They need the real, they need our testimony! Without the consent of Philemon and Baucis, Faust's work is "impure." The great reformer is disturbed by some trees, those real limes of the elders, from the patch of land that they did not want to leave. The bell of the small church exasperates him. But when Mephistopheles comes to tell him that he has destroyed everything from the face of the earth, Faust withdraws in horror. (The horror of the despots and dictators!)

Now, the old Ladies come around him: Lack, Debt, Care, Need. Goethe makes only one of them, Care, speak to Faust and tell him, in the name of all four, that he has been blind his whole life. Won't these old ladies come around the communists as well? Don't they also need us, just like Faust? I feel like telling them, "Beware, so that you don't fall one day under the investigation of the old Ladies!" To avoid it, they need our mercy and our testimony. They need Alec's joy and youth.

---

*   "Destiny is politics," in French in the original.

†   The part of the world with the electoral agents is formed by the Western democracies, while the one with the central committees (the leading organs of the Communist party) by the Eastern communist states.

‡   "They" refers to the Communists. During Communism, people often referred to the Communists with this impersonal "they." "They" were giving potatoes at the grocery, "they" were interrupting electricity in the evening, etc.

UI

During the following days, I no longer do the two morning exercises, to avoid irritating Alec. When the meal comes, I pretend that I have something to do and I let him eat by himself. The third day he is taken to interrogations. What do they have to impute to him? He crossed from East Berlin, where his team had a game, to West Berlin; he got bored by the Americans' interrogations, and he came back willingly. They will hold him for a while, and then they will free him, letting him finish his degree in architecture (he's a senior) or making him a volleyball coach, as so many others.

When he returns to the cell, he is pale with rage. He forgot any anger he had with me, and he tells me directly:

"They will try me for 'treason against the state.'"

"Treason against the state?" I shout.

"That's what they told me. Between 8 and 15 years of prison."

It is awkward to think that, after all, it had to be this way, according to my own explanations: he was also a *possible* traitor for them.

"I no longer care about anything," he says. "If I get out one day, I won't finish Architecture and I'll go someplace to the countryside. Perhaps I'll find a young girl in a mountain village, with two cows as dowry. Can you imagine what this is? Living simply, in nature…"

He sinks into that shattering silence of an injured young being. After an hour, he looks at me with a gentle smile. It seems that life made him mature all of a sudden!

"Don't you want me to tell you a story?" I suggest this so that I can make him think of something else. "I can tell you a love story."

"But is it a true one?"

"Yes, it is from Plato's *Symposium*," I say quite imprudently.

He frowns for a moment and then relaxes.

"After all, if it's a good one…"

At that moment, the guard's face appears in the peephole. He orders me: "Get your luggage ready in two minutes."

He closes the peephole, and while I start gathering the few things I have, Alec becomes agitated.

"I'm sorry you're leaving, I am so sorry! What do you need? What can I give you? I want to *give* you something."

He only has two shirts and three pairs of socks; he wanted to patch up one of them the first day when we would receive needle and thread. Helpless, he frets.

"I want to give you a memory," he says, being emotional.

"Give me the third exercise movement," I suggest.

He's happy that I've asked something from him.

"Yes, look, this is how you do it: with your arms on your hips, you raise your knees rhythmically, touching your chest with them if you can."

He shows me the movement, which he executes so supply.

"I'll do this exercise, Alec, and I will think of you."

"Quiet!" the guard says coming in, and he drags me to him, dumps the metal glasses on my head, and leaves me holding out my hand, but I no longer find Alec's.

I am taken through all sorts of corridors. It could be just the same one, as this is the guards' habit, to confuse you, so that you don't know where you are taken. I may have arrived in the neighboring cell or some completely different place. Even if I were next to Alec, I would be in another galaxy. When the door slams behind me, I hear knocks on the wall, more and more persistent, from three sides. Poor guys, I tell myself, they want to hear news. It's good that I don't know Morse code at all; otherwise, I would not be able to resist the temptation to answer.

After one or two days of desperate attempts to get in contact with me, my neighbors calm down. I calm down as well. All of a sudden, a quite curious thing comes to mind: what an interesting problem of communication appears especially when you do not know Morse or some other alphabet. The person next to you is just like a rational being from another planetary system. How do you communicate with him? This is probably, at this time, one of the greatest problems of man: how to communicate with other rational beings of the cosmos. We have no common code, and everything must be invented, both language and concepts. It is fascinating. You must be thrown into a place such as this to realize that the real problems of the mind are not to be found in books. How is it that people don't think of such pure situations when they are free? How stupidly they get mixed up into tangential situations. The situation here may even be ideal.

In this particular case, my neighbor is a rational being, just like me; this is the only presupposition. Everything else can be invented. But no, there is one more difficulty here: I must first convince my neighbor that I do not know any code and that I ask him to not know one either, so that we would invent one together. It will be difficult, but I must try. If I succeed, then everything is just like an encounter between a human being and another rational being in the cosmos.

I wonder which of the neighbors I should choose, so in which wall to knock. I decide for the wall on the right, because the colleague from that cell knocked the most. In my walk of 6 steps that I can make on the diagonal of the room, I stop every time at the wall and I knock. At the second signal, my neighbor responds to me. I knock again, intently erratic. He answers with still too regular signals. I knock with my fist. He still answers with signals. How come he does not understand that I do not know any code and that I would want him to not use one either? I stop for a longer time next to the wall and I knock in all possible ways, rhythmically, non-rhythmically, hastily, slowly.

"What are you doing there?"

I turn around and I find myself before two guards that had opened the door's latch silently and come stealthily in the room.

"What are you doing? You're knocking Morse!"

"I am not knocking Morse."

"How come you don't? Haven't we seen you?"

"I give you my word of honor that I do not know Morse."

"Look at this bourgeois, how he gives his word of honor! Aren't you ashamed to lie, when we caught you in the act?"

In despair, an inspired idea takes voice within me:

"Please take me to Mr. Commander, because I have something to report."

The guards look at one another. Perhaps they imagine that I found out something from a neighbor and I want to denounce him. After all, they had to ask for permission to punish me for my offence anyway, so they grab me by my arms, one of them puts the metallic glasses that he had in his hands on my eyes, and they both take me to the commander.

"We caught this scoundrel knocking Morse, but he says he wants to report something."

"Leave him here."

"Mr. Commandant," I begin, "I confess that I knocked on the wall, but I didn't do it to communicate with my neighbor, because I do not know Morse, but rather to establish a code for communication in the cosmos."

"What?"

I try to justify everything, calmly and as persuasively as possible. I show that, next to the technical problem, which has already been solved by humanity, the extraterrestrial communication is a question of imagination and sustained meditation; I add that I fell upon an idea that authorizes me to believe that I am able to bring a contribution to adding a code. I would place everything at the authorities' disposal, without any claim, not even a claim to improve the conditions of the regime in prison. I only ask for paper and pencil.

"You, buffoon," the commander says, after he listens to me with a vague smile, "do you think that someone like you can solve this problem? We have academicians…"

"I do not contest that there are more competent people," I insist, "but they do not have time to consider such a problem and the idea may not have come to them. You see, this is something special; you need a flashing, crazy idea…"

I become enthusiastic, I sense that my eyes stare as in a vision, and I enter a trance. It no longer matters what the commander thinks, but I have something to say; I have something to say... The commander calls for the guard.

"Take him back."

I cannot avoid a pathetic gesture, of despondency. At the moment we are at the door, the commander says, "Here, give him these sheets of paper and a pencil. If he lied, I'll show him."

I return to the cell happy. The guard counts the sheets: there are 22. He gave me a pencil later. I begin to meditate impassionedly, but confidently. Thus, let us assume that the technical means of communication are given: the radio waves or any other waves that carry messages. It is true that transmission of data takes years or dozens of years at the speed of light. But it does not matter. As Pascal says, the whole humanity is just like a human being. So, what does this human being transmit so that he makes himself understood by another being of a similar level in rationality?

Something curious comes to mind from the beginning: any signal or *regular* group of signals risks appearing to the other being in cosmos as stemming from the processes of dead matter. After all, today, we also register various emissions of waves from the cosmos, but it is precisely their regularity that makes them seem uncertain, and we attribute them rather to material processes taking place there. If you want to show that you are a rational being, you must first prove that you are *not* under a mechanical necessity. The first affirmation of rationality is, then, the freedom to not be rational; or the first manifestation of logic would be coming out of the strict logic of mechanisms, so fantasy and, in a way, the lack of logic. The dialogue of two rational consciences would thus begin with each indicating that he *is* a rational being: he can signal arbitrarily. You must show that you have spontaneity; that you are a rational *subject,* not an object of natural laws.

This is a beginning, too. Perhaps it is the only beginning. We want, then, to show that here, on this celestial body, there is reason. Thus, we reveal reason on earth by its capacity to deny itself, just as the laws of dead things *cannot* do. We start, then, by bringing the rational chaos, by bringing chaos purely and simply, the one from which all things begin. (This is what I could not do with my cell neighbor, for whom I was knocking chaotically on the wall: I could not make him begin from chaos as well.) You can *surprise* your interlocutor and make him pay attention and be interested in speaking to you only in this way. You prove to him that there is a rational being here, because, if this being wants to, it can decide not to transmit anything. Just as you erase the board or the magnetic tape so that you can record something new on them, you must begin here by non-transmission as well, by a zero-transmission, so that you could later transmit something intelligible to the other rational being. Faced with a clearly affirmed chaos, with a categorical zero-communication, this person will be filled with wonder, and wonder is the beginning of knowledge and of contact with things and other beings.

The guard throws me a well-sharpened pencil through the peephole. It fells on my bed. I rush to take it, because it has been years since I held one in my hand. What an admirable zero a pencil is, a positive zero, just like the white sheet of paper from where I consider beginning the cosmic dialogue. Anything can come out from the use of a pencil: communication, non-communication… I write on the first sheet of paper, beginning with a large title: COSMIC DAYS. I'm thinking that the signal sent by humans, together with the answer received over years, could represent a unity, a day of conversation. "Cosmic Days," then. Let their emergence among people be blessed!

When I wake up the second day, I feel as on a cosmic day. I do what I need to do in my cell as if sleepwalking, and I begin writing down the results I had achieved. The first cosmic day came this way: I established contact with the extraterrestrial being and the possibility of communication precisely because we did not communicate at all. We thus gained two things: first, we recognized each other as rational beings, capable of communication; second, we agreed that we have not communicated anything yet.

We have obtained all of this by a manifestation of spontaneity as rational beings. Now, we have to come out of spontaneity or to control it, still as rational beings. I let you know that I am rational because I say, "tra la la," or "bum, bum, bum," but now I have to transmit something. Since the first day was with free signals, the second day must have connected and ordered signals. Everything begins *now*.

I stop for a while. After the exaltation that had overtaken me, this is the first time when I begin to have doubt. I was convinced that it was sufficient to put the problem well — according to the principle that a problem asked well is half solved — in order to get a result. But what if nothing comes out of this? I shudder for a moment, but not out of fear for the commander, but out of shame before myself. Still, let us not give up. Let's see. I have obtained the attention of the other cosmic being. Perfect; I should not tell him something; it will be something still indeterminate, but *regular* this time, like a signal that is repeated at infinity. (If he answers with the same repeated signal, it means he's not stupid.) In fact, I can begin even better, with a group of repeated signals instead of a simple signal that I would repeat. This will help me to isolate the group later and, since the other knows it, to make out of it an announcement-signal: that I exist, that it is I, the one on Terra; or that I *begin* transmission. I prepare then a first concept: the beginning. We will be able to begin every emission with that group of signals, but we will also say "beginning" by it, anytime we would wish so. Similarly, we could end every emission in the same fashion, and then we will detach the word "end."

Is it possible to compose an entire language with two words, beginning and end? I could introduce a few others as well. I can, let's say, invent a kind of negation: I could reverse one of mine or one of his structured succession of signals. It is not really free negation, or logical complement, as it is called in logic, but it still is *one* way of negating or canceling something. I can declare that it is *not* so; thus, I communicate something. I also can — what? I can introduce some notions of quantity: "much" and "little"; or notions of intensity: "rapidly" and "slowly"; or even the idea of unity (for example, with a regular group between two irregular emissions), the idea of plurality, and perhaps some mathematical operations. I would still have to find an abstract formula for them, namely that I shouldn't have to indicate every time that *this* is a unity, *here* is a relation. But let's grant that I find a kind of language for mathematical notions. What do I communicate with them? As some mathematician says, mathematics is the only science that does not know what it refers to. We should however communicate something: that there are trees on Terra, that there is hydrogen in the cosmos, or that everything can be reduced to electromagnetic fields. How do I get to this point?

I only need a few days to realize that I cannot obtain "cosmic days." There is no place for any excuse: that I don't have the means to experiment by communicating with my neighbor, that I don't have books, that, after all, everything depends on the answer of the other from cosmos. There is no space for "let me explain." I am worthless. I have nothing to say to humanity and, after all, I do not deserve to be free. Yes, I don't deserve my freedom. I feel that, if I *had known* how to solve the problem, the gates of prison would have opened; even if it had not been about the commitment, or the service done to humanity, etc., etc., the gates would still have opened. When somebody has some essential thing to say, the walls do not resist.

It's true, though, that there may have been some people who had some essential thing to say in Auschwitz or in the Soviet camps, and the walls did not fall, or they fell on them. But *now,* they would have fallen aside. Or let me say it this way: it is not always true that a human who knows or can do some essential thing comes necessarily to light, but the one who does not know or cannot do some essential thing deserves to stay in darkness. I deserve it. They* can go ahead and condemn me for ridiculous reasons, as they want to do, for having declared that socialism is for the rich, not for the poor, for example. They are right. They judge badly but condemn well.

I have filled almost half of the sheets of paper, and I should ask to have my pencil sharpened. But I am not asking it. I remember a dear boy, who once told me how he received a passing grade at the exam in mathematics, although he was not good at

---

*   The Communists.

it. He tried to solve the problem in all possible ways; he filled four sheets of a notebook, and at the end he wrote, "I do not know how to solve the problem." The teacher gave him a passing grade because he was honest. I have to do the same thing.

The next morning I push the button to be called to report. At my third signal, the door is open, and the guard and the officer on duty come in.

"Get your luggage ready."

"But I want to report to Mr. Commander," I say.

"Let it go and get your luggage."

"But I have these papers," I insist; "it is a rather important problem."

The officer takes the sheets of paper that I hand to him, looks over them for a moment, and then shouts, "ah, it's about that story!" He tears up the papers, saying, "do it!"

I am suffocated by a wave of revolt: what if I had written something valuable? And why did they give me this chance to say something? But then I understand all of a sudden: they had been afraid that, in my exaltation, I could have fallen into a crisis, into folly. That was all.

VII

They shoved me in a jeep with curtains. While they take me to I do not know what destination, I think of the whole human sadness that is comprised in "I do not know how to solve the problem," which you must utter not before a professor, but before life itself. We do not know how to solve even the small problems — they take care of themselves, after all — and we have no clue how to solve the equation of our lives. How uninteresting are we, psychologically, intellectually, and morally, each one of us...

To me, it seems incomprehensible how people gave so much importance to the inscription on the temple in Delphi, "know thyself." To know myself. Who? I, Hans Castorp?* Not to say Thersites, that wretch from the *Iliad*? Or I, Smerdyakov, that villain from *The Brothers Karamazov*? But anyone, on any human level, senses how limited and uninteresting he is as object of knowledge. It is interesting to know nature, it is interesting to know the good God or the Great All, as the Indians say, to know people in their variety and how anyone bears an infinity within themselves, but to know yourself? Taken at face value, this incentive represents one of the great stupid sayings of humanity — there are others as well —, and it is difficult to accept that it was uttered fully by the Greeks. This saying could seem of great value only to the moderns, with their interest for the human subject and person. For the ancients, it is surprising to see the importance (perhaps an importance of argumentation) that Plato gives to it, and, if we are to give it full meaning, we

---

*   Character from Thomas Mann's *The Magic Mountain*.

can only give the Socratic understanding: search yourself so that you see that you know absolutely nothing.

The interpretations that attempt to save this saying do not go that far, though, and the way in which they attempt to give a meaning to it provoke pity. The majority of the commentators say that by "know thyself" man is encouraged to see his limits before god, and, practically, the same thing would be said by the second inscription, "nothing too much." Others who are less sophisticated say that it is about a warning for common man, who must acknowledge his subordination to the others: "shoemaker, stick to your job." But there are really exquisitely sophisticated people, who claim, no more, no less, that, given that man's soul has several incarnations, according to ancient traditions, knowing yourself would be the encouragement to "remember" the successive reincarnations. This is where people have arrived in despair! Can someone know one's "previous lives"? And, granting that one may, would it be that fascinating to know that I was a shoemaker, then a not so courageous soldier, and then a wine merchant?...

If I remember correctly, a crazy Englishman was the only one who said something meaningful regarding this problem. He began noticing that there were several inscriptions on the frontispiece of Delphi; among them, there was this mysterious letter E, which certainly had a deeper, perhaps religious, meaning. Then, there was the inscription, "surety, then ruin." However, it is curious that all ancient and modern interpreters speak gravely about the first two inscriptions, without mentioning the third. This is the one that gives the key for interpretation! It shows the main clientele of the oracle: the world of Greek merchants, entrepreneurs, and businessmen.

Of course, from time to time, during more special historical times, states or potentates from Asia Minor, Africa, Sicily came to consult the oracle. The regular income, though, for the one and a half million years of the temple's existence, could only be provided by the inexhaustible requests of common people who needed an advice or solution. The inscriptions could only be for those people. "Know thyself" has no meaning for a state or for a colonizing expedition, but it has complete meaning for a ship owner or a merchant, who must know how far he can go. "Nothing too much," so do not get into too great adventures; and especially be careful and don't give surety to others, because you risk getting hurt. This is the extent to which a "great" saying of humanity is reduced if you consider not its possible meaning, but its object, so yourself…

The jeep had stopped for some time now, and the driver had come out of it; the officer who was staying next to me was about to get out as well. He was probably the one leading me to the next destination.

"Don't you dare come out of the car," he says. "Take a cigarette."

"I would prefer the newspaper you were just reading," I dare. "Forget about it!" he replies.

How ridiculous they* are! They are afraid that we may find out what happens in the world. But we do not need newspapers to realize that there is a calming of politics in the world and that, as long as they have it better, we, the detainees, have it better too. It is certain that, at this hour, some generous people from all over the world intervene for the freedom of those who are in our situation in all communist countries. I imagine that they invoke the UN Charter and Human Rights, even if some of us, the victims, pretend like me (how sincere is it?) that they do *not* have a right to freedom. Humanity gives credit to the individual. In every individual, it sees a human chance, and it may hope precisely from us, the victims of the times, to get a deeper human reaction.

However, in reality it is not us, the ones imprisoned, who are interesting today, as human specimens; it is not us who give that "knowledge of man at a limit," by which a human being has always been defined. We are only the last wave — let us hope that

---

* They, the Communists. As before, I left this general "they" unspecified because it was so prevalently used in Communism. For a short discussion of this, see my essay, "Birth-Givers of Beauty: An Excursion into Finding One's Given Place within a Constellation," in Aspazia Otel Petrescu, *With Christ in Prison* (Citrus Heights: Reflection Publishing, 2014), 5–18.

it is indeed the last — of an evil that came in the first half of the century. But there is something more interesting that takes place with the human person in the world: according to what even we, in our prisons, find out, a first wave of humanity is confronted with "wellbeing" on a large scale, without historical precedent, in the developed countries of Europe and America. There have been some encounters with material wellbeing in history for some groups, casts, or clans, but wellbeing maintained something perverted and perverting, especially since it was not about goods of civilization (radio, museums, etc.), but rather about delectation and gorging.* Now, for the first time, wellbeing has become something common and educational, at least in one part of the world and for one historical moment. It may be a form of health for humans. What will it produce? In any case, it could be a deciding exam for the European man, who has believed so earnestly in materialistic values.

All of a sudden, *half* of the communist ideal is degrading if the full satisfaction of material needs does not bring about happiness to man by itself. And the *entire* capitalist ideal is degrading. The fact that capitalism succeeded to arrive first at this point, and not communism, is less relevant. Today, something takes place *beyond* them: it is the exam that the materialist ideal of the European man must take and, together with his ideal, man himself.

The European man has eliminated everything. "Leave me alone, you god, you philosophical doctrines, you church or traditions. I know better what I need." Beginning with the 18th century and until today, *the individual* has gained rights that he had never possessed in history. The totalitarian regimes that survive are ashamed by the audacity that they have taken, for a moment, toward the individual, not only oppressing him directly, but also transforming him into an object, as they had wanted. For the last two hundred years, all revolutions, and especially all materialist transformations, no longer serve narrow and privileged

---

* Both terms have a Biblical overtone, reminding one of Dante's *Inferno*.

casts, but the individual in general. The brother Γ has won; even if it is menaced, from time to time, by some WE — some true collectivism, going even to Teilhard de Chardin's odd idea that we might arrive to the association of consciences in some superior brain — the brother I still is, for the moment, the great beneficiary. The individual has succeeded in being and continues to be (until the encounter with the Asians, who are completely lacking individualism) that for which everything is done. For — as Goethe says — what is the good of all this squandering of suns and planets (of historical revolutions and technic-scientific revolutions, we will say), if, after all, a human being is not happy?

So, after all, humans do not feel happy, according to the news we receive even here, in prison. Pray for the satiated modern man… He has, in his consumer society, something of the psychology of a socialite woman: "I don't like this champagne; do something to entertain me…"

I do not know if we, those who are deprived of the most elementary joys, could have a better encounter with joy. But we experience here something that other people, in their plentiful society, do not realize: it is the *first* encounter of humanity with a more generally spread wellbeing, and it may be that a second one will not exist too soon! In principle, an "era of respites" should follow; but it is not at all sure, in fact, that today's idyllic moment in both Europe and the Unites States will continue.

A terrible exam for the individual is then played — the individual as it is conceived and respected by Europeans, as opposed to Indians and Chinese. It is an exam for the universe of the individual ego, so for the small idiot that each one of us is. This restricted individual — for whom the encouragement from Delphi to know oneself had a shadow of meaning, if anything — has won the game. The small idiot is driving his car and leaves behind the boredom of the workdays to go to the boredom of the weekend. Pray for him.

And we, those people thirsty for all the goods of the earth, from our daily cigarette to the freedom to take a walk without a

---

*   "I" in the sense of the *ego*.

sentinel, we shout to that humanity that lives so idyllically: "Pay attention to what you do, for *you* are responsible, with your joy or disgust, for the European man and for humankind."

When our jeep finally stops and I am ordered to come out of the car, I address humanity in my mind once again: "Pay attention," and I make my first step, concerned.

"Pay attention, idiot," the guard tells me, seeing that I stumble and fall. "We don't need broken heads here!"

As fast as I can, I gather my things from the small suitcase that was opened, and I get a foot in my back, with the order, "to the wall, and wait there for me to take you!"

I go toward the wall, somehow ashamed by everything that happens to me, to a large extent because of me. The oracle was right: know thyself!

UIII

The guards no longer give me glasses, so I see the fort well.* There are so many lives that drag along in its belly. This time, I will be with more people in the cell. But will I find someone who would be as dear to me as Alec? I carry with me, as in an envelope, the third exercise that I learned from him. I will begin doing it one day, in his memory. Who knows, I may even meet him again...

In the high basement to which I am taken, I see all of a sudden that there is *no* Alec. Twenty-five or thirty heads raise up from their wooden bunk beds, on three lines, to see the newcomer. It is late in the evening. A voice tells me, "Come up here, I know you." Then, toward the others, "We now have another one who can deliver lectures." I climb to the third bed, where my friend is, a doctor who had met me on the occasion of a conference I had once delivered. When I begin to take off my clothes, I realize that it is cold: there is only one window, at the level of the ground, but it is big, and it is largely open even though it is cold outside.

"Don't you close it during the night?" I ask timidly.

"We spent the whole evening discussing whether we should close it or not. But a swallow came in, there it is (I see it on the glass cover of the light that is above the entry door, as if it were looking for a place to make a nest), and then nobody said anything else."

---

* Noica is taken to Fort 13, the Jilava Prison. It is one of the most famous political prisons because it was built underground. The darkness and the humidity of the environment added to the lugubrious aspect of the prison.

I am no longer cold either. I place my clothes at my feet, and I begin to talk to the doctor, whispering. He is not yet 40 years old, and he did not get to profess medicine because they* found out, some years earlier, during his college, that he had vaguely participated in a beginning of a "counter-revolutionary" movement. He became embittered during the years he has spent here. Communism? For him, the only thing of interest is what happens in Russia, and nothing takes place there. Today's world? A biological failure. The sudden growth of the youth's size is morbid; the defense of free eros is a sign of the degeneration of the species; the malady ascends to the nervous system, and there is no more healing there.

The following day, I witness the household activity of the cell. (Any newcomer is given one day to adapt.) Then, the "lessons" begin. People study anything, with passion: elementary anatomy, physics, history, theology, and especially languages. What strikes me is the need for accuracy of those in our situation. People who still did not know to connect two words in English knew perfectly not only the 11 nouns that form the plural differently, but also almost the entire list of English irregular verbs. It was not surprising that people knew exactly the seven wonders of Antiquity. But the people here learned scrupulously the list with the Roman emperors by heart, or the names and residency of the main families of the Renaissance, as well as the succession of the Greek and Latin Fathers of the Church. Someone has produced sensation in the cell when he recited the Chinese dynasties.

This need for exactness, not only for them, but also for the mentality of modern man, seemed so significant to me that, when the hour for conferences came and I was asked, as a newcomer, to also say something, I could not help but talk about Exactness and Truth in the contemporary world, a theme that has obsessed me for a long time. ("I'm glad Alec does not hear me," I thought.)

---

* The same impersonal "they" that has already been used.

"Just as it happens to us here, in prison, it also happens to the contemporary world. Everything has been undermined around us: here, we no longer know anything of family, we have no profession or activity, we don't even have an identity, except an elementary one, the one of our weakened body and of our ultimate moral nature, as much as it can hold. Some of us do not even know whether we were right in what we did, if we defended good causes and if we are here innocent or still with a touch of guilt. In this chaos in which we are all thrown, we want certainty, any certainty. Just like a man who grabs a pillar to avoid losing his balance, we are also looking for pillars, certitudes, and they are the exact pieces of knowledge. We want to know something that *is* and that does not change, something that does not depend on the whims of people or of masters, something as the grammar which even poor Stalin recognized as unquestionable toward the end of his life. The list of the Roman emperors is graved in stone. We and our lives are, though — at least for the moment — simple names written on sand.

"But this is how the world today feels everywhere. And the world is in prison. It no longer has heavens and relatives in heavens, it no longer has nature and divinities of nature around it, but it is alone, in a cosmic captivity, attempting to evade from Terra or at least to communicate with a neighbor in the cosmos, whom it cannot find. It has given up myths a long time ago, be they religious, philosophical, or uncontrolled dogmas of tradition. Instead, it has so many small local truths that it feels as chaos. And so it wants *exactness*.

"It wasn't always like this. Up to a certain moment in the past, cultures were only of Truth, not of exactness also. They placed man in a state of drunkenness, in a sacred ecstasy. Not only the mythic and religious cults were this way, but also the profane orientations. Pythagorianism is a form of sacred delirium; the pre-Socratic thinkers are as in a trance when they say that all things are water, all are air, or all are fire; and Plato requires enthusiasm for Ideas, which you recover *now* because "you have contemplated them in another existence." Everything is ecstatic under the magic of truth — until Aristotle, who is the first thinker who is awake, sober, oriented toward exactness, in the European culture. (Other cultures continue to be under the sacred drunkenness even today).

"Just like us, Aristotle no longer gets drunk with 'truths,' and he would feel at home in our world. He would like to see that, finally, the world wants exactness everywhere, just as he wanted it. More than half of his work is a collection of data from zoology and botany of this sort, 'the cicadas sing by the friction of a thin membrane that insects with a longer life have in the dent below the diaphragm.'* The same Aristotle was composing a list with the tens of constitutions from the world of Greek cities, and even — this is a peak of the spirit of exactness — the list of the winners in Olympics. Do you realize what this was? There had been centuries of Olympic games, and he wanted to record the thousands of names of winners, as simple as that.

"It is not surprising that so much exactness — beginning, of course, with the list of the ten Aristotelian categories, with the list of syllogistic rules, and the list of virtues — filled the eras. But it is also not surprising that Christianity, as any religion, attempted to bring back the sacred ecstasy and, to do so, it even adopted Aristotelian exactitudes to transform them into Truth. The result was what we all know in the Middle Ages. Man really woke up, or he was detoxified so radically by the Enlightenment that he did no longer bear any alcohol or elixir of truth. Then, the methods of exactness came into play, which the ancients did not have: the empirical sciences and mathematics. The ecstasies were done for.

"But the spirit of exactness was not content. Mathematics is the most exact thing we have on earth, and it is as solid as the pyramids, about which people say that they would last until the end of Terra. Now, imagine that someone would consider *consolidating* the pyramids. Well, if we exaggerate a little, this is what happened in our culture: thinkers questioned how to make

---

* To my knowledge, Aristotle does not say this. Noica's point is to illustrate this philosopher's kind of discourse. Using his terminology, I would say that the statement about Aristotle is true, although it is not exact.

exactness more exact, how to ensure something that is certain, so in this case how to substantiate mathematics. This is what so-called 'mathematical logic' attempted. It is true that it stumbled upon some paradoxes, but the spirit of exactness did not give up and it cannot give up.

"In fact, the spirit of exactness is active everywhere, not only in the exact sciences. History, for example, can no longer be done without exactness. Man cannot bear to not know exactly what and how it happened. A French historian from last century, Ernest Renan, wanted to see exactly were and how Jesus Christ lived. He went to the holy places and proceeded scientifically to the reconstitution of the Event.* You know what happened to him? He found the traces of Jesus from Nazareth, but he no longer found the traces of Jesus Christ.

"If this is how things are in culture, it could not be otherwise in life and in lived history. There is no more space for utopias, modern man said to himself, with the risk of finding them just as the logician found paradoxes. We have nothing to do with utopic socialism; we need a scientific socialism. This is where we are, in a culture of exactitude.

"But I should not continue to speak about this version of the spirit of exactness. All of us, those who live under communism, know what planning means, how controlled everyone's life is, the level of "exactness" all processes have, including elections or meetings, and how precisely the destinies of our children are programmed or want to be programmed by the 'engineers of souls,' as Stalin said. Toward what? Nobody knows it any longer, because this belongs to Truth — or to myth. For the moment, we need exactness in experienced history, just as we can no longer afford to lack it in the science of history and in all sciences. Even these latter disciplines do not know where they send us. A great physicist of our time said, 'We now know that we do not know where science leads us.'

"However, scientists must go forward. We cannot continue without exactness, but empty exactness is blind. We have seen

---

*   Capitalized in the original.

genuine communists cry: after the terror and the sacrifices that were imposed to one generation, and now to a second one, the result is bitter. We know that Ernest Renan cried, in his own way, at the end of his life: in his autobiography, he confessed that *ces petites sciences conjecturales,*[*] the historical sciences, did not take him anywhere. The experts know that the logician Frege also cried, at the end of his labors, when a younger logician, Bertrand Russell, showed him that his entire construction was flawed due to a paradox. Modern man proved to be extraordinary, with his spirit of exactness. However, in a way, he cries, and you must pray for him.

"It is true that, instead of admiring and deploring, at the same time, modern man, who replaced truth with exactness, we could consider the English solution. The English know what they are doing: they gave up exactness for the machine (which was invented by them also) and for the natural sciences, and they maintained for life and politics the 'seeing and doing' attitude, so the approximation. London, with its crooked streets, was projected by a 'drunken architect,' the English themselves say… But not all have the virtue to behave in a disciplined fashion in the middle of disorder. This is why English values survive, while the others were ruined by exactness.

"One cannot live without values and without an idea of truth. But people nowadays no longer want to get drunk. Or, if you want, they are also drunk: with lucidity. Let us pray for them."

"For the communists as well?" a voice asks.

I am unsettled, all of a sudden. They do not want to *forget* either. I had thought that Alec was not there, but he appears before me all of a sudden, in twenty-five or thirty human specimens.

---

[*] "These small conjectural sciences," in French in the original.

IX

Starting the second day, my roommates give me the task to pour the water for washing, because they see I am not strong enough to carry the buckets or do other tasks. From the beginning, I am surprised to see how differently each man washes his hands or face, and I only needed a few days to recognize, just by looking at their hands, *who* was the one who washed himself, and even his character. One can "guess" by the washing of the hands.

When work is done, some people in the room begin to corner me with questions regarding what I said the previous day. "What is truth if not exactness?" "How can you say that being locked up and being free is the same thing?" (I had no intention to say this!) Only the doctor with whom I share a bed seems to be content with what I said. "It's bad for everybody, so it's good, all in order." Other than him, I receive the approval of a young man without studies, on whose face you can see the wisdom of peasants. He declares that he does not understand too well what I said, but he feels that this is how things are.

I am saved from the duty of giving explanations only because it is "search" day. We are all taken out, in the corridor, and we are made to stay in a line, our faces to the wall, while our beds and belongings are checked. This scene, with the face to the wall, in the corridor, reminds me of something from a book. It's just impossible to remember which one exactly; only after a quarter of hour, when we are back in the cell, I remember the book, and I smile.

"Why do you laugh, you there?" one of the guards asks me. He had remained by the door, to see how we put our beds and luggage back together.

"I don't laugh, I smile," I say, stupidly.

"But you laughed."

"I only smiled."

"You laughed!," he thunders and wins the game, since I realize how absurd my resistance is on such a topic.

He starts again:

"Why did you laugh?"

I think I should avoid the risk of involving a colleague in this lamentable situation, and I say the truth.

"I remembered a similar scene from a book."

"Which book?"

"*Darkness at Noon* by Arthur Koestler."*

"By whom?"

I repeat the name, which of course does not tell him anything.

"And what was in this book?"

I swallow and I sense that I cannot go back, nor invent something.

"It was a scene like the one before, with prisoners who had to face the wall, in the corridor."

"So? What's to laugh about this?"

"Nothing, just that the scene ends differently in the book."

"How?"

This idiot bores me with his insistence. Let me tell him the truth and be done with it.

"In the book, the prisoners get a pistol in the back of their necks."

The whole room froze. For a moment, the guard seems to be paralyzed as well. Then he lets out a howl: "Instigator!" and he jumps on me, pulling me by the coat until he gets it off me. Then he grabs me by the neck, yelling: "To the isolation with you!"

The "isolation" is a dark cell, which has some sort of table or stone bed and a hole for a wc. When you are in isolation, one day you do not get food, but only a bowl with warm water at noon, and one day you get half of the portion. As I am only in

---

* Noica mentions the title as it was translated into French: *The Zero and the Infinite.*

my shirt, I begin to do some exercises, to warm up. After half an hour, somebody else is thrown in, also in a shirt only.

"Now you can laugh together," the guard says and locks us up.

I look at my suffering companion, and I see that he smiles indeed.

"It happens," he says friendly.

"Why did they punish you?" I whisper.

"They found a pearl button during the search."

"And?"

"You don't know? With a pearl button on a string, you can produce a spark, and then you can light a cigarette or the fire in the stove, if it is quenched."

He is already an expert, and he teaches me to sit on the stone bed, back to back, to warm up. He begins to tell me:

"I've been here for two years, and I still have three reasons for joy. We had meetings at my job — I was an economist — and we were getting bored, of course. We could not laugh even at the jokes told by the speaker coming from human resources — as you know, they had received the order to sprinkle the sandwiches* they read with a joke. So I taught 2–3 colleagues to laugh heavily three times: ha-ha-ha, at every joke. Our laughter caught on, and the whole room adopted it. For a while, it was all good, but in the third or the fourth meeting, the *politruk*† took notice. He investigated the case and ended up getting to me, since I was known as someone who enjoyed making jokes. Realizing that they wanted to arrest me, I ran away from home. I didn't want to hide at a friend's place because I did not want to get him into trouble, so I traveled by train all over the country for a couple of years. I got used to no longer pay for a ticket, and I felt at home in the train. Then I got bored, so I turned myself in. I was condemned as instigator and enemy of the popular order.

---

*   In the context, the term "sandwiches" refers to speeches.
†   The person responsible with political education. Every institution had such a person with this role.

"In reality, I don't only like to laugh, but I am also interested in the problem of laughter. I had begun to look into it even before prison. It's quite something, laughter in humans. Reading and meditating about laughter, I noticed an aspect that we don't always consider: man laughs especially, if not exclusively, about man. Laughter is social. But it is also something extremely personal, and I was particularly interested in this line, so that I could understand people. How does each laugh? I had begun keeping a list: there is Homeric laughter, out of all your heart laughter, laughing out loud, laughing from the tip of your lips, ironical or sardonic, sour, bitter, or yellow laughter; laughing in his beard, and laughing at someone's beard,* hysterical, idiotic, or intelligent laughter, clear or stuffy laughter, and so many more that deserve to be catalogued."

"Of course," he continues, "just as it is interesting to see about what people laugh, it is also interesting to see *why*. One can even arrange historical eras on this theme. The medieval man, as well as the ancient man, laughed at things different from us. When I began studying the problem, I fell upon the case of the ancient sage Parmeniskos, who realized at a certain moment that he could no longer laugh. He then went to the oracle to get back his laughter, but he did not. Only upon his return, seeing a clumsy wooden statue of Apollo's great mother, he burst into laughter. I don't even mention the goddess Demeter who, after the kidnapping of her daughter, Persephone, to Hades, wandered and no longer laughed, until she saw Baubo, the wife of her host, raising up her dress. There must be something in these legends, just as it remains a problem why yellow people laugh less than white people. But I did not go too far with my investigation; after all, the question of what people and eras laugh at is a problem of the history of human culture and nature, and it is beyond me.

"I am only interested in *how* people laugh. And not how they laugh in general, but each in particular. Since I imitate others well, I was making people laugh imitating the laughter of hu-

---

*   The Romanian expression *a râde cuiva in barbă* is used for situations in which one fools you.

man types — the star, the idiot, the boss — or of colleagues and people of the day. Then I looked into how the main characters of books laugh, and I want to read again, when I am set free, Dickens or Balzac, to see how their heroes were laughing. This is how I got to the laughter of historical figures. I wondered how Napoleon or the Duke of Wellington laughed, or Henry VIII, or Philippo Nerri, that saint of whom people say he was joyful. I could imagine the laughter of Francis of Assisi, because it certainly was the natural laughter of the man pure at heart. But when I wondered how Jesus may have laughed, I stopped."

We were both silent for a while. There was something interesting in this easiness that ended in gravity. The man I was next to seemed to be a "free" man. In any case, he seemed to be detached from all things.

"How could you bear wandering on trains for so long?" I ask him.

"At the beginning it was wonderful. Just think about it, to have no roots, no fixed point, no home, job, nor any destination — such freedom! I felt that all people are just plants around me. I had saved a small sum of money, so I could leave in any direction, with the overcoat on one hand and the suitcase in another. Of course, I was choosing the trains with a long and cheap route. I was like a spirit flowing freely among the other travelers, who were heavy with matter, worries, and purpose, as they were. I noticed only then the full stupidity of the traveler, the stupidity of a boulder thrown into a running river. 'Is this the train that goes to...?' 'Haven't I missed the direction?' 'Where should I put my suitcase?' He doesn't know anything, he doesn't understand anything, and his only human reaction is fear. Then, the boulder gets lighter, and it begins to roll as well, but it remains a boulder.* I was talking to people, finding out what was happening in the world and, at times, interesting things about them, but, after all, I was defying them with my freedom. They wanted to and had to arrive some place. They had a dependency; they were

---

* In Romanian, there is the expression "being as stupid as a boulder," in the sense that a boulder does not move and does not have flexibility in thought.

Greeks.* How terrified they were when the train was late, which was a blessing for me! I felt as if I had a personal airplane. I truly believe that man will not travel happily unless he has a personal airplane, just like the birds, and not in cages, as now, on railways, roads, or airways previously given.

"However, I cannot hide the fact that I was *participating* in the life of these non-flying animals that lack any gratuity: human beings. When there was some serious delay, I was making comments, gathering info, and ending by protesting with a greater indignation than that of the others. I had all the interest to delay; still, at times, I also felt the need to arrive *precisely* nowhere. At the end of the line, I was coming off the train, looking for a room close to the train station, recovering, and then going back on the road. Money was getting scarce. After a year or so, I started to travel without paying, *pe blat,†* as one says."

"How do you travel *pe blat*?"

"There are two kinds of *blat*: one is arranged with the conductors, the other one at your own risk. If you want to risk it, without any arrangement, you can only do it on short distances. I had to prefer the arrangement. At the beginning of the trip, before departing, I was walking on the platform, carefully watching the conductors. Depending on their human type, I would decide whether I could try it or not. I used to travel in second class, which was filled with people. But sometimes, a conductor would let me sleep in first class for a small amount of money. He took tickets from those who were coming off the train and put one into my pocket. If there was an inspection, I could say that I fell asleep and forgot to get down at my stop. Others took my identity card with them, so that they could say to an inspector that they were about to write me a report. It was good when there were overcrowded trains, but this could not take place all the time. When we were many travelers, especially students, it was

---

* The ancient Greeks.
† I left here the Romanian expression, *pe blat*. When one travels *pe blat,* one does so without paying. Due to the explanation in the next paragraph, I considered that leaving the original may be more helpful.

calmer: the conductor let us know when the inspection came. If there was only one inspector, I could avoid it. It was harder when there was an inspection 'in pincers,' with two inspectors from each end of the train, who caught you in the middle. You would hear them ticketing, and you would run from one to the other. In despair, you would get up on the roof of the train car and get down further in the back. One time, someone caught me by the hand, when the train was about to leave. It was the inspector. Another time, I was next to a group of Soviet tourists. I pretended I was also a tourist, speaking with them in Russian as well as I could. They realized what I wanted, and they saved me. They told me that people were practicing this sport in their country as well, and they call the clandestine travelers 'rabbits.'

"And, indeed, this is the bad aspect, that you feel like a rabbit. You need to have great awareness, and you cannot join longer conversations with anyone, you cannot read a book, you cannot lose yourself in thoughts. Even independently of the risks associated with traveling *pe blat,* my life had become a rabbit life. What did I still have of the freedom I have assumed? I only had the run. That's all: I could run anywhere. After two years, I started to miss chairs, carpets, and people, other kinds of people than the spectral ones I was meeting in train. I was missing trees that would not move and grass. I gave myself in."

"I don't think you found many carpets here, in prison," I say.

"No," he answered (and I sensed he was doing it with a smile), "but I kept a magic carpet, the taste for flying. Even here, among people so heavy with so many troubles, I feel like a light being. I try to make people talk, dream. Haven't you sensed how much and how well one can dream here?"

In three days, we were separated.

"Look for me when you get out," he said. "My name is Ernest. Ask for Ernest at the City Hall, the Economic Services department; all know me."

"How do you know they would take you back?"

"I'm sure of it. They need people like me; I am happy and I make people laugh. *Their* world is so sad…"

X

Everyone in the cell receives me with affection when I return among them. They had pitied me for my naivety with Arthur Koestler's book, and now they had a bit more confidence in me. I surprise myself by asking the doctor what happened to the swallow. "It gave up making a nest here," he tells me. Too bad — it would have been a proof that it was not bad here either, I tell myself.

The doctor tells me that, having run out of speakers, he had to give a talk. He talked about the demographic explosion, and he succeeded to unite everyone against him.

"How so?" I ask.

"I spoke openly, without humanitarian prejudices. I showed that, most likely, two demographic explosions will take place, not only one, and that, if the first will be bearable for humanity, the second one will be unbearable on all counts."

"Which one is the second?" I ask.

"I will tell you in a moment. We all heard something of the first demographic explosion and, even here, every newcomer who is more informed tells us about the worries that the Westerners have. Even under the hypothesis of limiting births from now on, the increase in population will become problematic by the end of century. This is what I thought: if this sudden increase in population risks being an evil for humanity, let us remember its cause. Everybody knows it: the decrease of infant mortality. What is more logical, then, than to suspend medical care for newborns for two, three, or five years? And natural selection would kick in."

"But it is criminal," I say.

"This is what our colleagues said too."

"Let me remind you what a contemporary scientist said, showing that all progress of humanity was done *against* natural selection."

"I returned to this problem," the doctor resumes, "and I acknowledged that, after all, it is about billions of *young* people who will know, with their energy, to find solutions. But what do we do with the second demographic explosion, that of the old people?"

"What do you mean?"

"Look, until now, the population increased rather from the outside, by the appearance of new beings. Now it will grow from the inside as well, since the old beings no longer disappear. It is almost certain that man's life will be prolonged until 120–140 years old. But doubling the age means doubling the population. Unfortunately, life will be prolonged — for the moment, at least — as old age. I was telling our colleagues that this looks like the story from the antiquity with one of Priam's brothers, who had obtained from a goddess eternal life, but forgot to also ask for youth, and so he remained an old man into eternity. Let us ask ourselves: three billion young people can be supported by humanity, but can humanity support three other billions, especially billions of old people?

"You see, medicine, with its entire cortege of auxiliary or neighboring sciences, has triumphed. In a way, it has obtained its revenge against the ironies it suffered so many times (just as meteorology today) at the hands of a Molière, for example, or of those who could not forget that the ancestor of the surgeon was the barber. Now, medicine has triumphed; but hasn't it triumphed *too well,* tending to prolong life beyond its natural limits? Something must be done, then. After all, by a consensus in the interest of humanity, medicine might *not* apply its means to extend life. Not all progresses are immediately uncovered: it seems, for example, that there are one-person aircrafts, but the army keeps them secret; or artificial rain, and so many other things. But the physicians, just like the physicists, do not keep any secret. If they can extend life, they will do it. Something must be done, then, to prevent them from doing so.

"Someone asked me, 'Do you want to put old people up in the tree and then shake it?'

"This irritated me a little," the doctor continued, "so I said: 'No, we only have to make them get up in the tree by themselves. After all, the problem will become relevant only after 20 or 30 years, when we will also be old. What I say is this: we must understand that we will be overpopulated and that we will pollute our spiritual, political, and cultural life, our public taste, and our history. Until we also find the solution to prolong *active* life, old people, in their wisdom, will have to take some measures themselves. For a period of time, it would be good to find some noble justifications or who knows what ethical and religious significations for the right to suicide after a certain age. But this problem can be raised in a different way as well: for centuries, youth has been urged to be ready to give its life for one thing or other, for the "country" most of the times but also for much more debatable ideals or purposes. Wars have been waged with hecatombs of young people. Can't we ask for some "heroism" from the old people as well? In the meantime, as I heard that some Japanese do, they can do competitive sport, but en masse and mandatorily. This could speed up their infarcts.'

"All people in the room stopped me at this point," the doctor admits. "The theologian over there, who now speaks with that guy, who seems a bit agitated, told me, 'We don't need to become beasts if we stay in prison.' He was right, in a way, I grant it. But you tell me: don't we have to call things as they are?"

I look at him and try to see beyond this surface of cruelty.

"Do you know what I would do to you when they release you and would have to give you a job?* I would send you to a geriatric clinic. I am sure you would be fully devoted to all people."

"Perhaps, out of my scientific interest in the problem of old age," the doctor answers smiling.

---

* Under Communism, all people had to have a job. Officially, there was no unemployment. After graduating college, for example, students were assigned to different positions depending on grades, their party connections, and their propagandistic activities while in college.

"What is that, 'geriatric'?" asked the young guy from the country, Matei, who had listened to my speech on exactness and who had listened to our discussion.

He seemed to desire to learn as much as possible. I translate the word so that he could understand it. I even start talking to him, being glad to be able to relax a bit after the conversation with the doctor. Matei has not been embittered by prison. On the contrary, he tells me that, being imprisoned for the second time, he came back here with some joy: he was coming to the "University"! He had not found out about so many books, movies, sciences, and languages at any other place. Now, he was learning 4–5 languages at the same time, badly, of course, but he was learning them.

"Why don't you learn just one or two, but well?"

"I could not, because I am not schooled well enough. But I want to be able to communicate with anyone, just like those sailors who used to travel much. I like people and their variety. Maybe I'll get to travel the world. But you can travel even if you stay put, as a merchant, for example. I fully experienced the joy of commerce, and this is why I got here twice. I cannot work in the factory or in the office; I'd do anything to work in freedom. I left home to the city when I was 14; at the outskirts of the city, on a field, a group of young guys were forming two soccer teams that were playing for money. I joined one of them, I lost half of the money I had on me, and I ended up at one of my teammates' father, who had a shoemaking workshop.

"At the beginning, when I saw that a simple shoe is made of 24 pieces with 24 different names, I got scared. Then it became monotonous. I could no longer stand the sedentary life at the shop. I tried something more special: to go on my own, with a minimum of tools and fabrics, in search for clients, as the buyers of old clothes do. I purposely followed one of these people for a full day. I think he yelled 'buying old cloooooothes' a thousand times, but nobody called him to sell him anything. I suspect he was walking too fast, or he was just beating the air, having who knows what other purposes in mind. I began differently: I was walking slowly, starting conversations with some child or some woman standing by the gate, asking them if they have any shoes to repair, and so I was beginning to have some results. You must *invent* your clients, create a need for them: this is the art of trade. At times, I was invited to lunch. In any case, I was talking to all sorts of people while I was repairing their shoes. All went well until I fell upon a shoemaker's family and I asked if they have something to repair. I ended up at the police and then condemned for illegal practice and vagrancy. When I came out after a short detention, I was sent to the factory.

"In the factory," Matei continues his story, "I think I understood why today's world, everywhere, is not good. I would not have stayed there for a long time if my work in the factory had not given me the right to take some evening courses and thus learn something. But, after all, I did not regret the factory. I first learned one thing: in a factory, in any factory, you cannot work with joy. This is something serious, I thought, for today's world; it is like a heavy curse on a factory. Joy is, I don't know, a bit crooked, and in a factory everything is in straight lines. It's not just the shoe factories, where nobody works any longer on a full shoe, but only for one of the 24 parts; but, as I said, it's bad in any factory. Man starts the machine, and then the machine moves man. Well, if the machine is so great, I thought, why wouldn't it do the job by itself?"

"This is what happens today," I interrupt him. "We have arrived at automatized industries."

"I heard this, too. I even think that this is when the benefit as well as the wickedness of the machine will be revealed. First, it makes you work without joy (my shoemaker master was at times whistling when he hammered a nail; here, nobody sings); then, the machine breathes differently than man, who may take a rest, sigh, or have a chat. But there is something else, some kind of pollution, as they say today, but not only of the atmosphere or the surrounding world (it's their business how they take care of it), but a pollution of the souls. I have never seen more envy than in factories, among workers. They do this much, make that much money; everything is measured. Why would others make money freely, they say. They began with the merchants, they continued with the physicians, and ended with the waiters and the barbers. Why should they receive a tip? They, the workers in factories, remained persecuted by fate, and this is how they will remain as long as there are factories in the world."

"Don't worry," the doctor steps in, "the numbers of workers in factories will diminish more and more, just as the number of plowmen in the country. Someone who was passing through our room said that, in the United States, more than 50% of the workforce does *not* produce goods, but rather 'provides services,' so in schools, hospitals, banks, and stores. But I want to tell you that people are not pleased there either."

"Perhaps the spirit of the factory entered them," Matei replies.

I wonder: how could the communists throw into prison people so pure of heart? Why didn't they try to transform them into followers? Matei tells me that the prosecutor called him a class traitor at the trial. "What will you do when you get out?" I ask him. "I will continue to be a traitor, if they don't leave me alone. Nobody gives them any trouble anymore. Why do they fight everyone else?"*

I get up to move a little. While I walk between the bunk beds, I hear fragments of conversation between the theologian and the guy next to him, who had seemed a little agitated. After a few years of staying in the cell by myself or just with one other person, now, that I rediscover a group of people, I cannot avoid feeling attracted by the variety of human specimens: Ernest, the doctor, Matei, of course Alec... I walk a few times through the corridor of beds, but the theologian senses that something makes me slow down every time I pass by them, and I listen.

"Look," he tells me at one of these stops, "come here to meet a totally special man, engineer Goldstein. He discusses theology with me because he wants to become a Christian. Perhaps you

---

* After the Communists came to power, many people were fighting against them by forming armed groups in the mountains. By the time Noica is imprisoned, almost all of these resistance groups were annihilated. It's possible that Matei refers to this kind of resistance when he says that nobody troubles them anymore.

can help me to understand him, because I don't really understand what he wants with this."

The engineer offers me his hand; for a moment, he does not look into my eyes, as if ashamed, and then his warm look embraces me.

"How could he understand what I want," he says, "if I don't know well what I should say? I would become a Christian out of my love for the Jewish people."

The theologian looks at me as if saying, you figure out what this means. I sit down next to them and I listen…

How strange these meetings in prison are: you don't sit next to a man, but next to an entire life. But there is something upside-down in time and upside-down with regard to life itself, as in the vision of the Prophet from the Old Testament, where houses begin to take on life. At the beginning, here, in a room as this one, a skeleton sits next to a skeleton. The first skeleton says something: it thus gives itself a voice. The second skeleton turns its skull toward it: it gives itself sight. The first one invents a hand, the second one, another hand. One skeleton brings in the world a mother, the other a brother. At times, the two skeletons begin to quarrel, they get fists, muscles, and they invent the fight. Life seems to be rebuilt here, piece by piece. You shake one skeleton a bit, and you see coming out of it, like from a mechanical box, love, a job, two children, a gun forgotten in the attic, capital punishment transformed into hard work for life. You shake another one, and, like under a magic eye, there are other things coming out of it, great cities of the world, images from a dream, then the beginning of a counterrevolution, a fateful hunting dog, and a defiance before the communists. Flesh and life slowly get attached to these skeletons, as in a game of cubes,* bringing buttons, mouths, steps, or attitudes. At times, there are not enough cubes, and the skeleton remains with uncovered parts: without a nose, without a way of walking, without tics, or

---

*   Noica refers to a game with several cubes which had sides of different colors. Children used them to construct various figures, by placing them on top of each other.

without a life goal; other times, there are too many pieces, and so, after you finished remaking one real life, you must attached to it one, two, or three possible lives, with their deliriums and the fullness of their "non-living." A shadow, like the skeletons here, takes in its hand the entire history of the world and throws it as in a game.

Engineer Goldstein cannot come out of the fascination with the condition of being a Jew, and he feels *responsible* for the destiny of his people. It is the only people that has transformed its most catastrophic defeats in victories, but also the only one — he says — which transforms a victory into a defeat. For him, it is unbelievable how a people that gave the Universal to the world can withdraw so much in its particular. It gave all goods to the world, and it kept for itself what is most bitter. The engineer doesn't "understand" his own people, and this fascinates him. All nations have a stable space, a history, their own creations, joy, and fatigue. His nation has nothing of these. It gave to all, but it only has a book as great creation, the Old Testament, which has been confiscated by other people, to make marvelous works of art, history, and wisdom out of it, as his people did not know to do. It built a Temple, and it was immediately destroyed. It had no full joy, but it does not labor to want anything, to hope, or to fight — for what?

"It gave," engineer Goldstein continues, "the two great religions of this decisive half of 2,000 years of the world; it gave Christianity and, indirectly but by itself, Islam. Let us leave aside Islam, which seems to have adopted everything that was fanatical in Judaism. But what a splendid gift has it given to the world with Christianity, in which it did not want to see itself in the beginning, when it could place its seal on it — instead of the Greek Jews, like Paul, or the Greeks themselves later — nor later, when Christianity was accepted by Rome and the Jewish people could have priority, as chosen people, by accepting it. It did not want to be the *first* people of the world; this is unbelievable. Did it want to be the only one? The only saved one?

"Then something else appeared. After it gave the religious Universal to our humanity, it has prepared the secular Universal for 2,000 years. What is this Universal? Being in diaspora, but home everywhere; engaging in trade, and not in agriculture; using money, and not goods; making calculations, and not value judgments; being rational, and not emotional; doing mathematics, having abstract thought, wanting an open humanity, through reason and masonry, and not one closed by religious fanaticism; translating in all languages, interpreting anything, bringing nations closer, creating 'Internationals'; perceiving the machinist era as a humanistic school, and not as a defeat and sublimation of nature; being done with nature on all levels: economical, political, religious, artistic, or philosophical; saying, *Deus sive humanitas,* and not *Deus sive natura,* as the heretical Jew Spinoza!

"All these have been obtained in 2,000 years. In 1945, after the huge sacrifices suffered under the outburst of the beastly nature against the rational man, my Jews have again conquered primacy in the world, giving to the secular Universal its purest version: the fellowship of humans as rational beings. There is the version of Marxist International, given by the Jewish spirit as well; it could have taken it in its hand, enlightening it. But there is also the less annoying version for the rest of the world of a supra-historical rational community. I am not saying that the president of UN should have been a Jew every year; but its permanent secretary should have been a Jew. It cannot be otherwise, if the Jew is the 'binder' of the world and if he is the only one able to interpret this new Testament.

"And what did my nation do?," engineer Goldstein concludes. "It made a nation state, it revived a local religion and a local language; it wants to reinvent a local nature; even more, after it had obtained a type of human liberated from animality, with a brain closest to the electronic brain, now wants to reintegrate Judaic humanity in animality, vigor, force, and combative spirit.

"I do not know whether, in this way, the Jewish are maybe planning a *third* Universal for humanity, in 2,000 other years. But I return to the first Universal it has given to the world, and I ask to become Christian so that I could pray for the soul of my people…"

XI

This morning they gave us 125 grams of bread instead of 100 grams. All morning lessons prior to going out to the solar (a small court surrounded by tall fences) are suspended in order to discuss the event together. The 25 grams extra do not mean freedom, not even enough calories, but they are 25 grams *extra*. Together with some other extras, infinitesimal as well, the 25 grams weigh heavily and feed us well.

There's something enchanting about the good in these communist regimes: it comes slowly, in pieces, but irresistibly, when it comes (unfortunately, only to a certain level). Every day brings its own increase: a weaker shove from the guard, a few beans in the soup, a newspaper forgotten as if by mistake, a "what do you think, that I like it?" (Toward the end of my stay, an investigator would do something unbelievable: shaking hands with me.) All these things were accumulated, great pleasure after great pleasure. It's happiness in installments. It's true that the evil comes similarly in communism, in installments, and it is infernal. Every day begins with its privation and interdiction, but you also sense for months in advance that you will be arrested. You see how the rock rolls slowly toward you, and you look at it hypnotized. Everyone says that they would have preferred the evil to have come fully from the beginning, not in small portions, and they may be right. But they also want the good to come abruptly, and thus, in their lack of patience, they disregard the admirable chain reaction of the good. Such a restrained eruption is a real school of attention to small things; it is an initiation into life. What price does life have if you do not have access to its infinitesimal?

When we are taken for the walk, they do not take us in the usual solar, but in a larger court, with some grass. Grass! It is a beautiful day and, to our surprise, we are asked to take off our tunics and shirts. They have never allowed this in the solar. Our livid bodies are now an offense to the light. While we look at one another astonished, some officers with a lady show up. She is a doctor who checks our blood pressure. Somebody heard that they would ask us if we want to go to work. It is clear that they do not force us, and this gives us good hopes. Nevertheless, almost all of us would like to go. Matei is the only one who rejects the idea: "I prefer to stay at the University. Such work makes people stupid. There, *I* am smarter than my colleagues, and I do not like that."*

When it is my turn, I find out that my pressure is 9 over 6. The doctor shakes her head. I hear her telling an officer, "They should all be allowed to recover for one–two months."

These sad figures and beings that we are wanted to fight not a revolution, for this is dreamlike, but the regime brought by the largest army in the world at that time. They would continue to do it, but just like Don Quixote who, when he was standing before the portrait of St. George or St. Martin, felt that they *knew* what they had to conquer, but he did not know, just as we no longer know well. We only know one thing: that we do not like *this*. It's possible that the entire world, the communists included, may fight to change or at least correct the regime, just because it uglifies life and the world. The others regimes follow it in its steps. Some people here reproach the free world that it has not applied communism within its conditions. But its fault is more serious: it has no model to offer, but only some temptations. Everywhere the world is enchanted by ugliness today. Dulcinea, whom Sancho, exasperated, shows to Don Quixote under the face of a country girl encountered on the road, truly

---

* Communist political prisons were filled with intellectuals from all fields. There are other testimonies that refer to the prison as to a university, precisely because people could listen to various lectures given by others, as Noica mentions as well.

exists, but she is bewitched in ugliness. Only now, when the fight no longer has meaning, when the free world also revealed its ugliness, a counterrevolution in the name of freedom would have grandeur: you would fight for liberating the world everywhere from the spell of ugliness.

"I would like to tell you the story of *Don Quixote,*" I said after the meal in our cell, when I am asked to speak.

"Look," the theologian intervenes, "we are sick of books and movies."

"But this book is about *us,*" I insist.

"We are tired of us too, with our DonQuixotisms!"

The theologian is the one among us who truly fought against the regime. He has an extra certainty and authority in everything he says: "We would like to know what is to be done. We want practical solutions. We know well that Don Quixote has deep words — I remember the advice he gives to Sancho when he is named governor — but, if he were the one to govern during those three days, he would have been worse than Sancho. This is the problem: what do we do, not what we are and what we say. How can someone create a good state?"

How miraculously do man's resources get recovered! They just gave us 25 grams of bread extra, and these convinced fighters already consider that they may have the responsibilities of victors one day. A state? A good state?

I turn toward the theologian: "I know only one stupidity greater than the ideal state: the ideal army. If the state and the army are *ideal,* we are done for. There still are Germans today who tell themselves that it was something extraordinary that their army resisted before the entire world twice. So what? If an army is so good that it instills every ecstasy, then it becomes a curse. If a state functions too well as a state, it is a plague for an individual. But all utopias about a state want this. Humanity was lucky that nobody tried to accomplish Plato's *Republic*: the totalitarianisms of our century are nothing compared to it. Any time I hear somebody complaining that he does not get a passport, I tell him that, in Plato's state, a man cannot get out of the city until he is fifty, and even then only on a special mission. The good thing is that the state will disappear one day, as the communists say. Unfortunately, no one knows when."

"This is precisely why we must create *bearable* states in the meantime," the theologian responds. "There is something incomprehensible regarding our states: we have all seen people going to war joyously, but we haven't seen anyone going to pay taxes with joy. Why? After all, it's about the same thing, the city, the state."

I find the theologian's observation interesting. I attempt an explanation: "After all, in war you feel you are a super-citizen, while you are a simple citizen when you pay taxes. The state should create super-citizens during peace as well. Or I should say it this way: the state is forced to limit the individual, but it should liberate the 'person.'"

"These are just words," the theologian says. "It is as Nietzsche said, that the state must be a nursery for geniuses. Very beautiful, but how? Let's say something concrete, not just in general what should be done."

I feel cornered. In fact, I have an idea, but I was ashamed to ever share it with anyone else, because of its naivety. My utopia, however, has a merit: it does not involve a coup it is applicable everywhere, and it only requires a few checkbooks and an administrative disposition.

"I have imagined a way," I begin, "and I must tell you about it, regardless of how fanciful it may seem: 'the unlimited credit.' I imagine a state with unlimited credit, one in which, at the beginning, a few hundred citizens, then a few thousands, anyway, God knows how many, will have the right to a checkbook."

"What do you mean a checkbook?"

"A checkbook, like a rich person who can pay any sum anywhere; just that, in our case, the sum would *not* be limited, as it still is in the case of a billionaire."

"But this is crazy. How can you give to a citizen the possibility to spend more than a billionaire?"

"He will spend less than one or two salaries, but he will have the *unlimited* on his side and will shame the poor billionaire."

"Still, he does not dispose of the money like him, you say."

"He does not, because this man doesn't need much; it is sufficient for him to know that he *can* dispose of anything, so that he has no worries and takes care of his job."

"And what does society gain out of this?"

"This is where the problem comes: society begins to define itself, or to get some balance and backbone by those it credits. It begins to know what kind of people it wants to bring forward. Don't you find it curious that we elect Miss Austria or Miss Europe, but not the successful specimen of a society? We have beauty prototypes. Couldn't we have a prototype of human nature? Perhaps one of the works that risked unbalancing American society was the anarchy of the prototypes. To what should we aspire? What success should we obtain? From here, all those idols taken altogether from the ranks of heroes, of adventurers, of the 'kings' of shoe polish or of the newspaper sellers who became presidents of a country. But these idols could not be prototypes, because their success was limited and often strictly personal. The only open success there, which is at everyone's disposal, is that of money, and this is sad. In the old world, the prototype seemed to be given by aristocracy, but it also was limited and, in any case, it was lacking a truly human message. So, if a state has responsibilities beyond the administrative and national ones, it would have the one of producing and supporting chosen people."

"Pensions for merit or favors have been given at all times," someone says — everyone was listening to us already.

"But it is not about pensions, but *investments*; not payments, but credits. The selection should be done among young people, between thirty and thirty-five years old, so at an age when their human promise has been affirmed, but unaccomplished. At the beginning, we would choose 200–300 young people who would receive all freedoms together with the material means. We should less prefer young people with exceptional talents — artists, mathematicians, physicians, or poets, people who create their own place by themselves, through their singularity — and instead beings with *complete* human gifts, intellectual, moral, and practically creative. From any field, we would choose people who would have demonstrated up to that age that they want and they can give a creative meaning to their lives, with dignity. We would authorize them to choose their place, to change it whenever they think it is needed, to travel wherever they feel they should, to capitalize on their thoughts and raise their children as they wish. We would give them the checkbook and tell them, 'decide for yourself and do what you want.'"

From that moment, something extraordinary took place in the cell: my idea stopped belonging to me. I don't know how, but it was transformed into an object for play, for quarrel, for imagination, or for ecstasy of all. Perhaps under the effect of the extra bread or of the sun and of the hopes brought back to life, perhaps under the magic of the "unlimited" credit, people seemed taken by a hunger for this idea like I have not encountered before. They were all making and destroying projects. Something seemed good for my idea: I clearly sensed that *everyone* considered themselves targeted, wondering whether he would deserve or would have deserved a checkbook. This was, of course, the source of their positive or negative reactions.

"I would not accept a checkbook," someone says.

"You will accept it if they give it to you."

"I will not. I want to gain *my own* money."

"What is that, your money? This is the only way in which it would be yours, if you deserved to be credited because of the life you had until you were thirty years old."

"Being credited, so being a guinea pig? I want to be free, sir, I want to do what I like."

"But this is precisely what you are allowed to do with the unlimited credit, to finally do whatever you like."

"I would like to buy a yacht."

"You would *not* like to buy a yacht, but only to go around with it from time to time, which is perfectly honorable."

"No, I would like it to be my yacht, to equip it as I see fit, to stain it as I want."

"Possibly, but then you are not thirty years old yet."

"I'm already forty."

"No, I'm telling you, you are not thirty yet. You would not be thirty even if you said that you wanted a castle according to your taste or paintings by Rembrandt and Turner, which only you, and perhaps a few friends, would admire! Something has changed in the world. We know today that man's taste, his capacity to delight, and his reason are not limited to a class, and even less by one man; and we know even more, that you don't like your things *if* others don't like them as well."

"It's true," Matei intervenes, "I also found that, if the bride is not liked by others, then the groom does not like her either."

"Okay, but do you realize the anarchy that would result if some people would be allowed, even paid, to do what they like?"

The theologian, who after all had triggered the whole discussion, intervenes here: "I think that our friend, when he dreams a state that would tell a few hundreds people 'decide for yourself and do what you want,' recovers — without knowing or without wanting — St. Augustine's saying, 'love and do what you want.' This saying also seemed to be crazy; but we know its meaning, that precisely the one who truly loves no longer does 'what one wants, but only what one must, because any love is after all love of God. The people whom society would credit unlimitedly would have an unlimited responsibility.'"

"But how to choose? Even if there were only three hundred at the beginning, you must know their lives, their promise, to see if they are not badly married — because the wives or, respectively, the husbands of those with checkbooks, can destroy the whole game —, to appreciate if their human gifts truly are of interest to society, etc., etc. Who chooses them and how? By notes, just like the ball's queen?"

"Allow me to tell you how I think the beginning would be done," I try to intervene. But, to my joy, somebody takes it from there, for *my* opinions no longer matter.

"Let's suppose," he says, "that the choice of the first three hundred was done, regardless of how it was done. Among those, fifty, forty, or thirty were not chosen badly. You see, the *nucleus* for the development of the 'state with unlimited credit' would be established. From this point, we know who would credit others, who would make those who prove unworthy fall from the condition of credited people, who would control, discreetly but firmly, others, as they control themselves. Actually, public opinion would also have a role…"

"Thank you. Having a star on my chest and being controlled by anyone, whether I eat at a better restaurant, what I eat and what I drink, just because I do it on their account?"

"You don't need to have a star on your chest, because from *someplace,* from the inside, not from the outside, the sense of measure would appear."

"I would even enjoy checking annually the accounts of a 'credited person,'" someone, an accountant by trade, says.

"But then it is not really a privilege to be credited," the one with the yacht says. "If all people have with eyes on you, and then you also have the internal eye, what kind of a life is this?"

"It is a human life, or we are all worthless," the doctor, with his categorical judgment, decides. "If we are not able to handle the responsibility of being humans, under the request and with the support of society, then…"

"Then let us do like the existentialists," someone jumps, "complain about the human condition."

"No, then we deserve to commit mass suicide," the doctor decides.

"Well, well, all of these things are beautiful for the individual, or for the person, as you want to call him. But what changes do they bring to the state?"

"What do you mean what changes?," someone says. "They change everything. For a capitalist state, it is a terrible corrective, I would even say a whipping: think of how much people fret to gain what they need, and even more than they need, but never enough, according to them, leaving all the rest — honesty, humanity, culture, creativity — to be secondary or to 'come by itself,' while here this *rest* would be the primary and money would come by itself, without struggle and always as much as needed. It would be an even greater corrective for a communist state: here, where people are dispossessed by force, and so, regardless of the level to which their right to possess would be restored, this right would no longer interest them. Here, then, where man is directed in all ways, like a minor, it would be such a great blessing to give him *unlimited* credit not only at the financial level, but also at that of freedom and human dignity!"

"I consider even another aspect," a professor says. "Even if the credited ones would not be that great, their educative function would be extraordinary. Parents would raise their children having in mind the purpose of getting the checkbook, if the number of the credited ones is not limited; and I think that many young people, after the excesses of their early youth, would consider how to get qualified when they approach thirty. The society would have princely conditions to aspire to."

"But, after all, what would these princes do?"

"That's exactly what I like, that we do not clearly know *what* they would do," somebody else says. "We do not know what man can give under a request that would not be professionally narrow. The state usually closes people's lives, as if telling them, 'You will do this, *you* will be that.' Now, it would not only tolerate man's freedom, but it would also support it with its means. Man was free only at the level of the individual. Now he would be free at the level of society."

"In fact, it would be normal to choose the society's political leaders from among these elements that are credited by it..."

At this moment, when the game seemed to be won for the "state of unlimited credit," a subtle and gloomy thought comes to engineer Goldstein's mind.

"Thus, you build a state that would free people who, in their turn, think of a new state? I grant you that these people are good. But what guarantees that the state which they would create is not evil?"

A shiver goes through my body at the memory of the *tyranny of the good ones* in history. What do we know about man when he is inflamed by the fury of power? I would like to withdraw my project, but it is already too late. The theologian says, "Gentlemen, this state is in any case a good discussion theme. I propose to create committees to research every aspect it has: the mode of its constitution, its administrative problems, the function in economy and production that such free and mobile specimens would have, their educative role and their leadership, the limits of the unlimited credit, etc.… Don't you think that, not having something else, it is good to discuss it in an organized fashion?"

Engineer Goldstein comes close to me: "They did not allow you to narrate *Don Quixote,* but you still talked about Don Quixote."

XII

Engineer Goldstein is not right: I did not talk about Don Quixote; at the most, I have involuntarily injected Don Quixote into some of the people in the room. But if I think better about it, I did something else, something that seems more valuable to me: a success of the "secretariat" order. By "secretariat" I mean the organized self-affirmation through others, up to losing oneself *in* others. I have no other way to call this than "secretariat."

All virtues have something too personal within them: goodness, equity, courage, wisdom, or altruism usually involve someone else, but they define you. This is why any virtue is impure: it risks vanity. You remain a person, because *you* are the one who gives, just as you are the author of any deed in general. You do not become dissolved in the Great Everything. Here, though, with the secretariat — so by making others move — you get dissolved in the small everything that you have made possible.

In *Don Quixote* it was unfortunate that a team would never appear. The ideal, though, is the team, as an autonomous creation which would continue to give fruit *without* you. I name the capacity to create such a thing a virtue, because it comprises both offering and renunciation; I see it above the other virtues not only because it defeats, more than any other one, a person's pride, but also because it is open, like life. There is no longer a moral automatism in play: request — response (here's the poor, here's the alms). Here, there is something that is born, grows, and is able to not die if it is a good thing.

The secretariat... People attribute to Stalin an uncanny sense of humor, in a good and in a bad way. There have been three eras in the history of humanity, he apparently said: the matriarchate, the patriarchate, and the secretariat. It's true, after all, from the matriarchal agrarian economy to the society of managers, or su-per-technicians of tomorrow's world. But the perversion of this truth appears when the secretary becomes the leader, when he is *first* secretary:* king. In fact, "secretary" must be the one who hides, who gets "segregated," in the sense that he does not come out. Saying *first* secretary is a violation of language and spirit. General secretary, yes, but first? You would have to say *final,* secretary being precisely that diffused energy, that lack of identity of the center, that multiple One, already dreamed by the ancient thinkers and operating now in perfect modesty and submission. What will come out of the work that I have put in movement?, a good general secretary wonders. We live that splendid histori-cal hour of secretaries who, when they do not have the imper-tinence of being the first, represent the ferment and the cement of today's world.

Thus, in small, I realize I make something cooking here, in the cell, with my idea. I will have a few happy days, and, I would say, morally clean. *Others* will make my "state with unlimited credit." Then, may my thought be done and may it be lost in their will.† I remember Alec again: would I have caught him in this work? Through others, perhaps, I may have succeeded what I alone could not obtain from him: making him think at twenty-two years old that he may deserve the unlimited credit one day.

Out of joy, I decide to "bring" Alec among us, in this deliri-ous room, doing the third gymnastic movement, the one he had offered to me as gift at our parting. It is the right hour, immedi-ately after the morning wash.

I head toward the open window, I place my hand on my hips, and I raise my right knee. It does not reach my chest, as Alec wanted. I raise my left leg more firmly, and it touches my chest, but the violence of the movement seems to bring me an internal turbulence. I am overtaken by pain in my stomach, and I sense more and more clearly that something happened to my intes-

---

*   Noica alludes to the leader of the Communist party, whose position was called "first secretary." All local organizations had a first secretary as leader.

†   An allusion to the Lord's Prayer.

tines. I sit on the bed; I get up with difficulty when the guards change, and I sit back again, tensed.

"Something happened?" the theologian asks me. "Why didn't you ask to go to the doctor?"

I ask someone to signal. The guard comes to the peephole, and I say, "please take me to the doctor."

"Stupid, if you didn't ask at the guard change... Now stay and suffer until tomorrow!"

I stayed and I suffered indeed until the second day. "It's probably an intestinal occlusion," the doctor in the cell says, hearing what I feel.

I am worse and worse, and out of consideration for my suffering, my cellmates do not resume the debates about the state with unlimited credit, although it would have been the only thing that could have risen my spirits. The entire promise of secretarial happiness disappeared all of a sudden. Will they resume the discussion? Will they not?

When I am taken to the prison hospital the next day, I can barely walk. I realize that the surgeon who would operate on me is a fat guy. I do not know why, but I trust fat doctors. Perhaps I suspect that a fat surgeon makes fewer useless movements and operates with more certainty. He palpates my swollen stomach and says from the beginning: "intestinal volvulus."

"Volvulus," I think. Such a beautiful name! I remember the high school years: *Volvo–volvi–volutum–volvere*. "Volute" comes from there. How distinguished do physicians speak and what a delight to listen to two young physicians...

"Are you afraid?" the doctor asks me, seeing that I mutter something.

"I was thinking of 'volvulus,'" I say.

"Yes, it is quite serious. But how the hell did you do it?"

He lowers his head on my chest, as if he wanted to listen to my heart, but he asks me in a whisper, so the guard could not hear: "Did they beat you badly?"

"No," I say, "I did a more violent gymnastic move."

"That's what you needed, when your intestines were failing because of weakness," the doctor says.

"This is what Alec had taught me," I say as if for myself.

"Who is Alec, your wife?"

"No," I answer, "Alec is a man's name. He is a younger colleague who taught me to do this gymnastics movement."

"He was not too inspired," the surgeon says. "Well, let's see
what can be done."

On the surgery table I am given oxygen to inhale, and this
puts me in a good place all of a sudden. The lower half of the
body is anesthetized. In the white globe of the lamp under
which I am, I see an open abdomen, in which people work; but
this happens *there*. I feel better and better under the oxygen and,
in a sense, in the clear awareness of being detached from my
bodily being. In the meantime, the surgeon, who is assisted by
another doctor, says, "You see, it is twisted three times. If he
delayed a few more hours…"

Detached as I feel, I wonder about this obsession with *le
roi se meurt*?* Why this universally human lamentation, which
could be filled with meaning only by the extraordinary talent of
Ionesco: "we're dying, we're dying!"† All of us, standard people
made on a production line, feel as if we are a king, and the king
laments that he dies. Perhaps the disaster would be if the king
does *not* die. The disaster would not be for humanity only, as the
doctor from my cell was saying about the demographic explosion of old people, but for each one of us.

How come the king doesn't see that, starting with a certain
hour of his life, he has already died in entire regions of his being? It is not grave that we die physically every hour of our lives,
as it was said, but rather that we start dying spiritually at a certain moment, so that it would be unbearable for ourselves if we
did not have an end. If you are certain of your human talents,
content, you realize that your life becomes repetitive after a certain moment, as a broken mechanism, either in one space or

---

*   "The king dies," in French in the original. Noica refers to Ionesco's play *Le
Roi se meurt*, translated in English as *Exit the King*.

†   "We're dying" renders the Romanian expression *ne stingem*. Noica either
refers to a translation with which I am not familiar or he translates directly
from Ionesco's French.

another of your spiritual life. And what is death if not the fall into a repetitive inertia? The poor king in us finds it more unbearable that it repeats than that he is told, from the outside, "stop already!"

If you are Don Juan and make the *same* declaration of love, you are dead. You have the same way of brushing your teeth, of approaching people, of tackling new situations in the world; you give the same advice and you delight in the same sad joy. In some zones of my life, I realized I am no longer capable of novelty. One day, I will feel that I am making the same kind of secretariat and that, in this way, I have died at the same time with what I thought was best in my life.

Besides, "death" is not only the entering into repetition; it seems to me that it also is the retrieval of the same thresholds or limits. You try to understand something in some field of life. You give up because you feel you have reached a threshold. You return later, but you stop at *the same* threshold. There are people, for example, who cannot get over a threshold in learning a language or in the initiation into a science. Their intelligence and memory do not diminish, perhaps, in time, but they do not increase either. I started mathematics three times, but every time I stopped *there*. There is a "there" for each, so a border of his spiritual being, of his capacity of reception and, after all, of his human condition. As someone said, "scientists must die so that science can progress." Otherwise, they would keep it in place, with their authority and limits.

Well, if there are limits, there is death. You do not have the right to live beyond your own limits, which are forms of passivity also, not only forms of your affirmation. For, starting with a certain moment, you are receptive to a limited number of things only, and, regardless of how much you travel, you no longer "see" anything new. There is only one thing that would entitle us to still request the extension of our lives at that moment: poor curiosity. A friend of mine used to say, "You deserve to live so that you can read the newspaper every day." But is it still worth living?

Perhaps things will be different. By this techno-scientific revolution, we will have extra memory and something extra in our faculties for knowledge and assimilation. We will learn languages while sleeping, we will make more and more unexpected associations of ideas, we will register the most diverse sensations due to the machines that are adapted to our organism. *Perfect,* then we will have the right to live longer. But we do not have it now. I defy anyone *today* to produce headlines about a survival over eighty lawful years.

Oh, I know very well how interested Pascal would be to see today's world, the world of calculators, which he first imagined, and the world of moral reflections, illustrated still by him; I know how impassioned Archimedes would be by a book of elementary physics or Faraday and Maxwell by electronics. But I do not feel personally my inner boundlessness and I do not think that anyone senses it, after the precedent of Lord Rutherford, who gave the model of the atom, but who said that the atomic energy will never be released; or Einstein's example, who was also blocked somewhere in physics. As for today's philosophers, historians, or economists — they enter a terribly broken mechanism, a blind repetition starting at one moment in their lives!

I vaguely hear people talking. The surgeon who's operating on me explains to the other doctor: "I think he'll be fine. I had to cut only 12 cm of his intestine. Look, the problem now, when you sew the intestine back, is to make sure that the small veins from one side come in the prolongation of the small veins from the other side. You have to proceed so that the organism would not register that you have made a resection in it."

Isn't the entire civilization, I think, a way of *cheating* nature? "So that it would not register…" I wish I could sleep now, in full euphoria, under the oxygen I inhale, but the nurse does not allow me. Perhaps, in order to cheat nature effectively, you should not put it to sleep because later, when it wakes up, it gets upset because you hacked it. Maybe this is why people's victories today are approximate: they have truly narcotized nature and made it so that it "did not feel it," instead of touching its face with a finger from time to time, talking friendly to it, just like the nurse does with me, so that I don't fall asleep…

XIII

[This chapter was sent by its author five times out of the country — by mail, just like all the others — but it never reached its destination, and the manuscript that remained in the country was lost as well.*

The author remembers that he was describing here the two years that he spent alone in the cell, first because he was convalescent, after coming out of the prison's hospital, and second because he was too weak to participate in the work of "reeducation"† that was being conducted in prisons during those times, in view of the release of the political detainees which was requested and obtained, in principle, by U Thant, the secretary of the UN at the time.

In the beginning, the total solitude was a delight for the author. But what a curse it becomes when you realize that, by yourself, you cannot give your life a fuller content! Perhaps the spiritual techniques of the East know how to populate solitude — through the forests of India of even the prisons of Eastern Europe — but the author of these pages did not know them. He could not do much with the *Spiritual Exercises* of Ignatius of Loyola or Descartes' *Meditations,* which he had in mind. Then,

---

*   See explanation about this chapter in the Romanian Publisher's Note of this volume, p. 13.

†   The "reeducation" was one of the most terrible tortures that took place in Romanian prisons. Its purpose was to change the souls of human beings, to transform them into machines that follow the precepts of the communist regime. For more information, see Virgil Ierunca, *Fenomenul Pitesti* (Bucharest: Humanitas, 2011). Fr. George Calciu also speaks of it in his *Interviews, Talks, and Homilies* (Platina: St. Herman of Alaska Brotherhood, 2010).

with a few straws from the mattress on the concrete bed, which was ripped in a corner, he tried to do geometry, like Pascal when he was a child, or to recover some formula, that he only knew only a little, such as vector calculation, for example. He did not succeed much, again.

At that moment, man asks for forgiveness because he exists. "Lady," you say, "or Mother Nature, delete me from the civil list of those who exist and give forgiveness to the spermatozoid that made me possible, that it ran to take the place of another spermatozoid, which was destined to have a more worthy life than mine!"

In one of these moments, the guard opened the peephole and gave to the author of these pages the first volume from Marx's *Complete Works.* He would continue to give him the others too, volume by volume.]*

When I came out from the hospital, even if I was alone in the cell, it was clear that something had changed in the world and that the change was toward the good. I was given paper and pencil, in the beginning in order to write my biography. (Perhaps there was something else to find out!†) I hastened to write it, but I soon saw how empty our lives are. Even if many write their memories with pleasure and with a secret vanity, it is a terrible torture to remake your life in your mind, with its lost occasions and stupidities. How interesting is one's own life! Describing it, I suffered more than when I was beaten.

I remembered even with pleasure one of those beatings, which had been administered so that I tell "everything," just like now — but with different means, while I unfolded a dull life of an intellectual on two hundred large sheets. I had been laid on the floor with my face down, they had placed a piece of leather on the soft parts of my back, and a sturdy guy who held a thick whip with knots in his hands was giving me two strokes at a

---

* Addition by the Romanian editor.
† This phrase is, of course, ironical. Noica was already heavily under investigation.

time. I don't know how, the first one was more bearable, but the second one, which fell around the same place, was very difficult to bear. They had not given me more than eight or ten strokes, but my entire body seemed to revive and — I am almost ashamed to say it — when I returned to the cell I had a better digestion than ever.

The connection between the spirit and the body is strange. Any time I have a better idea, I experience happiness in my whole body, including the stomach. But now, when I was writing my biography, I had such indigestion! The only thing that I wrote with pleasure was the first half of the first page, somewhat provocative in a socialist regime, in which I described how I came into the world. "I was born as a protest: my mother waltzed for a night at a ball in order to lose me, but I was stubborn to come into the world. This is why, perhaps," I added, "I am so stubborn and sometimes impertinent." The rest of the autobiography was prose. I think this is one of the harshest punishments, to make people write their autobiographies — and this is, actually, what happened, in these parts of the world.

Going over my life, I realized then how vain European philosophy is, the only way I studied and in the spirit of which I was writing. It does not teach you anything, even if I still think that, without it, you cannot think anything in an articulated fashion in all cultures of the world, anything that would "belong" to the rational. (Goethe's saying makes sense for anyone: "I cannot do without philosophy, and I have nothing to do with it." Unfortunately for him, he became attached to philosophy after the death of his friend Schiller, and he was going to pay for this. European philosophy does not even teach you to meditate because it does not offer you any spiritual technique.)

With Descartes' *Meditations,* which I knew well, I saw that I had no use of them from the beginning. Then I thought of Ignatius of Loyola's *Spiritual Exercises,* trying, by vague memories, to do the exercises of organized imagination which he expects (seeing Christ concretely, with the sweat on his forehead, bearing his cross, etc.), but they could not take my anywhere either. They were probably good as meditation effort, just for the fixation of imagination (*le péché de distraction,** as the French Catholics say) and to avoid letting memory, which is so tyrannical and capricious, throw before you, in your conscience, all its horrors or, I would say, its dirt. There seems to be a devil in us which, when man is alone and not busy, comes to mock all our helplessness. One or other disgusting memory refuses to withdraw in the swamp of the unconscious and, the more you want to *not* think that specific thing, the more you make it resistant, just like today's bacteria with penicillin.

It may be that other European schools of wisdom have given more adequate spiritual techniques: Steinerism, Guénonism… But how poor did they prove to be! If I at least knew yoga. But what has always scared me in Indian thought — which gave the number zero to mathematics — is that it rather annuls than edifies. Well, an opinion, of course…

Here, in Europe, we know almost nothing of spiritual life. We will soon meet Asians, some great, some common, who know something about spirit (not only about intellect) and who, on top of it, can easily assume everything that we believe we have better than others: our mathematics, physics, and technology. Mathematics, what an anti-mystery! It is a religious mystery upside down. All cultures had their mysteries and their initiation, with symbols loaded with meaning and a good ambiguity. We are the only ones who discovered (or capitalized) the symbol emptied of meaning, the pure symbol, a mathematical sign. This play with figures and signs (later with structures) was a simple play at the beginning, as Pascal tells us, who, being invited by a mathematician of his time to meet in I don't know what city in France, replied in this way, "Sure, happily, but we should speak of serious things, not of mathematics."

Something happened afterwards — beyond or even before the application of mathematics to physics and technology — and this probably was the capture of the only mystery that could still operate in this profane world: the capture of *infinity*. Our mathematics were accredited and applied, beyond the Antique

---

*   "The sin of distraction," in French in the original.

geometrism, only because they domesticated the infinity (with the infinitesimal calculus), and then because they cheated with it (Cantor and set theory). The ecstasy of mathematics begins only with the taming of infinity. But, you see, it is an ecstasy that is handy to all, even to the tribal people who have rings through their lips.

Still, it's just a manner of speaking to say that mathematics is "handy to all." When you ask him to go more slowly in his demonstrations so that you can follow him, the mathematician does not understand that you need a certain *animality* in order to do mathematics well: a "bossa," as was said in phrenology, the so-called science of the spirit, or an extra-cranial protuberance, or who knows what wrinkling of the gray matter. You need something like the animality of the pianist or of the painter. The most "rational" thing of a culture requires the most irrational talent. (Woe to the people of Israel — as engineer Goldstein said — who sold this superior animality for the animality of first order. If things continue this way, I can imagine an hour when the Jews — at least those from Israel — no longer know the multiplication table well.*)

As for one like me, I can say that I will die with the sadness of not having been a mathematician. I am laboring now, in my solitude and with the rests of sheets of paper I still have after I finished and delivered my autobiography, to do a little mathematics by myself. Doesn't Plato say that divinity, once alone, only geometrizes? I try as well, as a small man, to discover, or at least rediscover (like the child Pascal), a little mathematics. I know, for example, the beginning of vector calculus. I take a few straws from the mattress, because the sheets of paper are done fast, and I cannot hope that I would receive more, even if I would soon be proven wrong, and I begin working. I get stuck on the first theorems. How could Descartes get analytical geom-

---

* Noica speaks here of how various cultures include a certain animality, the one of the artist. He believes that this animality is necessary for doing mathematics as well. His note about engineer Goldstein refers to what his cellmate said regarding Jewish culture on pages 81–83.

etry out of nothing (just as *dans un poêle,*[*] as he said himself, in a small room with a stove-oven, where he was quartered for the winter, like an… officer), from nothing, that is from playing with coordinate axes? I resume, because I know perfectly its beginning, but I stop again, even if I still have space to write a few recovered formulas on the margins of a few sheets of paper. I then move to the moderns' "topology." Maybe there's something to try with it. I know that topology is the "science of the rubber" (or it was so until it became an abstract discipline by excellence), so a science of figures which, while twisted in any fashion, still retain some constant relations. But even now something is constantly denied to me — like a greatly coveted beautiful woman. I perfectly know that, after you have "had" mathematics, they are no longer interesting ("Who knows what one plus one is knows everything that the human spirit can know in this regard," Descartes used to say), just like the poor women who are nothing else but beautiful. But what suffering to *not* be able to have them!

One day, as a blessing, I am given the first volume of the edition of Marx and Engels's complete works through the peephole. I gather that I would be given all of them, one after the other, if I want. I soar into lecture — reading, the only form of spiritual life of the European! — and, even if the translation is made from the Russian version, where the pages with the deep ideas from the *Economic and Philosophical Manuscripts* are missing, I am delighted. Do I really like Marx? Am I in the situation of kissing the hand that hits me? Or is it that inner poverty, my incapacity for doing geometry, meditating, and creating something out of nowhere, makes me experience even this reading as a blessing, as long as it is *printed* paper, so, for me, a European, about truth and life? For centuries, the printed book has said to the European man, "I am the Way, the Truth, and the Life"…

I feverishly read the first volume, and, from its beginning, I understand something that seems to be essential for the success of Marxism and for its lamentable ideological failure with those

---

[*]   "In a stove," in French in the original.

who are *forced* to learn it. This doctrine can only have sense for those without culture, to whom it gives a few slogans, in our case for the masses of workers in factories and only for them; or it has meaning for those who have stayed too long in culture. It's either something too elementary or something too refined. It does not stand at the middle level. But, after victory, the doctrine is taught precisely at this middle level, and this is why it is a catastrophe in consciences. Instead of allowing people to *end* in it, they begin with it, continue with it, and remain at it, being forced to pass exams and to learn laws (listen to this: laws in philosophy!). Or, at times, believing that they understand something, they explain the dialectical contradiction in the sense that one thing can be and not be: "Here, comrade, the hat is; if I hide it behind me, it is not." I tried to tell such a propagandist that, for the dialectical contradiction, he should rather use the saying of a French humorist, Allais, I think: "How sad it is to know that a glass half full is a glass half empty." He replied that this is a saying for drunks, which does not match the proletarian morality.

XIU

Objectively speaking, and without kissing the hand that hits me, there are bewildering things in Marx's work! I even regret now that this doctrine will disappear by itself in the era of automations, with the disappearance of the workers from factories and of the miners. It was valid only for them for a moment (so for an era); for the others, for the peasant, the clerk, the freelancer, the intellectual, and the merchant, it only represented something in the line of "resentment," as Max Scheler said, so in the line of irrepressible dissatisfaction of seeing someone else and entire classes better equipped than yourself for happiness and comfort.

There are pages where Marx shatters you. How troubling is his notion of "alienation" from the manuscripts of his youth — and I saw it later, because those pages were intentionally taken out from the edition I had received. Today everyone invokes them, but how many of us stand under their direct seduction and, after all, their ambiguity? He describes there the three or even four... no, a cascade of man's alienations, all of them being impressive in the light of living conditions of modern man.

In the phase that capitalism reached, he says, work produces not only goods, but also the worker as a good. The object produced by work opposes it as something foreign, as a force that is independent from the producer. As he produces more, he falls further under the dominion of his own product.

One is tempted to ask, to whom does this happen? Only to the worker or also to the one who gave him work, poor guy? If everything happens as in religion, where, as Marx says, the more man puts into God, the less he keeps for himself, then you could say that the exploited puts into play here only his work, while the exploiter puts his soul. You should probably deplore both, the slave and the master, as Hegel does; even more, since a "self-alienation in a product" takes place, as we are told, a worker could still shake away the deception if he started to run back into his poverty or wherever in the world. He could return to his dirt (if he is allowed to have it or if it has not been transformed into a golf course in the meantime). The other one has sold his soul completely, as it has been seen in so many cases, for example in so many rich families, where the father is not the only slave to his goods, but the son must also be modeled, rather mutilated, according to the requirements of possessions.

However, Marx has no mercy on the poor possessor. In the historical phase he was in, he had to denounce the exploitation and the alienation of the individual forced to work. Concerning him, Marx shows clearly that there are no less than four kinds of alienation, taking into consideration that the production activity is also at stake, not only the result of the production work. First, he says, the effort brought by the worker is something exterior to him, not having to do with his essence, and it represents the mortification brought about by forced work. Second, the type of work that industrial capitalism established is such that it does not allow any freedom to the worker, except the one for his animalistic functions, or eating, drinking, and procreating. On the other hand, and third, a common man is a universal being, a genus, who considers his entire nature to be his inorganic body; however, his work now alienated him from nature. Similarly, and this is the fourth point, it alienates him from the human genus. Thus, a worker, Marx says, is alienated: in relation to his nature and to his self, and then in relation to nature purely and simply, and finally in relation to other humans.

Perhaps we simplify things or we summarize them imperfectly, but how deep and open this investigation is! This is probably why it was not included from the beginning in this edition of the complete works, which I was given to read in translation. However, even in this version, you fall upon amazing things in the first volume. I would have never read — just as its own adherents don't — the article titled "Debates on the Law of Thefts of Wood." I find its psalmic beauty here, in prison. When the author says that you possess the tree, but you do not truly possess its dry branches, when he adds that the poor (who steal wood for winter from others' woods everywhere, not only in Germany) have a certain *kinship* with the dry branches, which gives them a genuine *right* over them, then what will you say that is to be found on this page? Is it something economical, as an impulse to revolt, or is it rather the religious poetry of the psalmist?

Of course, his polemical books, like *The Holy Family, The German Ideology,* or *The Poverty of Philosophy,* filled with heavy German irony, can no longer be appealing to anyone, if they ever were. There are, however, thoughts and entire pages that remain imprinted in your mind. Today, how true seems to be the affirmation found in the first work cited, that the class of owners and the proletarian class represent man's *same* alienation from the self; the former sees itself satisfied with alienation, while the latter is annihilated by it. In this thought, we almost have the pity for the possessors that I have mentioned. Similarly, from the same work, the idea that "all progress realized by the spirit has so far been to the detriment of humanity, which arrives at a situation that is more and more inhuman" is valid for those well established, but not for the multitudes, if it is about the progress realized by the European spirit in the line of well-being only.

I would not pass easily, as the official commentators do, over deeply significant thoughts, like the one (which, it is true, was deleted by the author) from *The German Ideology* in which he declares courageously, "We know only one science, *the science of history,* which comprises together the history of nature and that of humanity." Isn't this, after all, the novelty of Hegel and then of Marx, that they have placed everything within fluidity? Then, further in the work, if you are not satisfied with the cheap historical-materialist explanations, such as this, "the lack of sugar and of coffee (due to the blockade) raised the Germans against Napoleon," you are impressed, instead, by a few pages long thought to propose that the separation between the city and the village represents the greatest division of labor. He believes it can be overcome by the new system, and that this division exists only under the conditions of private property, which leads to the "urban animal" and to the "rural animal"! (But you wonder, hasn't the new doctrine actually increased the *urban* animality?) I would not just pass over all of these things — for the bad, but also for the good in Marx's intuitions — just as I would not easily go over the stunning, dark prophecy, so close to confirmation, "There will be a time when individuals (precisely the urban ones, *my note*) will take on themselves also this product of the species, *language.*" I don't know how, but, of all philosophers, only Marx, as much as he can be called a philosopher, has something of a prophet in him — and this is a novelty. Plato looks too much into eternity, and Hegel too much into past history, which he actually integrates admirably. Nobody has opened the door to the future. Instead, this one, regardless of how modest of a philosopher he is...

But the most surprising thing — leaving aside so many pages and places of first order, starting with the *Manifesto,* which has not been surpassed by any other — is that people easily ignore, almost with compassion and indulgence, the ten years of journalism at the *Tribune* in the United States. It's true that his articles are not directly edifying for the proposed ideology, but they are fascinating as cultural and historical *documents.* There is something so complete in them, between 1853 and 1863, as they were written weekly, as a report about the situation in Europe for the American reader. Also, there is something so tumultuous and alive in them that you could say that they are about the *Intimate Journal of Europe,* of a Europe that could spread its "imperialist" maneuvers over the body of other continents. Beginning with the Gladstones and the Russells of England, with Napoleon III or the Crimean War, passing on to the poverty and lethargy of India, to the Taiping Rebellion in China, Russia's absolutism, reactionary Switzerland and the revolutionary United States, deepening then the struggle of Europe to have something unique on Terra, with the industrial revolution, but also bringing great risks together with great hopes — what is the dramatic conscience that this minuscule and incomparable Europe does not have, as if it were a fiery man overwhelmed by the spirit of adventure! But if continents also have a conscience, then Marx was, at least for ten years, the devilish chronicler and spokesperson of this conscience. Whoever does not read the *Intimate Journal* of the middle of the last century ignores himself as European.

I don't plan on emphasizing everything that I liked in his pre-classical work, from before *Capital,* or on trying to encourage experiencing it with joy, especially in the case of those who study it because they are commanded to do so. I would only mention that the gold in this author is rather found in his small works, in simple manifests, portraits, or clarifications, gold that he himself wastes in the sand of action.

When multiplied, as he liked to be, beyond specialties, but with the vocation of the expert, a fighter for all, but in the name of *his* ideas about all, suffocated in an England which is the only one that stands him and which was, in fact, the only bearable one for him, how could he be gathered together in a well calibrated work? After all, he did not have time to write works and, as Nietzsche later, he wanted to be a fatality, not an author.

But one can see in him great thoughts and formulations even in a trifle of a speech!

In "Speech at the anniversary of *People's Paper*" from 1856, he says, "It seems that the more humanity subjects nature, the more man becomes the slave of another man or of his own vileness." And then, "All of our inventions seem to take us to only one result: to endow material forces with spiritual life and to reduce human life to a simple material force." Hasn't this happened in Marxist states, but also in the consumer society, exactly after a century? And here is, finally, Marx's verdict in this speech-manifest: "The new forces of the society need only one thing: new people, who know how to master them, and these are the workers. Just like the machines, the workers are an invention of our times.... History is the judge, and the proletariat is the executioner of the verdict."

It was not this way, or it *was* this way — I no longer care now, as I am behind bars. But I wonder one more time, faced with the intellectual emotion that his work awakes in me at certain moments: am I not actually kissing the hand that hits me? But no, I am clearly interested only in something completely unexpected, the prophet in Marx, the prophet as upside-down philosopher, and his monotheism, the man of only one idea, who can still see with it far in the concreteness of history, and who could say to someone like Chekhov, it seems (see the article "Herr Vogt"): "After all, it does not matter whether this pathetic Europe disappears — which will actually take place soon, unless there will be a social revolution — and whether America will exploit, then, the old system on account of Europe."

Actually, there is something else that interests me. It is the fact that I see in him, in this victorious man for a moment, a true brother Alexander, another one. *Pitié pour les forts!,** I feel like shouting one more time, from here, where I am. Have mercy on a thinker so great that, in those parts of the world where he is invoked too often and too incorrectly, he has become the laughter of children. Have mercy on the way in which his victory turns against him. Give up cheap mockery, those who feel you are his victims; give up describing him, according to the stories of his neighbors in London, as a poor common man in his relations with his wife of noble origin, or mocking him because he grew a beard in old age (and what a beard), after he had laughed in a letter to Engels of the German prophets from the exile after 1848, who had grown beards. Have mercy because of the curses that will accumulate one day over his head, the unhappy victor.

The Russians will curse him because he blocked their historical affirmation for so many decades, as no absolutist czar had succeeded in the 19th century. The Jews will curse him, his co-religionists, about whom he declared more infernal things than any anti-Semitic man. The workers will curse him because he deceived them for a moment that they are a unitary and supranational class, that they have a complete human identity, and that they are the only ones who can be the salt of the earth and of history. Even the communists will curse him, because, with his claim of speaking "scientifically," he forbade them the ac-

---

* "Mercy for the powerful," in French in the original.

tive idealism, the power of creation, and the access to novelty. Nature will curse him, because he has ravished it with his furor of industrialization, in the first hour of heavy machinism. The machines will curse him, as refined as they will become and as prepared, as brides, to marry the being of man, instead of being maneuvered by the rough hands of the workers. The gods with their religions will curse him, because he disdained them by portraying them as simple opium for the people, when they were aspiring, and at times succeeding, to bring to the world everything that he had desired, plus something of which he no longer knew or no longer wanted to know.

Then someone will come to say, "Forgive him, he also lived under the folly of the Good. Pray for the soul of brother Karl. Pray for *the Big Brother*."*

---

*   "The Big Brother" appears in English and in italics in the Romanian original.

XU

I receive paper and pencil again; I have read seventeen volumes from the complete works of Marx and Engels, and then the five of *The History of Philosophy* published by the Soviets and translated in Romanian (a lamentable page of European culture, pathetic especially for Marxism), and I have written like crazy four works, which I transcribed nicely in pen and gave to the character who was assigned to watch and "reeducate" me. Months and years passed this way. Two? Three?

In the meantime (I would find out later), almost all the other colleagues in detention were undergoing reeducation. On the surface, the reeducation seemed very gentle; in reality, it was very serious for people's consciences. They were given some books concerning the regime's accomplishments, they were shown propaganda movies, and they were even, toward the end, taken out in buses, a whole morning, and brought to see the industrial units, the new neighborhoods in cities, or the state cooperatives in the country. As I was to find out, the serious thing was that some detainees, who were converted faster, became propagandists themselves, and thus discussions were forming, in which people were accusing each other and they were getting into a pathetic situation: *either* some were exaggerating and becoming fierce defenders of the regime, *or* others were stubborn in not acknowledging any change toward the good of the country, refused everything out of "dignity," and were getting ready to come out of the prison more hostile than they were when they came in.

I was exempted from all of this (I was probably left on the side, since I was too weak after the surgery or because I was to be reeducated — who knows? — in a more special way), so I was enjoying staying alone in the cell, with the Marxist books that I received, paper and pencil, and, toward the end, even some magazines, among which there was one for the popularization of science, which I loved passionately. From it I found out some extraordinary novelties that had come out in the world in the meantime, in the context of the techno-scientific revolution.

I cannot forget, also, my encounter with Russian (an encounter that, to my shame, I had only then), because I had asked for a book for learning Russian from the beginning, in my desire to have a *printed* book, so the right to read something, anything, and so the privilege to exercise my memory. I suspected, and rightly so, that they would not refuse me such a book. But only when I had it in my hands I realized how our stupid — although apparently legitimate, at a certain moment — fear of Russians and of being annexed had made all of us, young and old, not to learn Russian, but also to *not be able* to learn this language. I had seen, when I was free, how even the most eminent students did *not* learn this language (which had been taught for eight years in high school). At the end of high school or college (where Russian was mandatory as well) they were even saying with some pride that "they did not know anything."

As much as I could learn it by myself, Russian seemed to me extraordinary. I no longer had here the worry I experienced concerning Marxism, that I ran the risk of praising those who beat me. This time, it was about the language of a people, not of a regime, and so I gave way to my linguistic interest for one of the most powerful and grand affirmations of human logos. Everything seemed remarkable and imposing in Russian, beginning with that force of stressing Russian words, which can receive the stress even on the fourth syllable, or even on the fifth before the last (while in classical languages, the stress could fall only on the third before the last, and in French the stress falls invariably on the last, in others on the second, and in others finally on the first, which terribly narrows the phonetic domain of speech, and, in the case of languages with fixed stress, it even narrows the domain of the modern poetical miracle of rhyme); continuing with the quasi-absence of the auxiliary verbs "to be" and "to have" (the Russian says, "with me gramophone" instead of "I have a gramophone," which can easily lead to the feeling that the gramophone is "with me" by chance, but it could be with you or with somebody else, and one could infer from here, with some naivety, of course, the easiness of applying communism to a people that speaks and feels this way); going, finally, over so many lexical and grammatical aspects of the language, to end with that splendid "aspect," literally, the aspect of the verb, with the Russian imperfect, which confers, of course, great beauty for formulating a thought and for narrating facts — everything, as I say, seemed impressive in Russian. Its *good* indetermination (from the absence of some articles to the imperfect) made me feel the infinity of which Gogol, I think, spoke in the *Dead Souls,* describing a troika that was advancing in the endlessness of snows.

After some time, they began to interrogate me approximately once a week, in the interrogation office, where a distinguished and intelligent character, who was dressed as civilian (not knowing how to address him, I called him Mr. Counselor), came at times alone, and other times with his adjudant, a captain — whom he was probably teaching directly how to "handle" people —, and gave me real lectures about the current situation in the country and in the world. I found out that president Kennedy had been assassinated ("a great misfortune for humanity," the counselor said) and that it was "still us," so the socialist concentration camp, who were the first to launch a man in the space. It was the hour when the socialist concentration camp still hoped to finally reach the other world in prosperity, and my counselor passionately unfolded the perspectives in that direction.

I was not indisposed by the fact that, according to him, the rapport was reversed in the favor of the East, nor by the pomposity with which he brought arguments and proofs for this, but rather by the idea that a man, who seemed remarkably intelligent and informed, was wasting his time with me in order to "indoctrinate" me. Didn't the regime have something better to do with "chosen" specimens, such as the counselor?

This feeling that the regime continued to use human intelligence badly, while it valued so impatiently all the other "prime matters" of the country was confirmed when the counselor called to ask me how I was feeling, if I had good enough nutrition, and if I wanted, for example, a can with good sardines, "you know," he said, "the delicious ones," and he was licking his mouth, believing that he would make me crave them. In reality, I have to say that he rather provoked pity, because I could clearly see how a superiorly gifted man was made to do such a lamentable service of "capturing" victims. Without any ostentation, I answered that I would rather have a jar of yogurt from time to time, since I was literally a *papă lapte** regarding food. (I realized on the spot that there was no virtue, no "strength of character," in my answer, but the simple fact that a rather anemic nature does not have many appetites. I think that what we may consider "virtue" is often connected with a vital deficiency or insufficiency and that, in general, you must be very content, as a moral being, when your weaker human nature or just your circumstances protect you from temptation. Christianity is perfectly right when it says, "avoid temptation," don't search for it so that you can prove to yourself that you are strong. The ascetics knew a few things regarding this, and Nietzsche's opposite saying, to *look for* temptation, *gefährlich leben,* which I liked so much in my youth, appeared now in all its ridicule. In order to not commit adultery, at least as a man, it's good to not have a couch — just like in the anecdote with the Jew who, finding his wife with another man on the couch, sold the couch.† Also, not

---

* "Milk eater." This is an expression that is also used for someone who is weak, who does not follow his interests, who hasn't grown.

† I am not familiar with the anecdote. In Eastern Europe, people often tell anecdotes and jokes in which the characters are representatives of "categories": a Jew, a Russian, an American, a Christian.

having a studio and not seeing too many beautiful women on purpose. Otherwise, *vivere pericolosamente,** as Mussolini had translated Nietzsche's saying, what happens to you on a small scale is what happened to this dictator on a large scale.)

The counselor did not consider my refusal a defiance — it was done in all modesty, after all — and moved on to the matter at hand: he asked me to write something against my friend C. But how can I write, I asked; here, in prison? The counselor quickly passed over this problem — which indirectly assured me that things are getting better, perhaps ever toward freedom — and added, "he is a great enemy of ours." I told him that my friend is a man who is detached from all people and all things, even from life, and that I was even afraid for years while I knew him that he would take his own life. "He is a *great* enemy of ours," the counselor ended, emphasizing it.

I returned to my cell, downcast by the entire scene and, I have to confess, worried that, after my refusal, they would surely take back the books, the paper, and the pencil... The next day, the counselor's adjudant, the captain, called me. I went, being resigned at the thought that I would receive the verdict for my refusal. The captain received me amicably, and he gave me an orange.

It had been years and years, even before I was imprisoned (due to the shortages in my country) since I had *seen* an orange. My hand was shaking when I took it — due to craving? Due to the feeling that they were resorting to such methods, almost Chinese, or to "Scottish showers,"† to force us to give in? I put it into my right pocket, out of shame (rather for them), so that the guard would not feel it when he would take me by my left arm to take me back into the cell, having the glasses on my eyes. I relished the orange in the cell, with the voluptuousness with which the counselor believed I would have relished

---

*   "Living dangerously," in Italian in original.
†   Noica thinks of psychological methods of torture, and he draws a parallel between the event with the orange and the cold showers that were, at times, performed in prisons.

the sardines. When I only had the peel in my hand, I wondered what to do: throw it into the WC in the corner of the cell, or give it to the guard through the peephole? I then remembered that, a long time ago, my mom used to make preserves with orange peel thinly cut, and so I started to bite small pieces from the peel, until I ate all of it.

At the end of these *happy* days, I was called with some solemnity and placed before a significant person, as I was told, who let me wait in the office around half an hour. I was in that splendid state of life when you are indifferent, but in a positive sense, not negative, to anything that may happen to you: it is good if it goes this way, it is good if it goes another way.

This person was a colonel, actually the chief of the interrogators who had taken me in custody years ago. The circle was closing: I was coming back before him.

"What would you do if you were free?" he asks me abruptly. For a moment, a thought crossed my mind: "I would read the 18th volume from Marx and Engels." I was afraid, though, that he would consider me defiant. In fact, the question had brought me into a state of real emotion, so that I asked for a cigarette from his younger subordinate, who accompanied the colonel and was smoking. He gave me the cigarette immediately, and I started saying that, of course, as any other detainee, I had the illusion that I would be free one day, despite the long conviction that I had received, and that I asked myself what I would do. I would do anything, I answered, from a very modest position as a substitute for elementary mathematics or foreign languages, in a small, forgotten village, to a higher intellectual use.

Since the cigarette started to give me courage, I began developing the idea that I could even be used as a "coach" — I dared to say — of Marxism. After all, I pointed out, nobody is interested in who the coach is: what matters is performance. Just as in sports, there is need of some instructing in philosophy as well. Being in the field to some extent, I knew well that one couldn't do Marxism well without Hegel, Kant, Aristotle, and the others. I could instruct someone in all of these — I praised myself — as I could also open his appetite for mathematics or some science, preparing him in this way to be truly receptive, at an adequate level, to Marx's philosophical message.

The colonel listened to me, registered my answer positively, and told me, "you will be free tomorrow." He added, "Do you want to remain connected with us? Or is it against your conscience?"

I remained dumbfounded for a moment. So, they had not changed: on the one hand, they had the generosity to free us, on the other hand they were asking us to become their agents. How could these two match?

I could easily use the door that he had kindly offered me, "it is against my conscience." I preferred to tell him something equally true, that I was not planning on having any social life. My family had left a long time ago, perhaps they went to Australia, and I could no longer have friends, since I harmed the close ones. "I no longer have a country, colonel," I answered. "I am detached from all."

The colonel went out, but his subordinate remained another moment. "How can you say you have no country? We make so many efforts to bring this country to another level, we even defy the Soviets when they ask things that are not convenient to the country, and you say that you have no country?" I had a weak moment — probably because of the stress to which I had been submitted — and I burst into crying. In fact, weren't *they* the ones who had detached me from anything, even from my country?

I returned to the cell with the refrain "you will be free tomorrow" singing in me. The next day, nothing happened; they only came to take my books, paper, and pencil. I remained this way another day, two more, four days. The fifth day, I thought, "they mocked me; they are using the Scottish showers again." The morning of the sixth day, I asked to be taken to the prison's commander. I wanted to ask him to give me back paper and pencil, trying, in fact, to see what my situation was. After some time, I am called to the commander, but I don't get to formulate my request when a civilian approaches me and begins taking all possible measurements. The next day, I am taken out again, and

I am given a new suit and a pair of shoes. When I am taken from there, after a last night in the cell, now dressed in new clothes, to see my luggage in the deposit (everything was worn out, and this is why they had retained me longer, because I had no presentable clothes), I take almost nothing from the suitcase, and I leave it there as well, because it was broken, and I keep only the coat, also worn, although it was still summer. With the coat on my arm and with a small bundle of laundry, I come before the commander, who hands me a banknote, the equivalent of around ten bus tickets. I look at the prison commander before I come out of the door. We are both caught in a smile, and I remember William Blake's verses:*

> *There is a smile of Love*
> *And there is a smile of Deceit,*
> *And there is a smile of smiles*
> *In which these two smiles meet.†*

---

*   The verses appear in English in the original.

†   [Romanian editor's note] In the preceding editions, the text ended here with the note "1965."

XUI

Whoever did not have the luck to be imprisoned between immediately after 1950 and immediately after 1960 (of course, as long as he also came out from there with sane body and mind) could not have had the shock of the change that had taken place in the world during that interval and did not fully enjoy the triumph of our era, even if it was risky or evanescent. It was something without equivalent in known history, something unique not only regarding the *generalized* prosperity in one part of the world (a prosperity that consisted not only in food, drinking, and sumptuous living, as other times, but also in radio, television, electricity, with the entire cortege of benefits of the "red fire," or in tourism, museums, and culture), but also something unique, especially regarding the technical-scientific revolution.

There was something that seemed enchanting, as I was coming out of the darkness of the prison, which was still somehow lit. I was surprised to see that the people I encountered, or those in the West about whom I was hearing, were not overtaken by any drunkenness coming from the victory of our era. On the contrary, they often met such success in the wrong way. They succeeded in consumption or entertainment, but not in *contemplation*.

What a thing to say, that there would be an opposition between contemplation and action! I would include it among the great solemn platitudes of humanity. There is, of course, an opposition between passivity — the passivity of the spectator or of the receiver of unexpected gifts — and action, but there is no opposition between *contemplation* and action. It's true that the opposition seems to come from the ancients, with their *bios the-*

*oretikos.** However, understood simply, it is another great stupid saying, as I said, just like "know yourself" or "self-love," so the love of the self which would command all things, as the French moralists and not only they pretended. (How much self-love can you have? If a smiling Brigitte Bardot were to come toward me, I would be delighted for a moment, but then I would set aside any self-love and I would call someone young and handsome, like Alec, to take care of her.)

For six months after coming out of prison, I couldn't read any book from my field (not even Marx's volume 18), but only books and magazines about the technical-scientific successes from the middle of the 20th century. In a few years, the world had changed or was opening toward extraordinary changes; however, those who had not had the privilege to be locked up did not realize this, as a child does not realize that it has grown.

What seemed to me unbelievable and terrifically engaging was that the technical-scientific revolution *had succeeded,* and beyond all expectations or imagination (even those of Jules Verne's kind). Until this revolution, man had succeeded in nothing. The humanist culture especially, but the scientific one as well, had not succeeded.

In the case of humanist culture, what had *philology* promised around 1800–1820 (the finding of an original language!), and what did it obtain; what had *history* promised, when it became aware that it is a science; or what ordering had *philosophy* promised, not only with German idealism but also with the French ideologists, and what did it succeed? For man and for the spirit, this failure would be truly a scandal if it were not somehow grandiose and if it did not leave man *open* to continue to pose the problem of the word, of society, and of thought.

What about positive sciences? Of course, they have brought some results, laws, and knowledge without equal in the history of the world. However, unfortunately — or fortunately! — they, even physics, did not succeed in giving the complete and certain inventory of all knowledge, as they had promised. Around

---

*   Contemplative life.

1900, the great physicist Lord Kelvin said that there would not be much to find in physics (and he even deplored the physicists of the 20th century), except "perhaps" some aspect of the problem of X-rays and of radiation. Around 1920, another great physicist, Rutherford, said that nuclear energy could never be liberated. And now, the physicists no longer know where their heads are from so many novelties, so that someone like Heisenberg asked at a philosophical congress that others also make an effort of imagining the new because the physicists are no longer able to do so.

What is left to say about sciences like astronomy, with its quasars and pulsars, great dark stellar masses, which decide, however, by density and attraction the fate of the rest of the world (so that the astronomers Hoyle and Narlikar showed that Einstein's theory of relativity is too *narrow,* since it does not take into account the rest of the universe). And what could we say about biology, "the science of the 20th century," where, on the one hand, the new devices for detection, such as electronic microscopes, and, on the other hand, the new theories and notions, such as those regarding the genetic code, have resulted into grandiose answers=questions, so extraordinary open notions for humanity.

However, beyond or parallel with everything that has been and has not been hoped for, the specter of a sad failure appeared, just as these admirable mathematics that place everything in order are a kind of failure, or at least are so to you. When they place at their basis a crass but extremely fecund "theory of sets" (actually, a kind of theory of heaps), they get to give account to all mathematical disciplines, to finally get confused themselves, no longer being able to explain anything. When the same admirable mathematics (the revealed mystery of our world, our God without beard and rod) attempt to place logic at their basis and to ensure, by axiomatization and logicalization, that they have order within themselves (so they don't only *place* order among things), they fall upon paradoxes, such as the ones which, as I showed, made logician Frege cry last century, or which made logician Quine today say that, after all, it is better that the logicization of mathematics did not succeed, because mathematics would have destroyed mathematicians and, perhaps, with the perfect machines and devices, all of us…

Thus, everything is a "failure" in our culture; or, if you prefer, nothing kept its promise. Only *technology* has kept it, even more than it had been asked. It's true that it also gave some stupidities, small machines and devices that you don't really need (the over twenty devices for cutting the tips of cigars), or some which *create* artificial needs, and so they disturb your human nature, but this is something else. Technology has given miracles, and not so much for consumption (as another physician said: around 1900, humanity had everything it needed to be happy materially), but for contemplation, *that is** for the action of thought, as for a deeper vibration of our spiritual being.

We have registered the amount of light that has appeared in the world after the coming out of darkness with such an intellectual voluptuousness. Light allowed itself to be concentrated in so-called "lasers," in order to favor all sorts of possible activities, such as transmitting information at a distance, transporting energy (with the risk of transporting explosive energy as well), surgeries of the eye's retina, etc. But at the same time, we saw well, only now, that light is no more than a narrow band on the register of electromagnetic waves, where so many other waves, and in the first place radio waves, came to transmit not only suave or hoarse voices, songs and thoughts, or political discourses filled with anger and madness, like those from the 1930s up to the years of my going to prison, but also transmitted messages toward unknown worlds from the cosmos, or perhaps brought messages, from extraterrestrial beings, about which we begin to wonder whether they "look for us" in space with their waves, with a language that we do not yet understand. I felt as if I were intoxicated by so many novelties, mechanisms, and devices, which, if we don't spoil our entire success, may lead one day to directly capturing solar energy, and thus solving for good the problem of the need for energy on earth, just as, using pho-

---

*   In English and in italics in the original.

tosynthesis, we would also solve the problem of nourishment once and for all.

There are admirable things brought into being by cybernetics, this strange mixture of mechanism (as a final and subtle effort of mechanistic conception of solving all problems with only two values, with *yes* and *no,* with 0 and 1, reducing at times the noblest chapters in mathematics to a simple question of addition done vertiginously, with millions of operation on a second, thanks to the electronic flux) and "systems theory." Consider the very evocative structures of any "cybernetic system," which represent something of the order of monads, "closed and without windows," of which Leibniz, the god invoked by Norbert Wiener, the inventor of cybernetics, spoke.

What is left to say about the ecstasy that had taken hold of me? When I saw that man could literally implant himself in machinery by the refinement and the miniaturization of machines — he would obtain an eye that could see infrared, so in darkness, an electronic ear, an electronic nose — that man would perceive unquantifiably more than today, just as in Antiquity man dreamt to implant himself into animality, with the sphinx and the centaur, but not obtaining an expansion of his being, unless we consider his simple nature. I then realized that poor Nietzsche did not know well what he was talking about when he invoked the "supermen" and when he admired the intelligent and gifted beasts of the Renaissance as superior specimens. There was a new humanity — finally new, after 7,000 years — that was about to be born. And it was not a humanity created artificially, in a tube, like the human embryo of Daniele Petrucci, about whose attempt to create man in vitro I heard back then with emotion, but a perfectly natural humanity, which would only use the conquests already obtained by technology, in order to give man, with some extra amino acids, a surplus of memory, of intelligence, and perhaps of creativity.

But this is no longer science or technology, I thought. This is theology. While Byzantium was under siege, some theologians were discussing the problem of the sex of angels, and history laughed at them. Today, however, it is revealed that the problem of the sex of angels is one of the most extraordinarily current problems for humanity. Indeed, what kinds of people will we colonize on other planets or artificial planets: pairs of people, like in Noah's Ark, simple men, as could be perfectly possible, only women (and Joliot Curie says that this could be possible too, by so-called "parthenogenesis"), or androgens, angels, asexual beings?

I dream about all of this and I read about the experiments with the Planarian worms while I live at my cousin, being happy again, in a small room 2 × 2.*

"You see," I tell my cousin's, "we arrived at the point where we could make a Planarian worm which was submitted to some electric influences to obtain a 'conditioned reflex,' just like Pavlov's dogs. But this is not all. It is extraordinary that if another Planarian worm eats the first, it also gets that conditioned reflex. Do you understand what this means?…"

"Leave me alone with your ideas," my cousin responds, still with affection. "I am fighting with the bedbugs brought by the tenant imposed on me by the tenancy office, and you're telling me about the Planarian worms and other scientific follies."

He's right, of course. All of those who, outside,† are still fighting the long lines,‡ shortages, a place to live, or adding up years for retirement are right. But I feel that I no longer get along with him. I will have to search for my prison colleagues, the only ones with whom I could still talk — the only ones who have maintained, I hope, a door toward dreams.

---

* 2 × 2 meters, approximately 6 × 6 feet.
† Noica means "outside of prison," those who did not have the experience of being imprisoned.
‡ Since resources were scarce, people waited in long lines to buy their food supplies.

XVII

"Why don't you get new teeth?" my cousin, who takes care of me like a brother, asks me. (I started giving private lessons, I found some translations second-hand, so I fare well; I can pay for my 2×2 room in which I am sheltered and I continue contemplating — having good news from my family, which left long ago, and being forgiven by my friends who had been imprisoned because of me, but against my will — the miracle of the world in the middle of the 20th century, with its promises.)

"You see," I say, "there will be a time when man will have fewer teeth, perhaps even none at all. Even now, wisdom teeth, which had a great importance for the primitive people, no longer matter. We can even accelerate vital processes. Everything has changed since we gathered the genetic code. I'll give you to read Jean Rostand's study, *Génies sur commande?* He is a great biologist, popularizing, but still good. He shows that with "twenty words," with the twenty aminoacids, one can fabricate a being. Man's memory and intellectual faculties will depend, it seems, on the quantity of RNA. Man will be able to transform living beings according to his will, and he will transform himself as well."

"If he wants to!" my cousin exclaims.

"Of course, there are many reasons to waver, but, in general, what man can do, he does not delay doing, regardless of the risks. In fact, I read someone's study about the so-called 'inductive substances.' You know that people talk now about transplants; those with a kidney have already succeeded. Let's see if they will succeed with the others as well, especially with heart transplants. We don't need to speak of those for the brain, because they are very distant and also absurd. If you change a human's brain, with his memory and intellectual faculties, then he is *another* human for sure. However, something great was discovered with the inductive substances: the cells taken from the patient *himself* and cultivated in the laboratory can give all the necessary organs. So there is no more need to take organs from others or from donators. It was even said," I continue, "that all moral problems, as well as problems of physiological incompatibility, with the rejection of the organ by the organism, would be solved. A certain doctor, Gurdon, made an experiment to confirm this, and a frog was born from a frog skin. This thing made someone say, 'Any human is virtually composed by some milliards of specimens of himself.' Isn't this beautiful?"

"It's great," my cousin answers, "but there also are some atomic bombs, somewhere, in deposits, and, in fact, even with these biological experiments there are some risks that are terribly similar to what is said in the Bible."

"My dear," I tell him, "I am the last one to contest the wisdom of the Bible, let alone its beauty; however, humanity cannot be stopped from taking a step forward."

"To stagger…"

"Maybe yes, maybe no," I answer, "but let me vividly participate for the moment, at least as a sports fan, in the festival that we all experience now. You know that I work with philosophy. Well, I have never believed that one can think and speculate more fantastically than philosophy has done. But I now see — and not only in pure science and in technology — how unexpectedly one can think. You heard, for example, how much people have discussed in philosophy the subject of analysis and synthesis: with analysis you decompose something, with synthesis you compose something. Do you know what I find out from the physicists now? That there are particles which decompose in sub-particles out of which they have never been composed! That the new particles are born only at the moment of disintegration. Isn't this crazy? Which philosopher even thought of something like this? What should I say about isotopes? That a great part of chemical elements are composed of a compound of two or several isotopes? So, that you are not *you* unless there are more 'you' like you! But have you heard of *breeders*?* They are some devices or atomic piles, which, consuming energy, end by producing more energy than they consumed, which makes dead matter become *also* fertile! In fact, this is also the cosmogonic theory of the English Hoyle with the Indian Narlikar: they claim that there is a 'C-field' that permanently replaces the energy that is lost in the universe by expansion. And what can I say about…"

"*À propos,*" my cousin interrupts me, "since you speak of the English… Have you read Orwell's book, *1984*?"

"I had looked for it earnestly 'before,' but I didn't find it…"

"Here, I'll give it to you," he tells me. "We'll talk afterwards."

I give him back the book the next day.

"I could not read more than one or two hours from it. It's suffocating."

"It's suffocating with truth, isn't it?" he asks me.

"Rather with *falsity,*" I answer. "I would argue this way: either Orwell is not right, so it will never happen in the world, in the year 1984, as he says, and this means that he uglified the world's face with his book and awoke useless fears, *or* it will truly be so, let's say even here, in our country — where it began to be this way — and then, with my small experience and with what I heard from others, I can tell you that the splendid thing about man is that, *some place,†* he survives even to such pressures. And *this* is the important thing, not man's disfiguration! It is important what remains out of freedom — not only for the one from whom it was taken, but also for the one who took it from him. What remains human in those hours of complete dissolution of the human matters, just as it matters what man still has as property when all was taken from him. After all, regarding man, it is as it was said about culture — you know it — that it would be 'what remains after you have forgotten everything'… This is what seemed extraordinary to me: that *something* still remains for man. And it may be that the thing that remains to man is *es-*

---

* "Breeders" appears in English in the original.

† Noica's point is that man can survive in some *interior* place.

sential; and in this case, Orwell's book will have to be burned in the public square in 1984."

"No one can talk to you," my cousin answers. "You know one thing only, even after everything that happened to you, that 'the bad is not that bad,' even that the bad reveals who knows what good thing, hidden until then. I will ask you, though, what you think about Solzhenitsyn; you said you were reading him a few days go."

"Yes, it was for Solzhenitsyn that I interrupted my readings regarding the technical-scientific revolution, because I had heard good things about him and I did not dislike it, as *material* — at least his first book, the one about Ivan's day. Denisov, or something like this."*

"Well, and then, did you still like him?"

"In a way, I liked him, I liked him very much, because this writer has something from the class of the great Russians; but, in another way, he depressed me, *for his sake,* I would say, and for the destiny of culture. He consumes his genius to denounce, just as simple as that! He somehow remained a physicist and a positivist."

"You mean you didn't like *The Cancer Ward*?"

"I liked it very much: there are extraordinary characters and situations there. But the author seems to be unable, or rather he *does not want* to make out of them a great work of art, a great fresco. He is embittered. He has to say *something* and to denounce something with his work, just like in the other book, *In the First Circle,* where he strives to see the last thoughts of Stalin, and with details for which he certainly had extensive investigations."

"Do you want to say that he is wrong to denounce?"

"For himself, yes, because he lowers his talent, if not also his genius. For the others, perhaps not. I have heard that he is called 'the good man' by his people. Probably their better conscience. But I wonder if he serves them and their cause to the end, the

---

*   Noica speaks of Solzhenitsyn's *One Day in the Life of Ivan Denisovich.*

cause of any just and good man. You see, culture is done with a little gratuity, a little detachment."

"But this man wants to say the truth. What can culture do without truth? Literature should leave me alone, if it does not fight for the values of truth and human justice under the pretense that it is interested only in beauty!"

"It's not that simple," I try to explain to him and also to myself. "When you are interested *only in beauty,* as a final piety to beauty, I don't know how it happens that you end up — just like the Ancient Greeks — with good and truth also. But when you absolutely want the truth and especially exactness..."

"What, do you make a difference between them?"

"Of course I do, even in Solzhenitsyn's case. I am worried that, being a physicist, as I mentioned, and also embittered, as I also said, this man with so much literary genius looked too much for exactness rather than truth. For if truth, at least for modern man, cannot be without exactness, exactness is not by itself truth."

"I still don't understand."

"I don't understand too well either," I confess sincerely, "but I *realize* it is this way. Look, we also have an ancient author, a prince who said, 'The one who has no stubbornness sees God.' I am afraid that Solzhenitsyn does not see God precisely because he has stubbornness and looks for exactness. Even more, something else may happen to him due to exactness: he may lose the entire truth, and thus harm not only his work — and, as it is right now, I don't think it will still be read in 20–30 years — but also those he wants to defend."

"What do you mean by this?"

"I would tell you this way. What if a good Christian today, in his desire to clarify *all* the episodes of Christ's life, wanted to know 'exactly' how Judas Iscariot's treason took place? What if he studied all documents of the time and looked objectively at things, on both sides? What if he arrived at the conclusion that Judas, denouncing Christ, did it out of love for Him, to save Him from crucifixion, hoping that he would save Him? So, if this Christian were stubborn about 'truth' and said to the whole world, particularly to the Church, that Judas was not really a traitor, what would you say then?"

"You would never convince me that this contemporary man does not fight heroically, and delightfully from a literary perspective, for freedom. And even for all people's freedom, even yours, if you want to know!"

"I believe this and I am, in a way, obligated to him for this, but it may be that he fights more for freedoms, plural, for his, my, and his people's freedoms, rather than for freedom."

"What is this?" my cousin says, exasperated.

"There are many freedoms," I answer, "and I am surprised that, in a country like Norway, where you have all freedoms, you do not have the freedom to drink alcohol, for example. There are many freedoms, but not all are significant. In any case, I sense that here, in our country, we have a deeper notion of freedom, that of *neatârnare* (*indépendance*).* This means two things at the same time: first, to not depend on another, and second, to not depend purely and simply (*not to be pendent*†), to not be too attached to the immediate things, to not be fixed into an idea, to have wings, so 'to see God.'"

"Listen, dear, I'll lose the train with your talking."

My cousin was about to leave for a vacation. Even if he was retired, he had received a "ticket for the baths" from someone who was still employed,‡ and he was to leave that day, taking advantage of favorable conditions to take a treatment.

The luggage for three weeks is already prepared, so in fifteen minutes we leave together for Gara de Nord,§ taking a trolley-bus. On the way, I relate to him what I had read in Arthur C.

---

*   "Independence" in English. I kept the Romanian term and the French translation in the text (they both appear in the original). In Romanian, there is also the word *independență,* but the literal translation *neatârnare* has some flavor to it.

†   In English in the original.

‡   During Communism, people could receive tickets from work to various treatment places in the country.

§   North Station, main train station in Bucharest.

Clarke's book, *Profiles of the Future.*[*] The author writes about how travel will be done in the future, focusing on vehicles on "air cushions." The wheel will be done for, he says, once what he calls in English *Ground Effect Machines* will come into being. People will create vehicles that will compete with the automobile as well as with the plane. Roads and highways, which occupy so much space and for which so much money was spent, will be obsolete, the author says. The new vehicles will be very useful, he adds, especially for the continents that do not have a good network of roads. In any case, it is about a real "road emancipation." We will travel smoothly on earth and on sea, above the waves. The harbors and the channels, such as Suez and Panama, will be outdated. The delightful thing will be, the author says, that there will be a perfect *continuity* between ground travel and water travel…

Our trolleybus stops abruptly, with a small explosion. It broke. We must wait for another, at the next station. Of course, the second trolleybus is overcrowded. Cramped among travelers, holding one suitcase (I hold another one in my hands), my cousin asks me:

"How is it going with traveling on air cushions?"

I take him to the platform. When he gets into the train, my cousin tells me:

"When I come back, I want to find you with new teeth!"

I smile and I leave, walking slowly on the platform of the station. On the other platform, which was for arrivals, not departures, I see an electrical engine, a new type, at least for me. I remember all of a sudden that, in high school, I had a colleague who liked to be here, at Gara de Nord, the main station of the city, to see the engines which were very varied back then. He liked them just like someone else would like racing horses. I remember that there were some engines called Pacific, with great wheels and fine spokes, like the legs of a beautiful girl. On the lateral plaque of the engine, it was written, "126 km/h maximum speed." I always wondered why 126 and not 125.

---

[*] In English in the original.

Someone grabs me by the shoulders and shouts, "Professor!" I turn around: it was Alec. A wave of joy builds within me. We hug, but I do not realize whether he has tears in his eyes, too.

XUIII

"How are you, professor?" Alec asks me warmly.

"Well, I got out, I live, I am content."

"I was sure of it," he responds ironically but with love at the same time.

We continue on the platform, arm in arm, and I ask him [what he's doing there].*

"I am going for an 'exchange experience,' as they say here. I came out of *the prison*† probably before you, I was reaccepted at the university, I graduated from the department of architecture, and now I am sent to East Germany for an exchange with the specialists in the field."

"Do you remember what you told me the day they told you that you would be accused of treason[?]‡ You claimed that, after liberation, you would go into a mountain village to find a girl with two cows."

"That's what I actually did at the beginning," Alec attempts to tell me. "I found the girl, but…"

"I know," I say finishing his thought, "you did not find the combination girl plus two cows. The latter are at the collective farms.§ In Switzerland you may still find them."

Alec does not smile. He becomes serious all of a sudden. He holds me strongly by my arm and whispers:

---

*   Addition of the Romanian editor.

†   In English in the original.

‡   Addition of the Romanian editor.

§   The kolkhoz.

"I'm telling this only to you. I haven't even told it to my parents. I want to get to the other side,* and I will stay there for good. I cannot live here."

"But I understand they allowed you to finish your studies. You probably have a job and will buy a car one day."

"Professor, understand that I cannot. There is nothing from my past for which I reproach them, not even the condemnation, but there is something unbreathable here, don't you feel it? I want to travel, to be free, to have the life I like. I don't think I will call for my parents. They are too attached to the country and to their friends."

He turns toward me:

"I'll get you out too! Yes, I'll get you out, I'll buy you from them. Don't you wish to? I need an older friend. I will keep you as a parent. You don't refuse me, do you?"

He takes me by hands without waiting for an answer, he hugs me, and then he turns and sees that people have begun getting into the train. He then drags me to his train car, shakes my hands one more time, and gets up into the train. He then appears through the opening of a window.

"Good. But tell me, did you do the third gymnastics exercise?" he asks me, thus showing me that he also remembers all of the situations from the cell.

I nod my head, smiling at the memory of the exercise that had provoked the intestinal volvulus.

"It was good, wasn't it?" he insists.

I hesitate whether to answer him, but the train begins to move at that moment, and so I shout sincerely, from the bottom of my heart: "Very good! Very good!"

The emotion rooted me into the platform of the station for some time, even after the train had been swallowed into nothingness, or in another galaxy, holding something dear to me heart. Why did I love Alec? Perhaps because he had the strength to not accept anything of what I was telling him — and still cred-

---

*   Alec means West Germany, which equaled the free world.

it me. I had felt from the beginning, in the cell, that he needed me and, at the same time, he had no use for my advice.

There is something without parallel in the affection of such a young man who challenges you: it is a call to be better and deeper than you are. He looks at you over his shoulder, but you're not offended,* for he still looks to you. In turn, you search for something in him besides what he shows you. After all, these young people are those who truly enrich the world, because they do not leave it into the satisfied wisdom of late years, nor into the satisfied indifference of the early years.

I needed him, just as he needed me. Of course, I could replace him; but could he also replace me? In fact, he did not even know my address and he assumed me into his life only symbolically, on a platform at a train station. I had to look for him in other versions, since I loved this free and daring young man,† this brother Alexander who, precisely because he provokes you, also bows before what *you should* be and seems to ask you to pray for him.

"Don't you see that it is unbreathable?" he had told me. The atmosphere here began to seem unbreathable to me as well, but not so much because the regime was suffocating our spirits, but rather because these people around me allowed themselves to be suffocated. A society that has been oppressed for more than twenty years should be able to come out of the fear of oppression, just as the people in prisons had liberated themselves of fear. But it bored me to see that people continued to be fearful.

I wonder what Ernest is doing, that joyful economist with whom I spent three days, back to back, in "isolation." I realize now, after I saw Alec for a moment, that I can feel well only with those who had obtained that detachment brought about by the

---

* The Romanian here could mean, "he does not offend you" or "you're not offended." I chose the second version.

† The relationship between a mentor and a disciple often appears in Noica's work. One of the most remarkable relationships between a master and a disciple in the Romanian culture is known as the School from Paltinis. See Gabriel Liiceanu, *The Paltinis Diary* (Budapest: Central European University Press, 2000).

years of detention. Something irresistible sends me from the station straight to looking for Ernest.

He had told me that he had a job at the City Hall and that he was certain he would be retaken there. I go toward the City Hall without any hope. Of course, at the gate, nobody knows anything about comrade Ernest. I ask to be taken to the economic department. One clerk knows nothing about him, but another one says, "Comrade director Ernest? He is in a different department, CDPCC."

What strange names, I tell myself.

I notice the use of "director." So, not only was he taken back, but also appointed a director. He may have accepted to be "reeducated" and may have made concessions. I would regret it, for he was such an independent spirit. Anyway, I must look him up, and I go to the address of the mentioned department. I find out that Ernest is "in the field," and I leave my name for him with the note, "the one to whom you once communicated your theory of laughter." I would come back the next day.

"But my dear," Ernest tells me when he receives me the next day, giving me a hug in his directorial office, "there was no need to specify who you are. I knew it well, not so much in isolation — because I remember that I was the one who spoke more — but rather from the others. Just imagine, after a while, I happened to be taken in the cell where you had been."

"What," I exclaim, "with engineer Goldstein? And with the theologian?"

"Yes," he answers. "And with Matei, with the doctor, with…"

"I wonder how the doctor is doing. He was embittered against all people and all things."

"But he's here, in my department, I brought him here as 'anthropologist.'"

"Unbelievable!" I exclaim. "I must see him. But what do you do? How could you become a director?"

"Do you have any suspicions about me?" Ernest asks jokingly. "Well, I'll tell you…"

He pushes a button and tells his secretary who was coming in, "I'm not here for anyone for an hour. I have to make a report with the professor for the Government's Department of Health."

And then he begins:

"I came out early. You know, I had no real guilt, nor a political past. However, they did not take me back to the Economic Department, where I used to work, because they had 'secrets' and, anyway, I had been a 'hostile element.' At the beginning, they assigned me as a simple administrator at the medical service of the City Hall. There, I found something that attracted me: a hygienist doctor had been recently assigned to take care of the city's pollution problems. He did not know where to begin, and so I gave him a few ideas. I told him he had to begin from odors. Since I have sharp senses, I offered my help, and we became friends. Anytime I smelled a pestilential odor, we both got into a City Hall car and went in the direction of the odor."

"How so, against the odor?" I ask, confused and amused.

"Yes, against it, to find out from which factory it came or which dump site at the outskirts of the city emanated it."

"And could you find it?"

"Most of the time, we could not. But why is that important? I liked to look for the not-found, just as I told you 'there' that I liked to go nowhere by train."

"It is admirable," I say enthusiastically. "Going against the odor! It is like in the ancient legends, when they went to the chambers of the wind and the cave of Aeolus, or like in the story where the prince goes against the dragon. I think it is splendid to find in the concrete, in a contemporary urban agglomeration, the myths of man."

"Isn't it so?" Ernest says, becoming passionate. "Now, when you tell me this, I realize why I liked it. Our civilization is not as deprived of poetry as it seems. With little imagination, our life would look differently. Today's writers continue to tell us about the great voids of humans, or about abstraction and nothingness. But I see all around us a plethora of things or of concrete situations. After all, just as we are surrounded by odors, we are also surrounded by electrical fluids, ideologies, traditions, or futurological anticipations. I sense that we do not live among inert things — and I did not like to find simple things, industrial units from where the odors started, or dump sites. I realized that the odors and the air pollution are made, I don't know how, out of nothing determinate, or out of countless small causes which, accumulated, make the air be pestilential. But, of course, when I come back from the 'mission,' I gave the report that we found the cause of pollution or that we were about to detect it.

"Then," he continues, "I got the idea to make a report, showing the importance and the complexity of the problem. Basing it on the data accumulated in my car expeditions, I added the points of infection and the possible *trajectories* to a map of the city with, and so the possible fronts of pollution (as one speaks of 'wave fronts'). My map made an impression, especially because the menacing arrows were colored in red. In the report, I asked that they hire meteorologists who would study air currents in the atmosphere of the capital in order to take measures for the present state, but also to determine where to place future industries.

"To be brief, the leadership became convinced that the problem was extremely serious — especially because it was also unclear — and I was assigned to recruit qualified personnel to begin the investigation. Later, I showed that there was need for other specialists as well — geographers, anthropologists, sociologists, and psychologists — and when I made a new report, which I began with long quotes from the early writings of Engels about the pollution of Manchester around 1840, due to the establishment of the first textile factories, all were convinced of the Marxist character of the problem. The CDPCC was created, and I was named director."

"I actually wanted to ask you: what is this, CDPCC?"

"It is the Center for the Detection of Pollution and the Control of its Causes."

"Impressive," I say. "And do you believe in its efficacy?"

"My dear," Ernest answers, "I have no choice, I must believe. I set in motion so many people — around twenty collaborators, plus the external ones, plus the relationships with diverse research institutes — and I awoke so many hopes in the leaders that I have to take things seriously. You know, after all, if it is taken seriously by others, even a joke becomes serious. Why wouldn't we find something if we look for it like this?"

"But there are devices to detect pollution, I suppose, aren't there?"

"Of course there are," Ernest responds promptly, knowing the lesson well. "For the air pollutants, you use 'chromatography in gaseous stage'; for the diverse pollutants, you use an electronic detector, the 'mass spectroscope'; to detect substances in general, based on fluorescence, the so-called 'spectroflourimeter' was invented, which does spectrofluorescent analyses."

"That's enough," I say, having a beginning of dizziness, faced with this technical ecstasy.

"You can also use scintigraphy," Ernest continues mercilessly, "for which some devices with radioactive isotopes were invented. They indicate the number of alpha, beta, and gamma pulsations on the second, respectively the quantity of radioactivity…"

I take out a soft groan and I rush to stop him, asking:

"But have you bought all of these machines and devices?"

"No," Ernest replies, "this is where I had the brilliant inspiration. If we bought them, these and others that I won't mention to spare you, it would have meant cutting my own carcass: our department would have been cut down to two–three technicians, and I would not have counted anymore. I proceeded differently. At a meeting with my superiors, I enumerated all of these technical means of detecting pollution, but I added: they impose great expenses, ultra-specialized people, which means other expenses, and they lead to incomplete or inconclusive results. Every city, I added, has specific conditions: certain currants, a special regime of rains, a proper ecological system, etc., etc. The devices can indicate no more than the actual situation of pollution, but a city in development requires information about its atmospheric, urban, economic, and human environment. If it could be said that there are no diseases, but rather sick people, I added during the meeting, that much more it must be said that there are no pollutions, but polluted things. Just like every human breaks his shoe in a certain way, a city breaks its air in a specific way. We should not spend large sums to make general investigations, but rather to get the *complete* picture of the situation of our patient, which would allow us to make him well and also to prescribe him the regime for his future life.

"I was congratulated," Ernest continues, "for the savings I so obtained and they also gave me, of course, the credits to put together the scientific group which, from meteorologists to psychologists, would study the special conditions here."

"Don't you think it would be more expensive?" I ask.

"At the end, yes, but this is how they like it, to do things indirectly, not directly. After all, I also like it this way, not because I have a good position, but rather because I do something out of the ordinary and which gives me, I don't hide it from you, some power over people. I told you 'there' that I liked to make people laugh. I evolved: now I like to make them be afraid. In this case, I bring upon them *possible* dangers. You should see them come timidly to consult me: should we plant a factory? Should we make a residential neighborhood?

"Just like an ancient soothsayer, who told the army commander whether to begin the battle or not, I keep some squareheads and their decisions in suspension. In this world, the one who counts is the one who knows or seems to know what others ignore. I would never exchange this life here for the one from the 'free' world. This is not because imposture would not be possible there — in fact, I don't feel at all that I'm an impostor; I'm telling you again: I may accomplish something. But I say this because there, with their system of measuring everything in terms of 'advantageousness,' there is no longer place for a sweet irresponsibility, like here. I am grateful to these regimes for making gratuity possible for man."

"I understand what you're saying. The game counts, not the problem. When I listened to you speaking, I was thinking about the story with the French bishop who, when he was asked whether God exists, replied, He exists since I am a bishop."

"I see you got it," Ernest says. "And since you got into the problem, I will ask you to tell me once what philosophy is. I know that you also are involved in very vague things. We may hire you here."

[1965]

Singing
for our
Supper

Walking an English Songline
From Kent to Cornwall

W. R. Parsons

For the songs and their singers,
and for everyone who supported this journey.
Especially for Ed, Saskia and Felicity.

Praise for Will and Ed's journey...

"A story that needs to be kept alive,
both in word and song"
BBC 1

"Ultimately beneficial for the country at large"
The Guardian

"Very merry men"
BBC Radio 4

"A small, but noticeable, magic has been spun"
The Telegraph

"Trying to revive the Medieval art
of the travelling singer."
BBC World Service

"A pure injection of energy"
Clare Balding

"The future looks good"
Headway EFL Textbook

Contents

FOREWORD

Song and journey, tale and land:
Joyful each goes hand in hand…

This is the true tale of how my friend Ed and I went for a walk and accidentally became almost-famous singers.

One autumn afternoon, we stepped out with overfilled backpacks, empty wallets, and a shared dream of ancient freedom. When we set off walking, singing was no part of my life. But our seven month journey from Kent to Cornwall was soon hijacked by traditional British songs, whose unreasonable power unlocked landscapes, won us friends, thwarted dark forces, filled our cookpots and guided our path.

I found wandering minstrels to be more wished-for and welcomed in twenty-first century England than we ever dreamed possible.

And so the good old songs led us on their merry way…

PROLOGUE

Pilgrims

Winchester to Canterbury

I first met Ed at school. He was a fuzzy artist who napped at lunchtime, and beside normal mild rivalries, we had little contact.

We met again on the Kentish hop harvest. We worked side-by-side at the mouth of a 1950's hop-picking factory, a barn-sized mechanical monster that flailed and bagged the East Kent Goldings hops we fed it. One sunny Wednesday, as the tractor rattled back to the fields with another empty trailer, Ed and I talked of walking the Pilgrims Way, the ancient track between Winchester to Canterbury. The idea bit like the wolfish hop. When harvest was in, we packed our bags. A year earlier I had inherited my father's walking boots. He travelled to London for the serious business of buying his Zamberlans, and they fitted me like a charm. Mum loaned me a cagoule, and my girlfriend gave me a woolly hat. I felt ready.

Everything Ed and I knew about pilgrimage came from old books, so we plotted fresh fundamentals. We'd only walk, taking no lifts or other transport. We wouldn't pay for accommodation, but we didn't want tents, as nightly identical nylon would limit immersion in landscape. Instead we opted for bivvys, waterproof covers for our sleeping bags, to let us be part of the world in which we slept. We'd buy food from independent shops, not supermarkets. And we didn't want maps, believing they'd limit spontaneity. We almost convinced each other to walk barefoot, but both feared the rot and stubbing. As for the contradiction in taking a train to Winchester to walk back to Canterbury, we were happy to empower our journey with the summoning gravity of home. And so we first walked the Pilgrims Way.

Arriving late in Winchester, we hunted for a wild-camp and soon struck urban gold. The cathedral's powerful sodium lamps, which normally glorify in orange the awesome Norman symmetry, were switched off for repairs. So under opportune darkness we hopped a fence, tucked our mats and sleeping bags into bivy sacks, and lay low on the stone skirt of Winchester cathedral.

Sleep came quickly, but ended similarly. We woke long before dawn cracked, the outdoor air sharp tonic to home-soft skin. Winchester was all at rest, not even the bakers' bun-haze yet up. After dressing in everything, we packed away sleeping gear to become early visitors, not trespassing sleepers. But since no-one yet moved, we risked being unlicensed breakfasters, and scrambled eggs on the gaz stove. As butter melted its path around the pan, we saw we'd slept by Saint Swithun's first grave, the place he chose to be buried before Winchester monks shifted his body inside the Cathedral. Swithun was a Saxon bishop, famous for miracles like fixing a basket of broken eggs. What had drawn us to exactly the same place as Swithun? Was it an echo of pilgrims past? Or is this just a really good spot? These were tough questions before tea. After breakfast, spying the morning's first jogger, we rose from Swithun's empty grave, leaving our broken eggshells behind. But with something between hope and cynicism, we didn't look back to see if they were made whole.

Following River Itchen out of Winchester, we walked east for Canterbury, spending three weeks lost, soaked, blistered, tired and hungry. It was an exhilarating, wonderful, whooping-with-joy freedom. Under an elder tree on the North Downs, with night storms crashing around me, for the first time in my life I felt that I was in exactly the right place.

When Canterbury arrived, we dodged double-deckers under the Medieval Westgate, then followed Bell Harry tolling up the high street. Through Christchurch gate, we entered the cathedral precincts and walked slowly toward a glowing gothic door, aching with the promise of a pilgrimage nearly complete. To be told: "No, you can't come in." An organ recital was due to start in half an hour, and although fur-coated gangs of concert-goers gathered in fuzzy support, our way remained barred. Thwarted, we slumped in shadows against the soaring cathedral wall. But we soon realised we weren't really sad at all. Our pilgrimage hadn't been about entering a building. The power we'd found was in the journey, on the path between the roads, where we'd met an uplifting land of kinship and connection. It felt like an unfathomably powerful upgrade of life. Ed and I both agreed: May the journey never end!

Of course, normal life intervened hard. I wrote my Chaucer essay, before studying the history of propaganda for a year. But returning to the convenience and busyness of life in one place didn't dampen my dream of the path. Rather, it intensified like a woodstove door almost shut. Humans have evolved from two million years of nomadic wandering, while our experiment with settled homes and agriculture only began twelve thousand years ago. Journey-making is what our bodies and minds are made for. So having found the paths open and the ways good, what else could there possibly be to do?

CHAPTER 1

Kent

Home to the Valley

Ed and I plan a walk with no end, a perma-pilgrimage. Friends and family are bemused, asking how we'll sustain it? We tell them we've got foraging guidebooks, sleeping bags, folding saws and woollen clothes - what else can we possibly need? "Money!" they cry, but we scoff. Food grows on trees, doesn't it?

I work nights in a homeless shelter, but spend all earnings on kit. Having learned from our Pilgrims' Way mistakes, we buy tarps to cover our bivys and keep rain off our faces. Cagoules are replaced with 'breathable' waterproofs. We compile an extensive herbal first-aid kit. And we bind a small book of collected plant-lore and bushcraft, the best of both our libraries, an internet without batteries. All kit we store in colour-coded dry-bags. When we finally hoist our fully laden backpacks, we're wonderfully overburdened, my pack weighing half my body weight.

On a warm evening in early September we walk west from Ed's family home. His mum weeps and his dad takes moving pictures of our first steps. Within the first hundred metres, Ed stumbles three times in his giant leather boots, made for Highland deer stalking more than strolling Kentish lowlands. I count his trips in an effort to ignore the awesome burden on my shoulders. It's hard to breathe under this weight. We shake over a gate, wobble up an avenue of lime trees, and win our first strange glares from dog walkers. It's far from a graceful start.

After a painful mile we reach the 'Grandmother Tree', Ed's childhood refuge. It's a field maple, a tree often found at boundaries. Ed suggests we've come far enough, and I happily concur. Climbing the tree, we spy on the gamekeeper with our army-surplus monoculars. Despite the aches and lack of distance, I feel like a triumphant seven-year-old, free at last after years of waiting. At dusk, we cook potato stew with fat hen, a meaty-leafed plant that grows widely here. The potatoes we carried from Ed's family garden, and as we eat we excitedly discuss how the weight on our backs will become strength in our bellies. This may sound obvious, but in the balmy autumn half-light, aglow with novel freedom, it feels like a revelation.

That night, I'm devoured by mosquitoes from neck to knee. I wake on fire with itches. Ed brews yarrow tea to calm my constellation bites, and though yarrow isn't much help for insect bites, I'm soothed by Ed's enthusiasm. We check the small book and learn that yarrow's Latin name – *Achillea Millefolium* - cites Achilles, the Greek warrior demi-God, who used this herb to save his battle-smashed companions. It's the sovereign herb for deep cuts and wounds (and for raising and breaking fevers), and was known in the ancient world as *herb militaris*. Yarrow's feathery leaves are everywhere around us. I never paid them much attention before, they always blended into the vague green world underfoot. Crushing a leaf between my fingers, I recognise the childhood scent of spiced high summer. Pleased to make my first new friend of the journey, I tuck a yarrow leaf into my hat.

We share this valley with sporadic sheep and thunderous horse-riders. But the main population here are pheasants, who chortle past our half-hidden camp like nervous overdressed tourists. We both carry catapults, but we're not that hungry yet. But we are soon thirsty. After breakfast of honeyed porridge, we run out of water. This valley lacks a spring or stream, so we consider popping back to Ed's house to refill our bottles, but we realise we might never leave again. So instead we find an animal trough, which at first glance is algal green. Yet under the covered hood lies a far cleaner reservoir, as well as the inlet pipe. In the UK almost all water is mains, so farm water is good as any other tap. We fill our bottles with thanks, and leave tenpence on the trough.

The rest of the day is spent in talk and play, and soon another evening falls. Though we'd meant to move on, the path ahead looms massive and unknown, with winter just round the corner, so we're happy to nestle in this gentle void between home and journey. But as night falls deeper, tendrils of panic rise through me. I fear a baseless future, though lack the words to express this. All I can say is "I feel closer to death". Ed consoles me, saying this is precisely what we've set out to overcome: "To shed old mindsets, and make the transition to a more connected existence, we should expect mental pain and be grateful for it." He's annoyingly right, and I fall asleep grumpy, but no longer glum.

The Valley to the Downs

At dawn, as we snooze in sleeping bags, the gamekeeper's truck revs and roars toward our camp before skidding away at the last moment. It's an effective way to say 'go away'. He must have stronger binoculars than us. We rise and make invisible all traces of our camp, flattening our sleep indents, re-turfing and watering the firepit. Then we heave our packs on our backs and stumble west.

At the first sign of blackberry hedges we stop to plunder breakfast, leap-frogging each other's pick-spot up the hill. These juicy fruits are in their absolute pomp right now, and with purple lips and seed-filled teeth, we congratulate each other for timing our departure to fruity perfection.

A mile along the lane, in a field verge Ed spots a shaggy-headed plant called amaranth or pigweed, an ancient middle-American sacred foodplant with a full offering of proteins needed for human health. Consulting the small book, we learn that pigweed in the USA effectively thwarts GM farmers' monocultural dreams of endless soy, by resisting all herbicides flung against it. Shaking the bushy plant heads, our hands fill with tiny black seeds, like pixelated oil. The small book says that amaranth traditionally offers invisibility when worn next to the bod, so we secrete some about us, then walk on. It's not till two hours later that I realise we haven't yet seen another human, in cars or on paths. Approaching a busy road, we hide behind bushes before crossing unseen. Herbal invisibility, we imagine, probably works best with a little help.

The chalk slopes of the North Downs rise before us, thickly wooded with ash and yew. We dive in, and at the first flat ground, ask silent permission to stay. Within a minute, a young crow craws unharshly. That'll do. We unpack and settle. Around us, mature trees still wear their plastic sapling protectors. Some are cutting deep into the bark they once guarded, and none seem to be biodegrading. We remove the worst offenders, and use the cleanest as a bread-mixing tray. Supper is a half-kicked giant puffball, fried with salami from home. With ash bread (flour, salt and water, cooked among the embers), it's a royal supper. For pudding we pluck yew berries from the tree above. While most parts of a yew are toxic, the flesh (aril) of the berry is not. Just don't eat the inner seed! The flavour is a sinister smoky sweetness.

After food, Ed sets up our day's collection of scraped birch bark to dry by the fire. Its red underbelly looks like bloody sliced meat. Birch bark is the most effective firelighter about, full of volatile oils that love to burn, and it smells like incense when lit. Our small book has been very clear that we must only cut bark from dead trees, so whenever we see a horizontal silver birch, out come the knives.

As we relax fireside, the wind in the trees tricks me into hearing rain, so I string up my tarp. Ed mocks my misinterpretation of Nature, but when water really does tumble, flung from yew boughs in heavy handfuls, we both leap busily. We've practiced tarping in Ed's garden, but this is our first wild setup. My shelter's a flappy shanty compared to Ed's slick hotel, but in his hurry he forgot to wear his jacket, so now he's damp under his dry roof. We agree an order of weatherproofing: first self, then kit, then camp. This may sound obvious, but even simple things need to be got wrong before you really know them.

It's half-past seven, and apart from the crashing storm, it's peaceful. From our tarps we sing the first song of our journey – *The boys are back in town* – but neither of us know the words, and it soon fades into bad guitar impressions.

The Downs to Wye

I wake feeling broken-boned. Last night my thin foam mat let every twig and pebble leave its imprint in my already tender back. I vow to clear the ground properly before my next sleep. The morning woods are storm-soaked, so we eat cold porridge before continuing up the hill. But the trees grow thicker as the hill gets steeper, and we're soon forced to retreat roadside. Stamping along the tarmac, I knock at the first house we see to ask directions, secretly hoping for tea and eggs. But no-one answers. Further down the road, we almost step on the wafer-thin imprint of a deer, made two-dimensional by thousands of cars' weight. It's so strikingly macabre that we linger, waiting for someone to show. But no-one else walks here, just confused faces flashing behind glass windscreens.

As the day progresses, my body increasingly aches. I find myself playing with excuses to quit this ridiculous walk, to just go home and get a normal job. Yet amid my trudging despair, I remember a clip of wisdom from the small book – that holding yarrow and nettle together brings courage. So I slip a nettle leaf beside the yarrow in my hat, and hope for the best. I can't say if it's the herbs that dissolve my doubts, or whether it's reaching Chilham village and relaxing in sunshine with mugs of tea. When the café owner says we can pick grapes from the vine around her window, we lean back and feast like picnic-bench Romans. Everything is golden again. Across the square we see the village pub where on our pilgrimage a year earlier we were kicked out for drying our socks in the fireplace. We'd felt very traditional, but the landlord hadn't agreed. This time Chilham is kinder. Perhaps we've learned the importance of asking permission?

An old school friend lives nearby, so we pop to say hello. Though she's out, her parents offer windfall plums and good advice. They can't believe we don't carry maps, and carefully describe the best route westward. But we're soon lost, wandering vaguely through fields of shaggy bulls and lump-headed sheep. A colonnaded temple at the peak of a small hill beckons us. Getting closer, we see a carving above the door of a ram's skull in hop-bines. We peer through the windows for glimpses of trapdoors leading to secret golden caves. But before we can delve deeper, a Land Rover revs and beeps on the hillside behind. We've been spotted! Wobbling at top speed into the wood beyond the temple, we enter a long-barrow of trees, a passage cut with symmetric dead-end alcoves thickly webbed by huge spiders. As Ed mutters about Shelob, we slow-hurdle the barbed wire boundary, and slide to safety down chalky clematis slopes.

A mile or two along the valley, we find flat ground. Nearby tracks are rutted with heavy machinery, but it's Friday night and we imagine contractors won't work on a Saturday. We settle under a young oak, careful to ensure we can't be seen from road or path. During our first pilgrimage we hadn't been so cautious, and one night our camp was approached by Barbour-clad locals seeking explanation. This was the first time we called ourselves 'pilgrims', which turned out to be the perfect password, transforming hostility into blessing. I was astonished how one word could so entirely change the reality we encountered, like a magic spell or information judo. But we're not Canterbury pilgrims anymore. I'm not really sure what we are. Wayfarers? Wanderers? Vagabonds? Whatever it is, we seem to be getting better at it. Before closing my eyes, I clear away all the twigs and stones from beneath my mat, and lather myself with mosquito oil, to be rewarded with my first good night's sleep of the journey.

Wye to Ashford

In the morning we walk for Wye. With its famous agricultural college, we expect crowds of young farmers in wellies, and are confused by the sharp-suited youngsters clutching laptops. Has farming gone so very high-tech? A passing professor explains that the college was recently bought by a London business school. He adds with a wide grin that this morning Wye found out that a proposed 'Science Park,' a mass housing development, has been officially refused planning permission. It would have doubled the size of this tiny ancient town, which no-one save greedy developers desired. We surf the tide of celebration to haggle at a butcher for outdated sandwiches, and retire to nearby Mersham deer-park for lunch. After food, we cut two walking staffs from a single bough of a fallen chestnut tree. Our small book says chestnut is 'the tree of persistence', which we're clearly going to need. As we whittle our new staffs on the deer-browsed grass, a school-teacher and her class crocodile past. The teacher is enthralled by the idea of a very long walk, but the kids are too hollyoaks cool to care - though a few sneak odd looks back.

After wild-napping under the chestnut, at Mersham pub we meet an old friend. After beating us at darts, Nat tells us his problem: "It's our village cricket team – we're a man short for tomorrow's game. And so are the opposition!" Recognising the quest, next morning Ed and I hit the village pitch in borrowed white sportswear. Drawing the short twig, Ed joins the opposition. Neither of us have played cricket for many years, but it's immeasurably easier without the girls at school watching in judgement. Playing for the trees, I score thirty-eight rapid runs. While fielding, I pretend to be a cat, stalking the outfield. When it's Ed's turn in bat, he swings big and gets bowled out second ball. I try not to cheer too loudly. At the cricketers' tea afterward, we gorge on white-bread sandwiches and individually wrapped biscuits before swapping sportswear back for wool. Nat has kindly washed our kit, but the lingering parfum of persil shocks us. We suppose woodsmoke will soon cover it. I leave Nat with a sleeveless leather jerkin I brought as armour for Sleeping Beauty thornwoods. My bag becomes instantly far lighter, and I wonder what other mythic junk I'm carrying?

We approach Ashford with sugar headaches, the ring road's flickering lights hurting our eyes as young men in low-slung fords shout unofficial welcomes. "Something about luck to you," Ed grins. To escape the fumes, we try to cross the ditched wetlands below the road, but the way soon softens into impassable marsh. A man walking his Doberman directs us to woodlands where he ran away as a child. As the sun sets we reach the promised hideout. Sitting to listen for signs to settle, we're answered by the scream of drinking youth. So we shift to more peaceful groves, before crashing into sleep.

Ashford to Tenterden

The sun rises with gentle strength, as autumn mists soak into fruitful hedgerows. We walk past a lady dragging her lawnmower round a heavily laden apple-tree, and offer admiration for the tree's bounty. Without pause, she invites us to help ourselves: "Take all you want. I never eat those apples, there might be maggots. I only eat supermarket fruit." Her apples have diagonally-snapping flesh and taste of minted cherries, so we happily load our pockets before following footpaths to feast by a lakeside lightning-blasted oak, where a fisherman with a clarinet tells us we have more freedom than millionaires. When the day fades, somewhere near Tenterden we camp among stinkhorn fungi. We make a pyramid fire following advice from the small book, using information taken from Ed's collection of Tom Brown guides. It's all about pre-sourcing the grades of twig, and building a structure that the fire can grow upward into. As the stewpot simmers, we sing a nursery rhyme called *Oats and Beans:*

> *Oats and beans and barley grows,*
> *As you and I and everyone knows.*
> *A-waiting for the partner.*

Among the crackling firewood and screeching

owls, the song's cryptic simplicity drifts into the darkness as just another natural sound of the night.

Come morning, after cat-washing in an icy stream, we squeeze between trees to find ourselves in instant suburbia. As we stare astonished at the sudden tarmac, twenty schoolkids burst from front-doors like spores from a puffball, and we follow the drifting cloud into town. On the green, a circus is coming down, small groups of capped men puffing roll-ups and gazing sullenly at damp canvas. Further into town, we peer into steamed-up café windows, but our original tenners have dramatically subsided. I can't even afford the merino-wool top I find in a charity shop. The financial aspect of our journey, we realise, was not especially well considered. We may need to make money somehow. But we have nothing to sell except our time, and that's not for sale. With rumbling tummies, we pass a busker playing a flute astonishingly badly. But the townsfolk passing his squeaks and whistles all grin and drop their pound coins of sympathy in his hat. We're amazed. Surely we could do better than that? So we discuss the radical possibility of street song. I'm initially uncertain. Aged seven, I embraced defiant songlessness to thwart my father's suggestion that I join a cathedral choir. But my dad died two years ago, I'm no longer seven, and this isn't about joining a choir. We could sing what, where and however we like. I find myself surprisingly keen, and suggest we start immediately. Ed however withers at my enthusiasm, saying he feels 'side-shunted into the ether'. So we look for somewhere for Ed to un-shunt. The only indoor space not requiring money is a church, vast, gloomy and col. We gratefully slot ourselves into the empty pews. Though Ed and I don't call ourselves Christian, I don't really believe in atheists. But architecture and accessibility aren't beliefs, and in such terms alone, England's roadside churches are the great treasures of our built environment. Added to which, they have plugs for hoovers and taps for gardeners. So Ed charges his phone while I fill our water bottles, before we both rest in the chilly songless silence.

Tenterden to Rye

Leaving Tenterden, we aim for the Isle of Oxney. Its name puzzles us, as water seems so distant. A bird-watcher explains that four hundred years ago this whole area was waterlogged, a famous centre of ship-building, until a great storm shifted the river: "Talk about climate-change," he grins, "I bet they blamed the sinners!"

Some miles further, we settle to camp among gorse bushes. But as we unpack, we find ourselves surrounded by the zany rolling eyes and eager pink noses of cattle. Knowing bovine curiosity can maraud, we swiftly re-pack and hop the barbed wire away. And then something strange happens. We both start walking with extraordinary swiftness, each step a great emboldened stride, our movements effortless like hill-streams. Are we on a ley-line? Have our boots been charmed into seven leaguers? "I can see sparks flying from your feet!"

Ed yells through slipstreams, and he's right, a shard of flint caught in my boots' tread is making sparks fly.

After an hour of inexplicable flow, we gratefully steer toward the harbour of a village pub. Reaching the porch, we're suddenly clumsy again with self-powered movement. As we stumble through the door, all heads turn and somebody shouts: "Suicide bombers!" "Boom!" Ed replies. Settling in, an old boy introduces us to the poetry of EE Cummings and the art of Kurt Schwitters. A teenage lad, here with his mum, explains the link between ghosts and aliens. When the pub closes, we're invited back to a family house for cheese on toast and Billy Bragg vinyl, after which we shift old bicycles to crash on garage carpets.

Far too early, we wake to hear the family getting ready for school. We rise to the street, and sit foggily curbside. As our hosts wave goodbye, they fling from the car window a gift that skitters over tarmac to wedge beneath my boot. It's an OS map. Unfolding this treasure, Ed and I can see where we are, where we've come from, and where to go next. It's an unfathomably vast upgrade. Now we have the eagle's vision. Now we can see the future. As we debate who should navigate, I'm extolling the merits of my half GCSE in geography when Ed suddenly raises his fist like a soldier sensing ambush. "Hold it," he cries, "we've just missed an orchard." Sure enough, twenty paces back, behind the bus-stop is an orchard of pear trees, whose juicy windfalls are just reachable by staff. Within an hour, the map has given us breakfast. I flick twenty pence onto a tree-root, and we gratefully crunch the sweet dewy fruit, as somewhere underfoot, Kent becomes East Sussex.

CHAPTER 2

East Sussex

Rye

Our new map leads toward the promise of Rye. We still walk tenderly under our backpacks, but it's getting better. Unlike our finances. Resting in a hedge to count coins, we find less than a pound between us. These blackberries won't last forever, so we talk again of busking. As far as we can see, the basics are a musical offering and a hat. Some street-musicians use microphones and backing tracks. Most play instruments. We've never heard two unaccompanied singers on the high street, but it's all we've got. We think about songs we like and know well enough to sing in public. We can only find four, all traditional songs from a sixties album called 'Folk Songs of Old England' by Tim Hart and Maddy Prior. A friend at university burned me a copy. It's an entirely leftfield genre of music for us, but we both sense a strangely nourishing power in these old songs. Of the four we agree on, *Oats and Beans* is probably a seed planting prayer, sung to the rhythm of the job. *Adieu Sweet Lovely Nancy* is about a sailor leaving his lover, and the perils faced at sea. *Fiddlers Green* tells of a dying fisherman's hope for the afterlife. And *My Son John* is a father's effort to secure compensation for his son who lost both legs while serving in the Navy. This song has a 'roo-dum-dye, rabba-diddle-dye' chorus which seems wonderfully ill-fitting for the topic. Perhaps this is the point - to make a jolly noise about a harrowing topic that's otherwise easy to ignore?

Our songs selected, the bigger question arises of whose hat to use? Ed makes a good point, his does get skittish upside down. It's made of hardened Mongolian cardboard, while mine is felted Welsh wool and sits well anywhere. While we debate, two elderly men with long white beards and tiny backpacks float briskly past. To our trollish heaviness, they seem positively elven. Inspired, we cease planning, and rise to follow our future into Rye. Halfway there, I realise we're already singing.

Over the field horizon, Rye rises like a Medieval moon. With its domed hill and pinnacle church ringed by black and white timber houses, Rye can't have changed much in the last seven hundred years. Following River Rother's loops, we ascend the urban slopes. Our OS map ends here, so in a secondhand bookshop we browse for the next chapter of our path. The Irish shopkeeper is all hard suspicious eyes, as though she can guess the limit of our spending power. I try and win her over by chatting of my dad's old bookshop, but it's not till she sees our packs and staffs outside that she thaws into smiles, offering us water and local history. We're told of French and Flemish lightning raids on Rye in the Middle Ages, when St Mary's church bell was stolen. Yet within a year, the men of Rye counter-raided to steal it back. It's hard to imagine today, invading France for a bell. When we leave, we're given a small notepad which we gratefully designate as our new songbook. Outside St Mary's church, now locked for the evening, I scrawl song lyrics in tiny writing. As well as the four we know, we add five more bangers from the same source: *Lish Young Buy a Broom*; *Farewell Nancy*; *The Rambling Sailor*; *Three Drunken Maidens*; and *The Gardener*. A passing man laughs at my 'prison writing'. Our songbook launched, at dusk we scout Rye for a spot to sleep. The veranda of the bowls clubhouse looks comfy, but it's a notch too cheeky, so we retire to the salt marshes below town.

Next morning, we spend our last few coins on a cup of tea from a roadside café. After sipping in turns, we're fully empty-pocketed. Now we really must sing. Last night we realised the importance of a sign. In a noisy world, people can easily block out sounds, but who can ignore written words? So on skip-delved cardboard I write *Singing for our Supper,* and Ed adds *Walking to Cornwall*. A passing builder, proving our artwork's concept, sees the writing and advises us to try at the market. So we head down and take a spot just outside the gate. Too nervous to linger, we fall straight to song. Almost immediately, we must double our volume to compete with the ambience. We're amazed that no-one tells us to stop. In fact, within a minute our first benefactor has stepped forward with fifty shining pence, saying: "Your songs are the finest I've ever heard!". I bet she says that to all the wandering singers, but it's a good start.

After looping our slender repertoire twice, we start getting funny looks from the fishmonger. And with the buses roaring, the butcher boasting, and the charity collectors rattling cans, it's hard to be heard. So we retreat to a nearby cobbled lane without car access. The hill is steep, so people pass slowly, giving us plenty of time to sing for them. We stay here for two hours, unafraid to loop, as no passer-by hears more than one or two songs. We settle into the system of Ed singing melodies while I make up harmonies. I've no experience at this, but as long as the last note of each line sounds good, the rest can do almost anything, weaving over, under and around the tune. It's surprisingly good fun. We debut *The Rambling Sailor*, about a man returning from naval service who hunts for women with pikish hunger. We also have a crack at *Lish Young Buy-a-Broom*, though we need to keep our noses in the songbook to stay lyrically united. This song is about a wandering singer who meets a broom-seller, to form a merry strolling couple until she sails home for Germany. I wonder if we'll meet broom-sellers somewhere down the path?

We stop singing when we're croaky and light-headed. My hat is heavy with silver and gold, and we've enjoyed lavish compliments and well-wishing, but perhaps best of all, we've been tipped the names of more traditional songs to learn:

Spenser the Rover and *The Harvest Song* sound great, as far as we can tell from the snippets sung to us. Our sign also worked wonders. We both witnessed initially unimpressed people read it and reappraise our offering with far kinder ears. But our next sign needs two sides, to be legible in both directions. All in all, it's been a hugely successful introduction to the ancient art of busking. At a fish and chip shop we change coins into paper and supper. As the sun sinks, with our hearts, pockets and bellies full, we walk out of Rye.

Rye to Hastings

Waking in extreme rain, we spend half the next morning learning *Harvest Song* from the warmth of our sleeping bags. It's an anthem about farmers getting drunk before work, and would have been great to sing on the hop harvest, bouncing on the back of a farm-cart as we raced down country lanes in first light. The song sinks in, the morning stretches on, but the rain keeps falling. So we finally rise and walk on. Under heavy deluge we aim for the village of Cock Marling. With his body and backpack draped under a green poncho, Ed looks like a military camel. I suppose I do too. Reaching the village, we climb from puddles into the pub. The landlord looks distinctly uncertain until we mention a man we met in Rye called Terry Walnut, who recommended we visit this pub. Suddenly we're everyone's friend, and when we try to pay for our mugs of tea, the landlord laughs and thrusts pints in our hands.

At the next village west, we shelter in Udimore church porch to eat pub-donated camembert with windfall pears. After food, we venture into the empty sanctuary and sing *Farewell Nancy*. When harmony hits in here, the echoing resonance of the stone building makes it feel like invisible choirs are joining our song. In excited shock, we agree to sing in as many churches as we can.

The rain eases toward sunset, and we get more lost than usual in vast cow fields somewhere above Hastings. After two hours stumbling through muddy darkness, we finally see lights, and escape through a school playground, then hop the fence into a garden-centre, where we sleep behind pallets piled with topsoil.

Our alarm clock is magpies. Members of the Corvine clan (crow, rook, raven), my mother taught me the habit of saluting them on sight. A group of magpies is called a tiding:

> *One for sorrow, two for joy,*
> *Three for a girl, four for a boy,*
> *Five for silver, six for gold,*
> *Seven for a secret never to be told.*

We're woken this morning by at least fifteen. I suppose we'll find out what it means. Leaving the garden centre before staff arrive, we roll downhill into Hastings, passing an exceptional unsteady gentleman who bids us good morning with an enormously powerful voice. By the stony sea, we take bubble and squeak at the Mermaid café, and quietly practice our songs on windswept benches.

A gang of bikers suggest we sing on George Street. We check it out, and find a grand echoing corner with passing and gathering room. As we prepare to sing, I shift my backpack to hear the awful crunch of an egg, bought roadside yesterday and yet unboiled. I'm alarmed by the hygienic and symbolic implications of an egg breaking inside my bag, but what can be done right now? I zip it away and get ready to sing.

Thankfully, I misinterpreted the signs. Whether it's the egg or the magpies, luck is very much with us. We've arrived in perfect time for Hastings Art Weekend, with public exhibitions unfolding all around us. An artist with an electric leaf-blower sends tumble-weed rolling up and down the narrow fishing street, and in the square opposite, 'British Bulldog' is played with clashing trolleys of unwanted antiques. Two green woolly singing backpackers fit in perfectly, and circles of clappers soon corral us. *Harvest Song* goes down a storm, our audience bopping merrily like they're bouncing on farm-carts, a move we suppose must have deep roots in English dance culture. Between songs we're invited to visit homes up the road, and even asked to sing at someone's wedding - though it's in Scotland next month, so we sadly decline. We're also given scrawled lyrics to *John Barleycorn* and *Diggers Song*, which both sound like bangers. Thank you Hastings!

We celebrate in the sea, and I wash the egg out my backpack. Nothing got got, as everything's in bags of bags. As we dry kit on the shingle, a man called

Paul arrives. He telephoned Ed yesterday asking to join our journey. Neither of us knows him, or how he got Ed's number, but why not? Along the beach this scruffy blonde man stamps, grinning and launching into immediate poetry:

> *Three vagabonds on the road of ley,*
> *In constant praise of love and play.*
> *I heard they seek the land of fay.*
> *They changed my life that very day,*
> *I pray they find the land of fay.*

Paul swings a suspiciously light bag from his shoulder. I learn he lacks a torch, bowl, water bottle and sleeping mat. We visit a camping shop, where Paul grabs essentials and we buy a new OS map. Then we leave Hastings as a gang of three, shouting boisterous farewells to cheering seafront drinkers as we walk into the sunset.

Hastings to Battle

Town soon turns to earth, and we wander happily in the peace of muddy darkness, until a dog-walker strongly recommends the local pub. Outside the Plough Inn at Crowhurst, we unify our intent to manifest good welcome. This means stepping in boldly, smiling, meeting eyes and offering greetings. It works beautifully. The grey-bearded giant behind the bar is visibly moved by our tales of journey, and pints of Harveys Armada (my favourite) line up on the bar. Ed and I sing, Paul rhymes, and the landlord passes round the darts trophy as a collection cup. When we leave, we're presented with a giant beetroot, and given directions to an idyllic sleep-spot in local woods, as well as a stamped addressed postcard to send to the Plough when we reach Cornwall. We depart richer than we arrived, and stride merrily into the woods. We're soon lost, and at the first flat ground we string our tarps and settle, drifting into smiling dreams as heavy rain smashes down and a screaming train zooms past twenty yards from our camp.

In dewy autumn pastures next morning, field mushrooms shine like supper-beacons, and pulse with life in our hands when plucked. Today we aim for Battle, where in 1066 Harold lost England. A moat of puddles guards the town, patrolled by families armed with umbrellas. In truth, among this damp leisurely countryside it's hard to sense the desperate fight whose outcome here determined so much of English history. We stop to sing hello to a purple budding alder tree, which our small book says offers protection at the front of battle. Apparently the first man was made from alder, and the first woman from rowan. In other traditions, alder is personified as half-hag half-maiden, who lurks in swamps to make travellers lose their minds. This story may be rooted in the illness of swamp fever, whose cure is to 'marry the hag', as the bark of alder is well-reputed medicine for this malady. We also learn that the pilings holding up Venice are made from alder wood. I tuck a cone into my hat.

Aldered up, we enter Battle. Squatting in the

Sussex clay, this town was built by Norman William to celebrate the very spot where Saxon Harold died. The abbey church's high altar was placed on the exact location of his death. This seems rather brutal for Christianity, but the Normans were 'North Men' or Vikings, famed for their violence, like the 'harrowing of the north' and the judicial cutting off of hands. I'm no fan of the Anglo-Normans, but I'd like to visit Battle Abbey. Sadly it's expensive and closed, double-whammy. Instead, we meet two musical brothers, and share songs and soup in their garden. I manage to tread barefoot in their puppy's poo, which wins me a soapy foot bath. Ed looks like he wishes he'd thought of it first.

Battle to Herstmonceaux

When we leave, our hosts walk a mile with us to the edge of their territory. We continue to Catsfield, following an invitation given in Hastings. But we soon get waylaid at another pub. For the second time this week, someone shouts 'suicide bombers!' as we enter. We laugh and bow. A minute later the shouter comes over to apologise: "I meant no harm, lads, will you take a drink on me?" We will. And soon we're singing, bashing out *My Son John* to happy applause, after which the whole pub bursts into song, in one voice all together. I don't know what we're singing, I'm not sure anyone does, but it's the best unified pub singsong I've ever encountered. As we leave, we're slid a tenner 'for breakfast'.

The glow of sunset has long faded, and it's now nine o' clock on a Sunday night. With headtorches shining, we finally spot the right gate and knock at a cottage door. Out pops Jane in her dressing gown and wellies with an 'Oooh' of welcome. She leads us to her woods and says to make ourselves at home. We string tarps and saw fallen wood, but something is wrong with our fire. Flames won't rise, despite having dry birch-bark and twigs, matches and breath. After twenty minutes we surrender, perplexed. Roaming badgers bark in laughter at the cold confused humans. Until I realise we placed our fire directly above an underground oak root. Shifting the charred sticks twelve inches to one side, with a single match flames leap brightly. It's a good lesson as more rain falls.

Early next morning, our hostess arrives with a steaming tureen of soup. "It's my own chickens, I kill and pluck them, and the soup's as honest as any." Though a professed vegan, Paul can't resist, and we admire his flexibility. After our morning feast, we walk through wet woods for Windmill Hill, where I spot a young mother tucking her toddler's trousers into his socks to help him walk. I try it myself, and find it drastically reduces trouser-drag on the knees. Sharing this walk-hack with the others, we all upgrade.

Soon we reach the Pevensey Levels, a legendary wetland of mist and smugglers. On its eastern boundary, a few metres above sea-level, stands Herstmonceaux, home to a castle and observatory.

Both are closed, so past rusty 'No Trespass' signs, we roam badger labyrinths of neck-high nettles. Our small book says that stinging nettles were used for millennia to make rope, clothing, animal food, paper and probably much more. It's a true companion plant for human life on earth. Also, nettle sting is a classic preventative medicine for arthritis and rheumatism, promoting blood flow and healthy circulation. And nettle is renowned as anti-tobacco medicine. The two plants never share ground, so nettle tea is a powerful aid for people trying to kick their smoking habits. I attempt the 'thank-you' method of easing stings, hoping through gratitude to turn pain to blessing, but I'm not sure how well it works.

Deeper in Herstmonceaux woods, we find flat unbrambled ground between three fallen trees, and ask permission to sleep. Stood in silence, I spy three twigs on the ground in the shape of a rune. I point it out to Ed, and wide-eyed he shows me the very same symbol as ivy growing on a tree-trunk. Then I see it as tiny twigs in a spider's web, and then as tree-roots jutting above the soil, and then as moss on a bough. Our vision blurs, and we realise we're surrounded by this symbol. It's everywhere around us. We can't decide what's more incredible, that Nature or a human arranged this? Among the mystery, we settle and carve the gifted symbol into our chestnut staffs and dreams.

Late that night, shotguns and champagne corks pop and blast in the fields below the wood, as some wild celebration unfolds. Peering from the trees, we can see only vague whirling shapes. I'd like to leap out singing, but caution warns otherwise.

Herstmonceaux to Jevington

In early sunshine, we leave the woods and take a full blackberry breakfast. Our small book says that when the devil fell from heaven, he/she landed in a blackberry bush and cursed it, so we mustn't eat the fruits after St Michael's day, the twenty-ninth of September. Checking the date, Ed says Michaelmas isn't till tomorrow. Reassured, we feast on.

The Pevensey Levels stretch before us. This is Will 'o Wisp country, where fog-blind travellers are led by treacherous twinkling lights to their watery doom. We're glad for the bright sun, but it's still hard to know where we are, as the flatness of this landmarkless land allows no sense of progress. After walking for hours, nothing around us changes. But deep in the wetlands, something does flare darkly in our group. Ed and I start to argue about who should carry a bundle of foraged chickweed, which weighs almost nothing. Our disharmony spirals and Ed storms off, silent and angry, leaving me to walk with Paul, who talks non-stop. I grow increasingly intolerant. Eventually we all stop and talk through our psycho-frictions. Ed says he's been successfully bashing it into the soil with his staff. I give Paul a fox's jawbone to aid cunning talk. We crunch the disputed chickweed with bread, butter and sachets of sugar, to share the burden internally. And then we sing *Fiddlers Green*, to patch our punctured friendship. Harmony restored, we safely leave the Levels and take tea in a pub advertising 'hand-carved roasts'. The manager brings out grey lukewarm tea, so we ask the waitress with brighter eyes. She explains that customers here are mostly pensioners, and the tea-machine is set to cold. Then she winks and pops to the kitchen to make us mugs from the staff kettle. The manager frowns, but everyone ignores him. On picnic benches outside, we sip tea and wax our boots, as a wobbly old lady approaches. "I think it's marvellous," she begins, and smiles stretch across our faces. "I think it's marvellous you men put your shoes on this bench where people sit. You have no manners!" she spits, before darting away righteously. There's no point explaining that the benches are already covered with bird-poo, that it will rain soon, that UV cleans so well, or that no-one else will likely sit out here till spring. She wants to fire a barb, not have a conversation, so we lower our heads and take it in the body.

Through Willingdon's jungle of bungalows, we take back-alley shortcuts to reach the South Downs. These small English mountains were born from an Alpine shimmy fifteen million years ago. A great fold of chalk arose, whose centre has long since eroded to leave two remnant nubs of chalk, the North and South Downs. Their name comes from the Celtic *Dun*, meaning hill, height or fort. East Sussex locals call the paths up and down 'twittens'. We stamp our first twitten, puffing heavily, at the top collapsing on a tump, a bronze age burial mound. I think Ed and I were racing, though neither of us says so and he got here first. Under rapid clouds, we lie chewing wild thyme and red clover plucked from this peak. It feels like our journey has finally begun. We sing *Adieu Sweet Lovely Nancy* and plant an acorn, though we don't dare hope it'll grow to more than a sheep-snack. Further along the prehistoric causewayed path, we find a ring of mushrooms and attempt a wild-nap, keen for the trip to fay; but sleep evades us.

The path leads to Jevington's pub, the Eight Bells, where the landlord requests songs and pours drinks. We may be new to our role, but it feels like we're expected. *Spenser the Rover* works a treat here, winning a chorus of deep 'arrs'. The song comes from this landscape, held by a local family called the Coppers. It tells of a Sussex man who leaves home to go walking, foraging and sleeping in the woods. This must be the totem song of English wayfaring, and we're happy to share it. But Spenser sets out because he has been 'much reduced', which doesn't feel like our motivation - though I suppose we're not exactly poster-boys for modern success. The song ends when Spenser returns home, there to find the peace he sought all along.

After song, a grizzled old boy teaches me secret Sussex poaching techniques. With an earnest smile, he explains that coarse black pepper and a big knobbly flint are all you need for catching bunnies. If you place the flint and pepper by their run, the rabbit will sniff the foreign powder and sneeze with a violent projectile motion. Your well-placed flint should stun or kill them. This is either a genuine poaching trick, or a classic wind-up for lads who don't know better. I collect a pocketful of black-pepper sachets from the pub's dining room, just in case.

When we ask about sleep-spots, the landlord recommends the bone-orchard (graveyard). We're about to head over when a sparkling couple stroll into the tap-room, and straightaway we know we'll be going home with them. Ella and Nick whisk us to their caravan, even carrying our bags. There we share songs and stories, before feasting on roast pumpkin and rice pudding. Long after dark, Paul sleeps on the caravan's spare bed, while Ed and I kip outside beneath the van, tucked away from the shire horse who shares this field. When I ask our hosts if they are late or early risers, they laugh and say they're 'airborne', which makes me grin all the way into sleep.

Jevington to Wilmington

After porridge and gifts, we return to Jevington village. Another stranger is joining us today, a man called Tim. I think Paul invited him. We find Tim nursing an early pint outside the pub, a tiny backpack on the bench beside him. He has no torch, water bottle, cup or bowl, which mildly irks me. But he does have a strong beard and strangely infectious enthusiasm. We sit and chat, and when a neighbouring table depart with half their lunch uneaten, we pilfer the plates to share the leftover largesse.

As a gang of four, we visit Jevington church via its Tapsel gate, a rare Sussex contraption that spins around a centre pole, designed to let coffin carriers rest their burden, and keep sheep in/out the graveyard. Circling the church, on the eastern wall I see the symbol we found in the woods two nights ago. Ed and I stare in wonder at this outrageous co-incidence. Tim asks if we're religious. "Are rocks religious?" is my evasive best.

Some miles of holloway later, we meet the Long Man of Wilmington, a hillside chalk giant carrying two long staffs. Like Dorset's Cerne Abbas giant, this carved man may once have sported a great chalk phallus, but local monks felt threatened. Some folk say the Long Man and his twin staffs represent the mastery of dualities, which can create a window of possibility in the world, aka magic. Or he could just be a wayfarer with two sticks? We step over the downtrodden fence to climb his outline, and pick greater plantain from between his chalky feet. Plantain is an infection remover, used by chewing the leaves and applying the green mush directly to stings, burns and cuts. Our small book says that Alexander the Great used plantain to cure his headaches, and Native Americans believed the plant was a gift from the Europeans, as it was so good at relieving rattlesnake bite. Plantain is known as 'Englishman's Foot', for it famously followed the British Empire around the world.

Another name is 'Cuckoo's Bread', from the Medieval legend that every seven years plantain becomes a bird, to fly in search of cuckoos it might serve. We watch awhile, but no cuckoos appear. I tuck a leaf into my hat, and we walk on.

Wilmington to Glynde

In Berwick village, we enter a pub quiz. But knowing nothing of John Grisham's novels, Amy Johnson's flying record, or the colour of the St George Cross ribbon, we come firmly last. Paul chats up the barmaid, who's impressed but confused by his poems. "But what's fay mean? And vagabond?" she whispers while he expounds. We leave the pub late, and in nearby woods, overgrown and brambled, Paul and Tim stumble torchless with drunken glee. Finding no convenient grove for all, we take individual nooks, Tim simply lying under his loose plastic tarp like a clammy blanket. In the pub this evening he admitted that he carries an apothecary's bundle of semi-legal substances, which might explain his twinkling enthusiasm. We wish him luck in the rain.

It falls mightily, but the rising sun soon steams away the waters of the night. While the others doze, under the hazel coppice I stalk a sleepy pheasant with my catapult, day-dreaming about being the great hunter bringing back fresh meat. Until Paul bounds over with a louder dream: "Will, I've worked it out, we're Star Trek characters. You're Ryker, Ed's Picard, and I'll be Worf..." The pheasant chortles off unimpressed. Back at camp, Ed is cooking porridge with fennel. I think he's trying to be the herbal equivalent of the great hunter. It's amazingly foul-tasting, but we're hungry, so down it goes.

> *He who sees fennel but picks it not,*
> *is no man but a devil.*

Ed quotes this ancient Welsh wisdom as we eat, and we discuss whether it means that the health benefits of fennel are so great, only the worst people would leave it unpicked – or whether it means that this Roman-introduced herb, as an ally of the invaders, should be uprooted at every opportunity?

On the edge of the Downs we meet free running horses, mohawked like city punks. They nuzzle soft hellos, and seem puzzled why we're walking when we could be riding them? It's hard to explain the ethics of private property to a horse. We rest in Alciston church, whose silence wonderfully holds our songs. And then we walk for Firle, a village owned entirely by one aristocrat. Despite my natural distrust of such monopolies, here the model seems to work, for Firle's beauty is well-held and rare. We spend time in St Peter's church, particularly admiring the John Piper window of sheep at sunrise. Then we cross the great rushing road to reach Glynde. Finding a dead robin in a gutter, we bury him in a wrap of mugwort between the roots of a roadside oak. After song in Glynde's neo-Italian church, we creep through llama fields into woods, where Ed cooks a wild-food melange of all the day's gleanings. I think it's the rowan berries that make it so odd, but again we're hungry and there's nothing else. Later, I encourage Tim to set himself up a proper shelter. With a pipe of African dream herb in his hand, Tim's reluctant to co-operate, but he admits gladness when lightning flashes. It's proving a stormy autumn.

Glynde to Lewes

Next morning, with legs like rotten tree-trunks we labour up the Downs, to meet a hillfort called Caburn. This was once a ritual centre for Iron Age locals, though no-one agrees what people did in such places. We cross the pinnacle ditch to soak up views of the wandering Downs, pierced by River Ouse curling to the sea. Suddenly, twenty-yards away from us, a man with great white wings lands softly on the hilltop. As we stare in shock, he folds away his paraglider. When we say hello, Rob tells us how he sometimes soars a thousand metres high on thermals from this very hilltop:

"Just the other day, I was up there in the sky as high as I could go, to the point where the earth looks flat and people are smaller than ants. When to my surprise I hear a voice, as clear as yours or mine, saying 'Timmy, Timmy, come here Timmy'. I look about, but there's no-one else flying. Now, I'm a religious man, so my next thought was 'It's the Lord!'. But surely the Lord would know my name's not Timmy? So I descend a way, squint my eyes, and sure enough, down on Mount Caburn is a lady walking her dog. Her voice had risen on thermals to meet me in the sky!"

Perhaps this is why the ancient British were so keen on hilltops – because songs offered here might reach the very peak of the heavens? I wonder if voices just keep going, to float through space as bubbles of song? Or whether they meet a final reflective layer in Earth's atmosphere, there to echo and harmonise with all the other hillsongs? Ed suggests this song-layer might repel meteorites. We join the lineage by lying on our backs and singing *John Barleycorn*, as gift from earth to sky.

Many families are out sauntering, and one smiling couple promise us pints if we reach the Lewes Arms within an hour. So we step to with purpose, and reach our destination with minutes to spare. But our donors are nowhere to be seen. At the pub door, Ed and I request a micro-holiday from Tim and Paul. We imagine urban adventures will be easier in smaller groups, especially wild-camping. We agree to meet tomorrow.

Inside, the Lewes Arms is steamy with Sunday lunchers. At the last empty table, Ed and I chat with two fellows who've just walked the Seven Sisters, the famously undulating chalk cliffs between here and Eastbourne. But when conversation touches traditional songs, one of the men groans: "Don't get him started on folk music, we're having the weekend off!" We roundaboutly learn that this walker has an OBE for services to

English Folk Music, as librarian of Cecil Sharp House, the national centre of traditional dance and song. We've never heard of it, and though we'd love to ask more, we respectfully shift the topic to talk instead of Vashti Bunyan and the Captain Swing riots. The walking pair then offer us a pie and a pint. "Each?" we ask in amazement. "Of course!" they roar, as though it's the funniest question ever. As we feast, we're warned of Lewes' November Fifth celebrations: "It's fiery mayhem, and you'll almost certainly get beaten up." The folk man admires our chestnut staffs, and tells us how to chamfer their bases, trimming the edge of the base to prevent the puffy flowering of wood that can lead to splitting. We instantly whip out our knives to follow his advice. The pair express surprise to see us wielding sheath knives in a town pub, but we assure them we have certificates, printed, signed and laminated, to explain our 'good reason' for carrying such blades. We made these certificates at home to confound curious coppers, but this is the only time they leave our backpacks.

Later that evening we visit Lewes folk club, upstairs in the pub. It's our first folk club experience, and costs four pounds to enter, so we wreak justice on the sandwiches. I blunder to the other clubbers that we met the librarian of Cecil Sharp House downstairs, and they gather in shock: "But why didn't he join us this evening?" they demand. I invent something about urgent folksong business in London, and they seem quelled. The folk club involves sitting and listening to a talk about the mechanisation of farming, before everyone taking turns to sing. We really like a song called *Pleasant and Delightful* about a sailor's farewell to his lover. This seaward cycle of departure and hoped-for return feels like a crucial story of the south coast. When our turn comes, we blast out *Lish Young Buy a Broom* at full raucous busking pace. Everyone joins the chorus at nostalgic half-speed, but we restart each verse with redoubled tempo. Later, there's a raffle we don't win, though the victor kindly donates us their prize bottle. At the end, we enquire after the town's best outdoor sleep-spot. We're recommended Lewes Priory, once a wealthy house of the Cluniac Order, now empty ruins. One side is open to the public, while the other is private. Preferring solitude, we choose the latter, and hop a flint wall to sleep beneath a vast beech tree. We imagine its mother beech may have witnessed the Reformation destruction of this place, when the monasteries and abbeys were suppressed by King Henry VIII and Thomas Cromwell in the mid 1500s. In the pub tonight we learned that a battle fought here in 1264 created England's first parliament, when Simon de Montfort and the barons defeated King Henry III. Ed and I lie low among the mist and memories. Apart from the distant tyre-squeaks and exhaust roars of youth in small cars, the night is silent.

In earliest morning light we rise. Last night a solitary beechnut beneath my mat caused great restlessness, never quite waking me up to deal with it, nor letting me truly rest deeply. After morning tea, I find the offending beechnut and pocket it. In exchange, some peregrine instinct prompts me to leave my chestnut staff here, leant against the beech tree. I imagine that many pilgrims left their staffs at this destination, back when pilgrimage was a thriving reality in Britain.

Beyond the priory, Lewes town is slowly waking up, and after breakfast we seek somewhere to sing. The high street bridge looks ideal, with Harveys brewery behind and River Ouse below. I fling last night's beechnut into the river, and we set to song. Almost immediately, a woman and her young daughter sit cross-legged in front of us to form a seed-crowd. The busk follows beautifully. Passing cars lower their windows to fling out coins. Tiny children stand close to listen, before ever-so-shyly donating their family gold. We bow deeply for every gift, and offer rapid thanks between the lines of the songs. *The Rambling Sailor*, about a seaman fresh ashore and prowling, works best here. "What's the song about?" a small boy asks, and I explain: "Well, a sailor has come home from the sea, and he wants lots of new friends to have fun with." The child nods sagely, and his grandmother guffaws uproariously.

On Lewes bridge we learn how the direction we face changes where our voices meet. If we both look outward, our notes never fully harmonise, each voice drifting down different streets. But if we face inward, our voices mingle about fifteen feet away, creating a song-zone into which people step to find themselves surrounded by sudden blasting harmony. I watch folk stop in shock.

After some hours of song, our hat is heavy and we're happy with our haul. Ed even finds a fiver in his boot. As we don backpacks, a man named Mike steps up, saying he hasn't heard *Lish Young Buy A Broom* sung in over twenty-five years. On the strength of this, he invites us to lunch. As we walk to his house, Mike points out fruitless pomegranate trees and gutterfuls of nipplewort among the Lewes backstreets. After sharing food and song, we donate Mike last night's donated bottle, and he teaches us another traditional song called the *Nutting Girl*, about the consequences of young women being overawed by sweetly-singing farmers. Then Mike shows us his secret archaeological dig, concealed under a pallet in the garden: "I've only found cat skulls so far, but I'm going ever deeper..." His eyes grow misty as he talks about the stories hidden in soil: "There's a dig in Boxgrove where five thousand years ago, hunters killed a horse, then sat in a circle knapping flints to butcher it. From the flint shards they left, we know that one of them was left-handed." I talk vaguely about not knowing what songs they were singing so long ago, but Mike grins: "Are you sure? Because that's not what I felt when I heard you two on the bridge today..."

Lewes to Brighton

We later re-meet Tim and Paul, who also enjoyed unexpected adventures with new friends. Tim now needs to return to London, as he has a concert tonight – he's an electronica musician. I suspect his exotic supplies may have run low. He hops on a train and we wave goodbye. Then Paul, Ed and I leave Lewes as sun sets, aiming to night-walk over the South Downs to Brighton, where the promise of friends and shelter awaits. As we depart town, a man with well-coiffed dreadlocks loudly tells his companions: "That's what I want to do – live freely, walking wherever I feel!" We see he's pointing at us, so we pop back to explain that the paths are open, and with a pack and some basic kit anyone can claim such freedom! The dreadlocked man looks rather irked by our interruption.

On the edge of town we find a late enclave of plump blackberries. Despite Michaelmas having passed, we fill our blood with wild fruit sugars. At the foot of the downs, soft rain spittles and we tog into waterproofs. In his zipless cagoule, Paul asks worriedly if it'll be heavy? Within minutes, it's the heaviest rainfall I've ever met in England. Visibility is less than a metre, with no airspace between falling water. It's like walking through a tap on full. When the wind joins in, even breathing gets tricky. Each step forward is accompanied by three steps sideways. We drive our bodies into the storm, trying to ride its ferocity onward. At the peak of the Downs, the most exposed spot for miles, lightning forks down on each side of us. Stoic, yet totally wired, among the madness I sing myself sane with a verse of *Black Jack Davy* - though I can hardly hear the voice in my head:

> *The skin on my hands is like leather or hide,*
> *And my face is hard from the cold wind,*

But my heart is warm with the song that I sing,
Will charm that fair lady,
Singing through the green green trees.

The storm grows ever stronger, and when we really must rest we huddle on the drenched grass to chew salami and soak up the show. Ed is damp, but my skiing jacket holds out well. Paul is swimming in his mac and Doc Martens. Some hours later the lights of Brighton appear, and we follow the flowing puddles into town. We rest in a multi-storey car park, sheltered from the now merely heavy rain, and a man sidles up to ask if we've got any alcohol? But all we've got is songs and he's not keen. Then we make our way to our friends' flat, and crash on their carpets.

Morning newspapers herald last night's 'Brighton Tornado', and we're proud to have found safe passage through its violent veil. We stay with our friends for the next few days, resting, eating, washing everything, and learning new old songs. Busking in Brighton's back-streets is glorious. *Pleasant and Delightful* works a wondrous enchantment here, summoning echoes of seaward partings. Not long ago, men were lawfully captured and forced to sea by roaming press-gangs. Many never returned, condemned to lethal service in whichever the King's wars. How safe and easy we have it in the modern era! As if to underline this, each night one of our friends returns from work in a gourmet pie-shop, bringing back bagfuls of plump unsold pies on which we fall like ravens. It's far from the cruel seas.

Soon we say goodbye to Paul the poet. He needs to reach Dorchester where his father lives, and having dawdled with us for two weeks, he must now walk twenty miles a day to make it on time. We wave him off into the Brighton sunset. Ed and I also try to quit town, but it's not so easily done. A chance meeting leads us to another house of beautiful people and parties. Brighton has a self-sustaining circuit of excess and recovery. Each night they flare and crash, and every day they rise to do it again. It's exhaustingly wonderful, but dangerously hard to leave the ensnaring potency of such constant joys. But finally, ten days after arriving, late in the day and tired from the good-times, we really do depart.

Brighton to Devils Dyke

Stamping cracked pavements through Hove and Portslade, I notice a shaven-headed man following us closely in the bizarre pace-matching way where neither party gains nor loses ground. Annoyed by my bad imagination, I turn to confront him with hello. The stranger instantly transforms from potential yob into meditative health-warrior, and he's thrilled by our journey and the vision of freedom it offers. We walk together into the colouring sky, talking of crystals and vipassana, dharma and bananas. Ed and I consider him a waymarker of our perfect timing.

Finally spying the footpath out of town, we rest on a bench to breathe. Over the road, young boys playfight with plastic whips. As we watch, a combatant breaks from battle to jog over and demand our plans. We tell him we're walking to Cornwall, and he returns to tell his foes. For five seconds, all warring ceases. It's our moment. We climb the narrow footpath into darkness, stopping only to snack on bitter pathside sloes. High above Brighton, the town becomes a thin band of light between the dark hills and darker sea, just another port disappearing behind us. At the top of the downs we reach Devils Dyke, a Bronze Age hillfort. In a hidden corner of trees we string tarps and fall to deep post-urban slumber. I mumble to Ed that we're now in West Sussex, but he's already snoring.

CHAPTER 3

West Sussex

Devils Dyke to Washington

We wake to sunshine slanting through green and gold hazel trees, arching like an organic cathedral. From my sleeping bag I see dog walkers parading the path beyond our camp. Rising quietly, I realise with delight that my Brighton head-fuzz has gone. It's an instant benefit of sleeping outdoors in oxygen-rich places. We leap the barbed wire and surprise a sniffing spaniel, then follow the crest of the Downs west until a twitten leads to the village of Fulking. Here we meet a man of very pure smiles but no words, and apples of dark red skin and sweet pink flesh. We fill our bottles at a spring roaring off the Downs, the stone fountainhead built by Victorian polymath John Ruskin. Then we walk west along the wooded ankle of the hill. Among the tall beeches I find a stand of hazel, and cut a rod to replace the chestnut I left in Lewes. Hazel in my hand feels flexible but strong, purposeful and focussed. I start tapping the trees I pass, hoping to leave an invisible kinetic tattoo, so the trees might remember our passing. We both wear rubber-soled boots, insulating us from the earth, so staffs are vital tools to meet the world beyond our bodies. Tapping an electric fence offers tingling proof that this works.

As the afternoon fades, I watch Ed trust his staff's balance to lean precariously and pick coltsfoot leaves. We recently learned that coltsfoot makes a great cough remedy and herbal tobacco. But Ed fumbles and tumbles, jarring his knee. He sits in shocked surprise as pain blossoms through his body, but he brightens when I suggest it's an opportunity to use his first aid kit. While Ed delves for arnica cream and a leg brace, I read from the small book that raw onion is sovereign for sprains. Yet we have no onions, only the yellow fat full moon under which we sleep.

Next day, Ed's knee is still flimsy, but he hobbles along happily. His staff is now vital walking kit. We talk little, and I spend time getting to know the hazel in my hand. I notice that when I slip into negative thoughts – not an entirely rare occurrence - my staff clacks on a stone or root, like an alarm to better direct my mind. Hazel is known as the tree of wisdom in Irish tradition, and is commonly used by dowsers to detect unseen things. But it doesn't help us find more blackberries, whose daily nourishment we already miss. Thankfully, rosehips have begun to replace them, each bright red fruit a sachet of violently healthy jam.

We cross River Adur, and sing her a quick *Oats*

and Beans, before meeting mullein, toadflax and mugwort on the opposite riverbank. Our small book tells us that mugwort is also known as 'mother herb', 'wild wormwood', or 'felon herb', and is renowned for smoking meat, repelling insects, flavouring beer, and enhancing dreams. Placed in shoes, the Romans used it to counter fatigue on long journeys. We try it out, and Ed seems to walk a little stronger. We also learn that Mugwort's Ukrainian name is 'chernobylnik', after which the town of Chernobyl was named. And John the Baptist wore a mantle of mugwort when he wandered in the wilderness. It's definitely another herb for the hat.

Toward evening, in a pathside horse paddock we spot a giant puffball, big as a head and white as a cloud. This is the jackpot of fungi foraging, so I leap the wire to gather it, grateful it hasn't been trampled. Horses are clearly wiser than humans. A mile later, we find a patch of trees with space enough for two. We ask the beech, birch and pine if we might stay? The crows craw welcome thrice, so we burn a little mugwort, then relax and cook the puffball with rock salt, wild marjoram and cayenne pepper. It tastes like chicken nuggets should. In the fire's embers we also bake pheasant sweetcorn. Anticipating soft human corn, we're shocked by the yellow bullets that emerge. They need so much chewing that our jaws ache with the effort, and our bellies, by Pavlovian trickery, cease rumbling. After food, I switch on Ed's phone to find a message saying I've won my MA. I talk tactfully about how meaningless it is, but I'm actually rather pleased.

After supper we learn songs, and I try a method of outsourcing harmony production. As Ed sings the melody, I imagine that an angel is somewhere singing a perfect harmony, and if I can stop thinking and trying, these unpredictable sounds might flow through me. The results are strange, and hard to remember, but I manage to keep a weird throbbing half-harmony for *Pleasant and Delightful* that feels wonderful but probably breaks the rules of music. Ed calls it the 'Devil's Interval', but agrees it sounds right. The song tells of a sailor who must depart tonight, so he and his lover embrace and swap rings, with the promise to marry when he returns. But warlike seafaring was a notoriously perilous enterprise in small wooden craft, and there was always a jagged edge of probable loss in such partings, despite the lovers' optimism. So it seems right to leave harmonies hanging, incomplete and unsure, like a seabound lover's name cried to the heedless waves. After song, we sleep among dying firelight, barking badgers and the leaping crash of lightning.

Early next morning we reach Wiston Park, a manor house surrounded by razor-wire and CCTV. Our map says there's a church here, so I buzz the intercom and ask, in plummiest accent, for permission to 'sing a brief devotion'. The gates rise yes. This manor is leased to the Foreign Office for conferences, and is generally off-limits, but the church being consecrated remains fair game to any visitor requesting access. Security approach with visitor badges, Ed signing in as Elwyn Streatham while I become Winston Palmer. The church is wonderfully at ease with its decrepitude, and we relax on a mouse-gnawed sofa in the side chapel. For fifteen minutes we try to coax out a trapped blackbird, who finally swoops low under the ancient doorway. When we leave, security guards enter to check if we've graffitied the altar or stolen the candlesticks. They ask what we're doing, I mention my MA and they visibly relax: "Oh, you'll be working here one day".

Back up the Downs, we walk three circles clockwise around a ring of beeches known as Chanctonbury, before resting in the centre. Sleep evades us, but when we emerge from the trees, the season has shifted from late-autumn to early winter. We shiver and jumper up. Westward, the village of Washington's beauty is almost overpowered by the road roaring past it. In the pub we drink thin beer and meet the village churchwarden who tells us that though he's afraid of flying, his dog often goes up in a friend's two-seater from the local aerodrome. The dog, dreaming of vistas his owner shall never witness, snuffles in accord. We ask about local sleep-spots and the warden recommends a field with shelter and water where the Tinkers (travelling ironware menders and knife sharpeners) used to stop. We gratefully seek this Tinkers' hollow, but get hopelessly lost in dark mists. Finding a flat spot that seems isolated, we lay down to sleep. But in early morning light, we wake to see a large manor house barely thirty yards away, wholly invisible in last night's fog. We quickly pack, surreptitiously as we can in front of twelve large windows, but we're too late, for the front door opens and an irate-looking man in tweed steps purposefully toward us, red-faced and ready to vent his ire. But when he's ten yards away we start singing *Pleasant and Delightful*. It's a strong shield. The larks that sing melodious shall not be broached. The angry chap flickers and falters, then abruptly turns back home to slam the door behind him. Two minutes later, we're back on the footpath, no harm done.

Passing through Washington village in shining daylight, we pluck five varieties of wayside apples from the hedge, from heavyweight yeasty monsters to sharp little twangers. That's breakfast and lunch sorted. The apple trail leads us to St Mary's church, where parents stand waiting for the local school's Harvest Festival. The efficient-looking headmistress, a large gold crucifix glinting at her neck, tells us that we cannot enter. "It shall be full," she smiles, looking past us. But it's a church service not a private event, so I appeal to higher powers. The flustered vicar agrees we'd be most welcome. Inside, marrows, pumpkins and apples deck every stone shelf. The sermon is about people without houses or fridges who sleep outside and need the children's tinned food and sympathy. When the organ blasts out *I Needed a Neighbour*, Ed and I sing with full vigour and heartiest harmonies, and the children raise their volume to match, till the whole building hums with raucous holy song, as well it should.

Washington to Arundel

Waving goodbye, we ascend the Downs again. From the top ridge we gaze north over the quilted dream of England, the sky stretching over us in impossible blue widths. The path is busy with bicyclists and strolling couples. Plantlife underfoot is remarkably thin, the grass a few microns long. I can see why people call the South Downs a 'green desert'. At supper time, we find a small woodland in which to cook. But first we must cross the ring of hasty poos, decorated with bramble-flung paper, left by folk caught short on their hilltop jaunts. Why don't they bury these deposits? It only takes a small stick to scrape a hole in the soil. No other animal, we reflect, requires such industrial paraphernalia to perform this basic biological function. Are folk not embarrassed? I suppose they are, which is much of the problem.

Deeper in the wood, we find the foundations of an old house, all mossed-over. We cook supper where the hearth once burned. I'm keen to sleep here, but Ed is more determined to move on, so we emerge to watch the purple sunset from Rackham Banks, before rolling down the Arun Valley to Amberley's pub. Our public house technique, like a new language, is growing with each practice. Tonight we buy half pints and chat with the landlord, getting outline permission to sing, before asking all the other drinkers if they wouldn't mind a song or two? Then we launch into *John Barleycorn,* a hymn to beer and the seasonal mysteries. We've been practicing it during hedgerow rests, and I've found an off-key harmony that I really like.

> *There were three men come out of the west,*
> *Their fortunes for to try.*
> *And these three men made a solemn oath,*
> *John Barleycorn must die.*

In the song's afterglow, the landlord brings us plates of moussaka and summer ale. We relax in the warmth of welcome, until I spot through the window two lads stood shivering with heavy backpacks. It could be us! So I leap up to usher them in. They step in hesitantly, and the publican asks the usual questions. But their reply to 'why' summons laughter from the gathered drinkers: "We're walking to send cows to Africa." The pub sniggers into its pints, the pair redden, then shuffle off to search for a campsite. "Too young to drink anyway!" the barmaid sniffs. We leave soon after, rather than taking the offer of sleep on the pub floor, and follow River Arun along wooden walkways into the Duke of Norfolk's estates, to find a cosy triangle of scrub woods for our night's hotel.

Ed wakes early grumbling about mozzies, so I gather greater plantain for him. It's the top remedy we have found so far, and far more soothing than yarrow. After an apple breakfast, we walk south toward Arundel. The sheep on these hillsides all have long tails, which to me look outlandish, though in truth they're simply unaltered. In Kent, lambs' tails are rubber-banded off shortly after birth. I realise I don't know why sheep have tails.

Under ever-screaming skylarks, we follow the hills into town. Arundel's name may come from the French for a swallow - l'hirondelle. The vast nineteenth century Catholic Cathedral is closed, though we admire its symbolwork of carved kings and queens jutting desperately out from the Bath stonework. Are they being glorified or entrapped? Arundel town centre is set around its war memorial. Unlike a grave, none of the listed bodies lie within, as World War One politicians believed repatriating the dead lads would be a PR and logistical nightmare. We tap the memorial with our staffs and offer a minute's silence among the car traffic. Then we visit the boutique food shops in search of outdated goods, a surprisingly fruitful quest. As we discuss the obscenity of waste with bakery staff, a gentleman arrives with a cake bought yesterday. He wanted ginger, but found this too bananaey. When his refund is transacted, the baker winks at us: "A cake with one slice missing. What'll we do with this?" It's an uncanny demonstration of cosmic support, the proof in the pudding.

After brunch in St John's graveyard, we share song with Arundel's sleepy backstreets. Launching with *Oats and Beans,* a long line of women swarm the street, all wearing purple shirts and red hats, devotees of a poet called Jenny Joseph. Their leader stops to listen closely, before nodding and flinging a coin. The others all follow suit, and in two bustling minutes our hat is full.

When I am an old woman, I shall wear purple
with a red hat that doesn't go, and doesn't suit me.
(Jenny Joseph)

Here in Arundel, we learn the benefit of standing rather than sitting to sing. An upright posture projects our voices further, and people treat us like active performers rather than background music. No more slumping on backpacks to sing! Post-busk, we watch seagulls circle the concrete-banked River Arun, until an Indian taxi-driver in a Mercedes pulls up to offer us a lift to any destination, free of charge. "I only wish to help," he says. We thank him, but explain our aim to walk every step of the way to Cornwall. He nods slowly. "I would walk too," he announces, "but I must drive this taxi to support my family." We quite understand, and everyone parts smiling.

After supper in a pub, we ask the landlord if we might sing? But he hasn't got a license, and apparently all public performances need licensing now. So we slip outside with a chap called Ray, who sings *A Kiss from a Rose* better than Seal. We reply with *John Barleycorn*. It's deliciously taboo street music, all the better for being forbidden. Back in the pub, we meet an eel-trapper who tells us how eels return to life after a week in the freezer, and how they make a yearly pilgrimage to the Sargasso Sea to breed. Later still, the table behind hands us a napkin full of coins, on the basis that they overheard me saying 'autumn is a kind season.' "So we know you must be poets!" they explain.

Arundel to Chichester

The day lengthens, and we nurse glasses of orange juice, trying to summon the energy to walk out of Arundel. A fellow drinker is fascinated by his perception of our organic good-health: "Orange juice in the pub," he murmurs, dazed by it, "women must find that irresistible..." But the truth is, after busking we're drained, our power having been poured into song. Ed says he feels tired of people, pubs and performing, and he needs time to recuperate. "But Ed, tomorrow is Sunday in Chichester. It's an unmissable busk!" I insist. He remains far from keen. Unable to agree a path forward, we sit in silent disunity, sipping our irresistible juice. Until we overhear two fellows talking about a famous pub called 'The Gribble' in a village called Oving near Chichester. Checking the time, four hours remain until closing. "It's ten miles away," I offer Ed, "do you think we can make it?" Galvanised, we rush through England's dimming light. Losing the footpath, we follow a Saturday night B-road, the semi-drunk drivers rattling perilously by. We stop only to bury a squirrel, and finally reach Oving village, our feet pounded by tarmac, twenty minutes past closing time. We never do find 'The Gribble', and half-believe it was a joke played on us. We got gribbled.

We shelter in Oving's church porch to eat supper. With a candle illuminating the silent stones, it's so cosy that we decide to stay. Our roll mats fit snugly alongside each other. It's the perfect pilgrim shelter, as though designed for the very purpose.

I would rather be a doorkeeper in the house of my God
than dwell among the tents of wickedness.
(Psalms 84:10)

Waking refreshed in our stone hotel, we leave a donation of coins in the shape of Vesica Piscis, the Jesus fish. A couple of hours later, we hit Chichester for breakfast, before settling to sing under the market cross. Chichester town centre is pedestrianised, and the market cross is ancient, both very helpful facts for unaccompanied singers of traditional songs. A teenage girl sits weeping behind us while we sing, before flinging a fiver and running off. I wonder if her love has gone to sea? A moustachioed man in a guernsey jumper tells us to learn a very old song called *Claudy Banks*, as well as an Easter carol called *The Leaves of Life*. We jot them in the back of our song book. An elderly lady with armfuls of plastic bags shuffles over to tell us that her grandson Milo has had nine operations. She asks if we'll pray for him when we reach Buckfast Abbey? We agree wholeheartedly. Then we catch the attention of Chichester's polyester-clad youth, a ganglet of playstation delinquents. One of them circles to try and steal Ed's walking staff, but I thwart him with growls. They giggle and caper, hoping to make us uncomfortable, but they're soon listening closely, the bigger boys quieting the small. "The woods are that way" one lad tries to mock, looking to his friends for support, but his elder replies: "I think they know where the woods are". We premier the *Diggers Song*, a celebration of radical seventeenth century farming by Gerald Winstanley, which almost starts a riot, as the teenagers leap and whoop wildly.

The club is all their law, to keep poor men in awe.
That they a vision saw, to bind us to their law.
Stand up now, diggers all!

"Oy! Catch!" one of the lads shouts, and Ed opens his song-shut eyes in perfect time to grasp the flying mars-bar. As we pack away our hat and sign, a family invite us to their home, the husband saying he trains Special Forces in anti-interrogation techniques. We're unsure if this is a unique learning opportunity or a delve into realms of knowledge best avoided. Either way, their home is many miles south, so we say no thanks. I wonder how our refusal makes them feel, and whether our role might be to accept every invitation? But such questions disappear when an Australian girl called Ruby appears. She and Ed made friends at a Brighton house-party, and now she's come to walk awhile. We leave Chichester via Bishop Otter's avenue of beech trees. As we pass, I knock on a door to tell the household they've left their car's lights on. They're grateful, but despite the wafting scent of spicy woks, I win no noodley boon.

Chichester to Lavant

In Lavant, at a wooden public house with an inglenook fireplace, Ed starts drinking Badger ale in pot after foaming pot, saying it's medicinally perfect to counter his toothache. The pub's menu offers only one bargain, bread and olives at one pound fifty, so we order six portions. Fed, we leave the pub's warmth for a chestnut wood with a prehistoric earthwork running through its centre. Ed and Ruby take the south side of this tribal divide, while I stay north.

In soft morning light, I wake to the sound of objects falling. One boings right off my tarp. Who's throwing what? As my eyes un-blur, I realise it's chestnuts tumbling from the treetops, pure falling food. I rise and stretch, then set to collect the manna, checking each shell for softness or insect holes. After I've gathered some kilos, I glance over the earthwork to see the others still slumber, so I wander into the local village. Ed and Ruby are only just uncurling when I return, their faces shy and sleep-creased. We roast chestnuts, and make a slow stew of quinoa, rosemary, garlic, fat-hen, apple, cleavers, and parasol mushrooms. It's one of our best meals yet.

After lingering all afternoon in the wood, Ruby must return to Chichester train station. Ed escorts her away, hands held in the dusky lane as bats circle the half-dark above. Suddenly they turns back, shouting: "Come on, let's go for one more pint." So we all swoop to the wooden pub. A Rolls Royce sales team are here, but they only talk about cars. We order pints and settle, when through the door boldly steps a gold-earinged man and his green-eyed wife, both dressed all in black. They throw their leather boots onto the low table and call for ale. Aha, we think, veterans! Chatting, we learn that Frank is an artist of international renown, here to paint the yew trees in Kingley

Vale. I confusedly wonder if paint might damage their bark, but thankfully don't ask. After beer and song, we're invited to Frank's home in Cornwall. "If you ever get that far!" he winks in challenge.

When the artists leave, Ed walks Ruby back to Chichester, and I wander to the next pub, where a jazz band twinkles madly. I offer to sell the chef some kilos of chestnuts, but he says the pub doesn't buy food from strangers, which I suppose makes sense. I take my pint with a sixty year old man who is growing ginseng in his greenhouse for the day he meets his future wife. Returning to the wood, I pass a green-clad man gripping binoculars with peculiar tightness, and I ask what's he's watching of a night? "I keep my wildlife to myself," he mutters angrily, so I leave him be. But closer to camp, I wonder more about this private viewer, and turning a corner I duck into the hedge to wait and see if I'm followed. But I'm not.

Lavant to Kingley Vale

Next day, Ed and I walk for Kingley Vale, said to be Europe's largest yew forest. The rain is soft when we arrive under the ancient trees, and we dive in to get lost. Yew is the only British tree that has kept its Gaelic name, and is our longest living tree, some estimated to be five thousand years old. According to our small book, a single yew tree forms many colonies of life. As one stem dies, new ones grow outside it, the young rising from the bodies of the old. A bit like humans. When night falls, we settle under curling roots. Both of us sense strongly not to bring fire here, so instead we eat a raw supper of greens and chestnuts, before sleeping at the ancient watchers' feet.

> *The lives of three wattles, the life of a hound;*
> *The lives of three hounds, the life of a steed;*
> *The lives of three steeds, the life of a man;*
> *The lives of three men, the life of an eagle;*
> *The lives of three eagles, the life of a yew;*
> *The lives of three yews, the length of an age;*
> *Seven ages from Creation to Doom.*

Morning merges forest and dream. Fallow deer wander silently past my sleep-spot, while deep in the woods the leonine oinks of rutting stags rattle the morning stillness. I rise chilly-necked, having left my snood (scarf sewn on a hood) somewhere in the recent past. Ed calls this my 'power garment', so I can't lazily consign it to loss, but backtrack to hunt it down. I eventually find it outside Lavant post office. When I return to Kingley Vale, Ed is relaxing on a bed of sphagnum moss, having spent the morning crawling down deer trails and foraging wild parsnips. I talk of my hope for a yew staff, and Ed scoffs, saying the yew branches here are far too deeply connected. But when I walk round the corner, the perfect bough, already cut from the tree, stands waiting for me. I leave my hazel in grateful exchange.

We climb the slippery chalk away from Kingley Vale. At the top of the hill, a row of five burial mounds watch over the flatlands and far sea. Here lie long forgotten heroes, kings and queens, at rest until they're needed again. We each lie with foreheads pressed into our chosen mounds, asking when they'll rise? "Soon," they whisper, "soon..."

Kingley Vale to South Harting

The wooded path leads north to the Royal Oak at Hooksway, sadly shut for winter. We knock at the back door, hoping to win unlikely hospitality, but the caretaker says sorry we can't camp in the garden. So we head for the Devils Jumps, another gang of five ancient burial mounds. Arriving in twilight, it feels unwise to walk on these tumps until the safety of daylight. Under nearby pines we settle to eat another raw salad. I miss hot food, but that's the cost of camping in sacred spaces. Night falls, and winter winds rifle through my sleeping bag to snatch away my body-heat. The easy warmth of autumn is passing.

Next morning, shortly after rising, we again meet the Hooksway pub caretaker, walking his labrador. He seems anxious about having turned us away last night, so we offer him dried fruit and *John Barleycorn* to cheer him up. A mile west, we pass a field of red-faced men blasting lead skyward with back-slapping guffaws. Pheasants, their living targets, tumble dead at each spat command. A beater, sucking cigarettes by the jeep, tells us that these pheasants will be buried not eaten: "It's sport, innit. This lot ain't 'ungry!"

We soon arrive in South Harting, a tiny village with two pubs. Peering through the windows, we choose the one without TV. As we take tea, the landlord says what we're doing is bonkers. Ten minutes later, he tells us he gets it. Twenty minutes after, he brings out free bread and cheese. An hour on, he asks us to stay and sing for an event this evening, promising to pay us in food and accommodation. The deal is turned on a slab of yesterday's roast-beef, which Ed ferrets away for tomorrow's lunch. That evening we entertain the local cricket club. They best like *The Rambling Sailor*, whose song locations we change to 'Chichester' and 'South Harting' to better catch attention.

> *Oh then I came to South Harting,*
> *And there were lasses plenty.*
> *I boldly stepped unto a one,*
> *To court her for her beauty.*

After song, our table is joined by a mercenary fresh home from Iraq. He looks like a steroidy stoat, and seems keen to be friendly, though with an odd undercurrent of complete disregard. Perhaps he's on some kind of anti-trauma drug? I suspect he mostly wants to impress the barmaid, as he rushes into the night to fetch us 'crucial kit'. He returns with a double-edged sheath knife that he says has saved his life more than once: "When the gun fails, you've got to know how to use a knife," he explains, his eyes shining dull and dark. We accept the gift with uncertain thanks.

South Harting to Buriton

After sleep in the pub garden, in morning light Ed and I climb the Downs away. Children in gardens wave, strangers stop us for songs, and clouds form a three-legged symbol that surely bodes well. We meet a small plant called redshank, whose black dotted leaves are said to have been caused by the dripped blood of Jesus. We sing it *The Leaves of Life*, the Romany Gypsy Easter carol we're learning. This song features Jesus dying on an elder tree, and ends with arcane plantlore about fennel and roses. Ed and I talk about how Jesus came back from the dead and took the form of a gardener. Surely this should make gardening Christianity's highest aspiration? So why aren't churches all gardens? Yet again, we have no answers.

At the top of the chalk world, we're trying to guess which path to take when an eighty year old man emerges onto the summit, not at all breathless despite the steep climb. He says he's lived his whole life in Buriton, and points the best route down. We slide to the village below, and rest by the pond to eat our wedge of roast beef with raw onion and crunchy bundles of chickweed. As we eat, the church bells chime disharmoniously, and a mother and toddler start a duck riot by flinging a whole loaf of crumbs in the pond. Among the joyful racket we rise to walk, but we're waylaid by a tattooed-faced man who offers us a strength test. We must touch the ground with one knee, without any other body-part touching the ground, and then we must rise up again. It's surprisingly difficult, but we both pass the test and our teacher waves us gladly onward.

Buriton to Petersfield

Walking toward Petersfield on cattle-ruined trackways, we're kept from a knee-high soaking only by the balancing power of our staffs. On the far side of one lake-like cowpuddle we see the first young hikers we've yet met on this journey. They walk east as we go west, passing with wordless smiles, like ships in the light. And then we're in Hampshire.

CHAPTER 4

Hampshire

Petersfield to Steep

On the edge of Petersfield, we give the mercenary's knife to River Rother, and with a sharp plop it disappears below the waters. Onward into town, the path leads through a remarkably neat estate of static caravans, each with a perfect garden floral display. Nearby brick homes look stained and squalid in comparison. Then over feral heathland covered with nettled tumps, we step into Petersfield town.

Looking for somewhere quiet to sing, we wander the town. A key lesson in street song has been that voices always lose to cars. Sadly, Petersfield is riddled with vehicle access. Until we chance on an enclosed pedestrian shopping precinct. It looks perfect. Under a statue of a shepherd and lamb we open with *Nutting Girl*, which warns about the consequences of intimacy with songful farmers, but delivered in such a jolly way that it seems unable to shock even the most conservative of listeners.

And what few nuts that poor girl had,
She threw them all away.

It wins more wry grins than donations. Until a yellow-jacketed man approaches, arms out wide, saying this is private property and song isn't allowed here. We nod and smile with the kung fu of polite agreement. He squirms under the unexpected pressure: "It's not my rules!" Shoppers instantly surround the official, disputing his duties, and our hat fills with pound coins of pity. An elderly lady tells us she's ashamed they can't have real music in their hometown. One man even threatens to call the police if we're moved on. We dispel the revolt by leaving, and relocate twenty yards outside the private gate, tucking ourselves into an estate agent's doorway. But a few minutes later, the yellowcoat again advances. This time we hold our corner: "We're on public land now, fellow..." He grins: "Can't a man donate some money for music?" he asks, depositing a handful of change in our hat of plenty.

Despite the cars, it's a steady busk. Halfway through, we meet a chap who vows to immediately join our journey, now, today. But an hour later, while he's at home packing, his girlfriend tells him she's pregnant, and so his swiftly made plans swiftly change. We also meet the daughter of a Pink Floyd guitarist who takes us home to play us music by a singer called Martin Carthy, which fairly blows our minds. We swiftly copy out lyrics to *Sovay*, *Geordie* and *The Begging Song*. After, she promises to show us the 'best pub ever'. Following recent experience, we scoff mildly, but she's not wrong. The Harrow Inn at Steep is a jewel among hostelries. The main room has only two tables, so everyone must sit together, which allows the long-established locals to jostle and play with visitors, a social immune system that's rare to see in such rude health. The landlady's family has held the pub for over a hundred years of matronal lineage, the pea and ham soup daily cooked to her grandmother's recipe. Alec Guinness and John Wyndham were regular drinkers here, and when the local council health and safety team tried to move the pub's outdoor toilet inside, the biggest petition in local council history was collected and plans were rapidly scrapped. We sing *John Barleycorn*, an ale spiritual, which goes down very well. Another singer in the house, a old boy with a transplanted pig's heart, responds by cracking out Hampshire songs he learned as apprentice to an auctioneer in the 1950s. In lisping drawl he sings of a 'lunaticky asylum', and the pub roars with joy. We jot down all the lyrics we can follow, as we drink deeply and eat roasted chestnuts. Later, another man tells me of his worries for his son, who's obsessed with being a troll in role-playing adventure games. I offer tales of Norse 'cinder-children', who lived in the communal long-hall eating scraps and cinders, doing nothing much while they grew up. Until one day a warrior asks: 'Will you come?', and then they wash off the ash and go to battle. If they return, they're counted as men. "In other words, trust that necessary metamorphosis will come." Though I'm hardly a good example, he's grateful for reassuring noises, and later slips me a wedge of notes as we shake hands. On the other side of the bar, I hear Ed talking to a local landowner about the importance of badger dancing. When the night ends, we're loaned the donkey barn, and sleep on beds of baled hay.

Tea and toast await in the shining morn. We tell the landlady we've an inkling to go to the local church. She raises eyebrows, saying the vicar is an ex-accountant: "But may your gods travel with you!" Despite our best hopes, the church service feels like bad performance art. The vicar is costumed with gold ringed embroidery, his sermon about Hebrew prophets is unpronounceably turgid, and the hymns are dirges. But when the bell tolls, everyone exhales and smiles again. Outside we're surrounded by curious parishioners, and a couple take us home for soup and mars bars. They tell us we must visit the font in East Meon's church, and we accept the quest. Backtracking through Petersfield, we upgrade our OS map and say goodbye to the girl who showed us the Harrow. She's now at work in Costa coffee, and slips us a wedge of pre-stamped loyalty cards as we leave.

Steep to East Meon

Crossing a dual-carriageway, we're marooned in the central reservation for twenty zooming minutes until we can safely cross. Some hours later, we approach the Templar village of East Meon. But on he edge of the village, we find ourselves in a holloway with six paths leading to its empty centre.

It's unclear why this spot was once so significant. A small mound called Barrow Hill watches down from the north east. Before moving on, we sing *Claudy Banks* at this strange meeting place. This song is probably the oldest we've learned, and tells the tale of re-meeting lovers, one of whom tests the other. Perhaps this forgotten six-way path outside East Meon was once the site of similarly significant rendezvous?

I steppèd up unto her, and caught her in great surprise,
My own she did not know me, for I was in disguise.

As the harmony fades, a squall of rain blows in, so we shelter under pathside root hollows that would make excellent beds. But the rain soon passes and we don't linger longer, for the day is already dulling and we have a font to catch.

We arrive at East Meon church in perfect time to find the warden locking up. He promises to return tomorrow morning, so we retire to the pub. After song, food and talk, we don't leave till long after midnight. Clouds race across the bright moon, and a lone owl screams, as we walk back to the church, hazily imagining we might spend the night in its open porch. Plomping down our backpacks, I instinctively try the door. To my entire surprise, it swings open wide. Ed and I step over the threshold, and before us stands the famous font, a lump of black marble carved with dragons that seem to dance in the flickering moonlight. We stare in delighted confusion, until we realise that we're not alone. Someone, something, is already here in the dark, and they aren't happy to be disturbed. A sense of imminent approach raises the heckles on my neck. They are coming closer. To run would invite chase, as known from childhood nightmares. So I whisper *Leaves of Life,* and within a breath Ed begins to sing:

> *All under the leaves, and the leaves of life,*
> *I met with virgins seven.*
> *And one of them was Mary mild,*
> *Our Lord's best mother in Heaven.*

As the harmony rises through dust and moonbeams, all sense of approach ceases. The hidden watcher becomes a silent listener. We relax into the song, letting it flower and fill this ancient temple with its strange invisible light. As the final notes echo and fade, we bow to the dragon font, and to our unseen audience, then gently step backward and close the door behind us. The porch is no longer an option for sleep, so we climb the hill behind the church to bivy on its flat pathway. In no time at all we lie as the long-dead, the pennyweights of song and miles pressing shut our tired eyes.

The sky is still dark when I'm woken next morning by a man talking loudly on his phone: "Yeah mate, there's two geezers asleep behind the church." I wake a grumbling Ed, and we pack up. Sunshine soon nurses the land, and we revive by East Meon's rushing stream. River Meon has its source nearby, so this water runs fresh, as yet uninjured by humanity's heavy deposits and demands. We dangle in the water filter and fill our bottles with cold chalky goodness. Soaking sunshine in our skin and fresh water in our bellies, we're soon feeling grand. A pair of tiny boys toddle over to ask what we're doing? When we tell them, they excitedly ask if they can walk to 'Cornwult' too? We smile and say of course! "But you'll have to ask your parents." Their parents look horrified, and bundle the children into a Range Rover before roaring away.

Back at the church, we try the great wooden door again. It's now solidly locked, so we eat oats while waiting for the churchwarden. He arrives as we're scraping clean our bowls. I casually ask whether he returned here last night? No, he replies, looking puzzled. Does anyone has another key? No, he says again. He holds out eight inches of ornate metalwork, hardly the kind Timpsons will copy while you shop. Why, the warden asks? I mumble about how pleased we are he's here.

The church by daylight is an entirely different place. The font no longer moves, but is now a solid lump of well-hewn Tournai marble. On the other side from the dragon is carved Adam and Eve. I think last night we chose exactly the right song.

For I must suffer this, he says,
For Adam and for Eve.

We don't sing here again, but pour River Meon water into the font, watching it slowly drain into the earth below the church, before sitting in chilly peace.

East Meon to Winchester

We head for Old Winchester Hill. Somewhere near the peak, our map promises a site called 'The Seven Wells', but we can't even find a damp puddle. At the hill's crest, the yew wood is hidden and sheltered, offering ideal furtive sleep. But we have miles yet to tread. Below the hill, Ed finds a crow in a trap, which he releases with apologies. Then we collect tiny super-sharp green apples, on which we feast by the willows of Warnford, with the now wide river Meon flowing slowly by

Past the lost Medieval village of Lomer, we stop at the Milberry pub, which boasts a three hundred foot hand-hewn well. This is a mind-blowingly deep hole, sound taking many seconds to travel all the way down and back up again. It's hard to understand the determination required to dig such a well using hand tools. I suppose the builders were really thirsty. The landlord says he'd love to climb down and explore, certain of finding treasure, but insurance won't allow it. He even tried to get the local firemen involved, but to no avail. I don't really believe his eyes when he says this, and suspect he has long achieved his deep delve. Ed and I lie flat on the pub floor and sing through the grille. *The Leaves of Life* bounces back best, and we harmonise with its echoes.

Back on the path, after climbing a stile I almost tumble over a pigeon, who lies in the path squawking with pain. When I'm certain it's dying, I stamp hard on its neck to hasten its passage. Life relaxes from its body, and we bury it with song in graveclothes of rosemary.

The day and our fatigue soon grow long. Ed votes to rest, but I pluck late zeal to continue. We seem to have agreed this system of a stopping veto, where the person wanting to push on always trumps whoever wants to stop. I'm not sure how wise this is, but Winchester is not far off, so we continue until we hear the unwelcome roar of the Twyford Downs bypass road. When sight meets sound, we're shocked by the abruptness of this rushing metal nightmare, cut into the soft green hills of Hampshire. The protestors were right, this should never have been built. No wonder Maggie smashed them.

We get sad and lost on our way into Winchester, and rest at a residential corner in the early evening drizzle. I rise to ask a passing family for directions, but forget I'm carrying a wooden stick. The family shrink away as though fearing highway robbery, but they soon understand my request, and smiling point the way onward.

Winchester is the furthest from home we've ever walked. It's taken us six weeks to get here, twice as long as our previous pilgrimage. Tonight we're hungry, and with song cash in our pockets, we pop into a pizzeria. Underwhelmed at the portions, Ed asks the neighbouring table if they don't want their leftovers? This upsets our waiter, so he brings us free garlic bread. After food, we sing *John Barleycorn* for Winchester's Deputy Mayor, or a man who says he is. When we ask him about walkers' accommodation, he loudly recommends we check the Guildhall board for hotel vacancies, before leaning in to wink and say we can probably camp in the North Gardens. We follow his tip, checking the Guildhall board en route. The only available room costs one hundred and fifty pounds, which seems a frightful price for a few hours of unconsciousness. But the North Gardens are open, dark and empty, so we string our tarps between riverside trees as rain starts to fall hard. The downpour grows mighty, its weight so intensive that despite being tucked in my sleeping bag and bivy, under a tarp tightly strung, I must keep rubbing my toes together to convince myself that I'm actually dry. Under the frenzied percussion, I lie listening to the ground getting drunk on it, before eventually slipping into uncertain sleep.

We wake to sunlight and the heavy pad of passing joggers. As slyly as we can in an open public park, we rise and dress. I'm dazed by yesterday, but smiling folk and sunshine soon revive us. After a rich café breakfast, we hit the high street. Singing in Winchester is astonishing. The songs are well remembered here. Hundreds of people stop to listen, of all ages and backgrounds. One small boy explains to his mother, after depositing the family coin in our hat, that we're singing 'forest songs'. We like that. Between each song, commenters queue to offer tips and suggestions. A surprising number of folk interpret our singing not as performance but as a public sharing session, and feel compelled into reciprocity. We collect their snippets of ballads, our notebook filling with the poetry of unknown titles: *The Farmer* and *When I Die I'll Live Again* both sound ace. We sing until a juggler starts spinning upstreet. He's very good, successfully stealing our songs' attention, so we fling him a quid and call it a day. With our hatful of fresh gold, we refill our food bags with oats, quinoa, stock and salami. At a camping shop we buy boot wax to ensure dry feet. Then we spend the afternoon in Winchester cathedral, which is beautiful beyond description. We visit the shrine where Swithun's second burial happened, but this was smashed by Henry VIII at the Reformation, so now no-one knows where Swithun lies.

At a fish and chip shop for supper, we're waiting for our haddock to fry when a fight kicks off outside the window. The owner slips from the counter to bolt the door and dim the lights. We sing *The Leaves of Life* in the fishy darkness, and the fight rolls up the street. After food, we conjure our options for the night ahead. The cathedral's sodium lights are now full-powered, and we've little chance of surreptitious sleep under their blasting gaze. A passer-by, guessing our quest, suggests we might try the local monastery? So we wander Winchester's stone lanes to the Hospital of St Cross.

Ducking through the hatch of a great wooden door, we step into another time, when the Church was a central part of English life. Jagged chimneyed apartments overlook a lush quadrangle, with a cathedral-sized chapel tucked in one corner.

It's a stone miracle, sat quietly by River Itchen. Though the day is already dark, it's not really late, so with hats in hands we bash a door with a hefty knocker. A man appears, and we ask the main question: "Any chance we pilgrims can stay in your monastery tonight?" "Zero chance," he replies, but he doesn't slam the door, so we ask further questions - which monastic tradition it follows, who built it etc. He confesses he has no idea: "I'm an army man, it's my wife who works here. She'll tell you what's what." He fetches his wife, and our hopes linger. She emerges to explain that the monastery is for Christian widowers who give up their worldly property to live in noble poverty. This place is apparently the original source of the 'dole' in English history, with 'Wayfarer's Dole', a portion of ale and white bread, having been given to pilgrims for over eight hundred years. Even the Queen Mother took the dole here. "But you're quite sure we can't stay tonight?" I push. "I'm sorry," she says, head shaking with certainty. But when I ask if we can take the dole, she wavers: "We only give it to people who ask, but now you have asked, fair and square. Look, I'll fetch the Master, he'll tell you what's possible and what's not." She disappears, and we hum harmonies in the chilly corridor. Ten minutes later, a tall bearded man steps sternly from the shadowy stairwell. He stares into our eyes for a minute each, before asking us to describe the route we walked to get here. We do so, and after further silence, his head nods. "Give them the dole," he says, "and let's put them on the bowling green. What do you say lads?" We say thank-you very much. The dole is a slice of

Sainsburys white bread and a disposable beaker of John Smiths bitter. I don't quite smack my lips, but it's nourishing. The Master is now excitedly expounding on the lost rites of pilgrimage. We're taken to the 'bowling green', an overgrown graveyard with a sycamore in one corner. It's on the outside edge of St Cross, separated by a thin iron fence from the footpath through the water meadows beyond. We string tarps from tree to fence-line, and nestle our bodies between roots. Long into the night, young folk pass our shelter like the ghosts of ancient wanderers, their handheld phones casting white light and thin bass into the chilly darkness.

At dawn, a gardener rouses us with coffee and fruitcake. We rise to catch the seven-thirty Matins service. Holy Cross chapel is cathedralic, and almost entirely empty. We sit with the resident Brethren, each clad in red or black robes. We're the only two in green. The Master explains our presence: "These are genuine pilgrims, the first we've taken in for over three hundred years." After Matins, we learn that the Jerusalem crosses the Brethren wear on their robes are the sign of the Knights of St John, who today provide ambulances for civic events all over Britain. This almshouse is a 'hospital' in the oldest sense, offering 'hospitality'. It was started by William the Conqueror's grandson, Henri du Blois, and it may be England's oldest charity. The original Master here was called Robert Sherborne, who has left his motto carved on sundry walls - *'Dilexi Sapientiam'* - 'I love wisdom'. Masons' marks are likewise scratched all about, hiding in plain sight the secrets of crusader-won geometry. Glad at our interest, the modern Master's eyes flash once more: "What if I offer you a place to wash your clothes?" We admit this would be welcome. "Then how about a cell of your own? We have one spare." So we settle in to wash, rest and eat. The monastic cell doesn't quite meet our hope for straw mattresses and stone floors, as modern regulations require double-glazing and microwaves. But it's certainly a privilege to borrow. However, after a few hours we're both clean and fed, our boots waxed and our ripped clothes sewn, and Ed is keen to leave. The Master laughs that we're walking into evening rain: "Go on then lads, get walking, and God speed you." Refreshed, we wander out of Winchester.

Winchester to Lyndhurst

Ahead of us is the New Forest, the famous hunting retreat created for William the Conqueror. But we want to find the Old Forest. I think we meet a fragment of it near Michelmersh, in the form of a huge beech tree, her branches elbowed with lumpy burls. One great limb has half-fallen to crush the lower boughs, so Ed and I spend the afternoon clambering twenty foot up with our small pruning saws. The heavy dead branch finally crashes to the ground, and the beech gives a great moan of relief as her pinioned arms spring skyward again. We feel like successful monkey surgeons. That evening, odd sounds echo through the wood, like hollow tree trunks being drummed by distant tribes. We don't think much of it, and camp a way apart for space to dream.

In the midst of slumber, I find myself suddenly wide awake but unsure why. Till I hear something dragging and thudding along the forest floor, shouting: "NO! NO! NOOO!" The cry of booming anguish echoes around the woods. It sounds powerfully angry and impossibly huge, and it's definitely coming closer. Lying wrapped in my plastic sleeping bag and bivy, under my thin tarp, I realise how entirely unprotected I am. Should I reach for my staff and knife? But this creature, whatever it is, sounds so big that I cannot imagine how bopping it with a stick will achieve anything helpful whatsoever. Paralysed by my total lack of options, I lie still and silent as it roars ever nearer and fiercer: "NOOOOO! NO!" The creature stops at the foot of my bed, the shake of its stamp shuddering through my foam mat. I'm deeply afraid, and entirely helpless. Then slowly, my incapacity to meaningfully act becomes comedy. I begin to relax and smile. If this is my end, then so it goes. The last thing I remember is my surprise to be falling back to sleep, while a monster is still roaring at my feet.

I open my eyes to gentle light. Birdsong dances on the silence, as my unfurling awareness flickers into life. I rise and stretch against the beech tree before looking over to Ed's camp, hoping he might have got breakfast going. And then I remember last night. What happened? Ed lies under his tarp reading, and I enquire directly: "Ed, last night...did you hear anything after we went to bed?" He sits up, alarmed and amused: "Oh God, you heard it too? I hoped it was a dream. It stopped right by my bed, shouting. I thought it was going to squash me!" Who or what did we meet last night? Was it a green protector of the Old Forest? Or a child abandoned by his parents, who grew into a monster with only one remembered word of human language, like a Hampshire Yeti? Or was it just a boar? I suppose we'll never know.

After breakfast of boiled eggs and steamed greens, we say goodbye to the Old Forest, and walk for the New. We cross River Test, where brown trout muscle against the flow, bull-headed in their peregrine hopes. We'd like to stay here longer, but the riverside is patrolled by fishermen, so we stop only to eat our lunch of bread, cheese, chickweed and raw onion, before flinging River Test its fair share and moving on. At a pub nearby, the landlord marks on our map where the New Forest gamekeepers live, so we can plot a route to avoid them. But soon after, our charity-shop OS map begins to show its age. Much has changed since 1978. We wade a stream where the promise of a bridge proves false, only to meet the impassable obstacle of a twelve foot razor-wire fence protecting a theme park. We may need newer maps. The subsequent detour forces us along fast main roads, where our self-protection strategy involves wriggling head-torches and diving into bushes as cars hurtle past. We can see them, but they barely seem to notice us. I's the first time I wish I was wearing brighter clothes. Finally escaping the tarmac, we rest in a circle of mossy oaks at Emery Downs. Removing backpacks, our shoulders steam in the icy moonlight. We camp by a patch of surprisingly delicious Horn of Plenty mushrooms, which look like dead men's ears but taste wonderful fried with garlic.

In the morning we hit Lyndhurst. Tourist cars crawl nose to tail on the only road into the village, and with long strides we overtake them all. Not one car carries a smiler. I suppose it's hard to be happy in a traffic-jam. Reaching town, we browse a charity shop in hope of merino. I find a compilation of Robin Hood adventures, which we take for dream fodder. Then in the village centre we sing. *The Nutting Girl* is becoming a new favourite. It's excellent at capturing peoples' attention, and seems designed for street performance.

> *Now come all each of you fellows,*
> *Come listen to my song.*
> *It is a little ditty and it won't contain you long.*

Mid-busk, a man called Michael steps up talking excitedly about Hampshire songs. He brings us a wedge of photocopied lyrics from his collection, and is particularly keen that we learn a local ghost song called *George Collins*. Michael then invites us to sing at a care-home for dementia sufferers in four days' time. This will be our first proper gig, so we celebrate with ale. Practicing quietly in the pub garden wins us handfuls of change. As we leave, a lady in a wheelchair grasps Ed's hand and stares into his eyes for two solid minutes, saying how much he reminds her of a lost friend. Then we walk into the trees, and sleep by the forest footpath.

In the morning, I cook apple porridge while Ed sits in conversation with an oak. When I ask what was said, Ed responds in his oakiest voice: "Do you know where water comes from? No, none of us do either…" After breakfast, we wash up with fire-ash, stream-water and a twig scraper, then walk through Lyndhurst toward the south-eastern corner of the New Forest. Some hours of pinewood wandering later, we find we've both got ticks nuzzling our bloodstreams, two each on our elbows and bellies. Sat cross-legged on the track, we coax out their hungry heads by twisting them anti-clockwise with tweezers dipped in myrrh. It's a pleasant grooming moment for social monkeys. Night follows soon after, and under pines we take food and shelter. As supper bubbles in the pot, I read aloud a chapter of Robin Hood. Tonight our hero is beaten up by a pedlar who turns out to be Little John's cousin, so the pedlar joins Robin's outlaws and everyone feasts heartily. We tuck into our hedgehog-fungi and cep stew, as New Forest ponies in the never silent night around us scream of ancient freedom.

At first light, I rise to find Ed brewing pine-needle tea, which tastes like disinfectant but Ed swears is full of Vitamin C. We breakfast on oats and raisins, then walk in hope for a hideout. Through acres of recently de-forested woodland, deep-rutted by heavy machinery, we pass boughless trunks spray-painted in 'do not climb' stacks, piled like corpses after battle. Ed and I talk of futures where human and horse work the woods together again, in slower, quieter and more careful ways. As we walk and chat, we keep our ears alert for the sound of vehicles on the tracks, and dive into wayside undergrowth whenever we hear the Forest Ranger's truck approach. With our big backpacks, it must be pretty obvious that we intend to sleep out, and we don't want to give anyone the right idea. Undetected, we finally reach an economically futile corner of slow growth woodland, all beech, oak and ash trees. A hundred yards above a clear-running stream, far from pathways and hidden by holly bushes, we choose our spot, and build small shelters from fallen wood and dead bracken, which for the next two weeks we'll call home.

When our care-home gig comes around, we hide our packs under bracken and walk to town. It's four hours away, but walking bagless feels like gliding. We arrive in perfect time to find Michael distributing rattles and shakers among the slightly befuddled residents. Switching on a CD of 1940's instrumental hits, Michael tableaus as a cheeky nymph, oboe in mouth, before leaping spritely, trilling from armchair to polyester armchair. The residents look alarmed, almost ashamed at his direct musical engagement, until suddenly the silent mob awaken as one, to drum and clap with astounding unity. "Music helps them," Michael explains, breathless between tracks, "it brings them to the here and now." The transformation is so miraculous, I half-believe it's a joke being played on us. This is technically known as a 'significant, immediate and positive engagement to live interactive music'. Music defeats even medical-grade apathy.

The crowd is well warmed-up when Ed and I step forward, and we too win a chorus of well-shaken drums. The acoustics of the care-home are almost the polar opposite of a church, it's a space built to prevent resonance. But it's still easier than singing against lorries, and we've learned how to be loud. The *Nutting Girl* is again our biggest hit. Afterward, an old lady grasps Ed's sleeve, asking if he's come to take her away? She won't take no for an answer, until Ed tells her how wet and cold it is outside. She harrumphs uncertainly, before slumping back to the sofa. "Well manoeuvred!" whispers a staff-member. But we sympathise with her hopes of escape. Though it's good to visit here, it's far better to leave.

Michael takes us for lunch at his home, where his children have cooked a vat of delicious soup. After food, Michael teaches us *George Collins*, which makes wonderfully little sense, with its white marble stones, corpses and kisses. But we like it a lot.

> *Arise, arise, dear sister he cried,*
> *Get a napkin to tie round my head.*

Joyful with song and full bellies, we easily accept Michael's invitation to linger in his house for a few hours while he pops out for an appointment. It's strangely pleasant to be left in charge of someone's home who we've barely met. Two hours later, when Michael's thirteen year old son Josh returns from school, he's not at all alarmed to find strangers rummaging the kitchen for tea-bags. He even digs us out the best biscuit tin. Later, Michael tells us that his friends were surprised by the trust he offered. "But I told them trust works both ways, doesn't it lads?" he laughs with wide open eyes. We sing and talk with the family till late, before announcing with yawns that we'd better head back to camp. Our sleeping kit is all there, and though we'd really like to slump on warm carpets, it seems inappropriate to ask. "Well, ok then, I suppose you'd better go," Michael nods. The family hesitantly say goodbye as Ed and I shiver into the frozen mist. Getting heartily lost, we don't reach our woodland camp until 4am. When we next meet Michael three days later, he explains he thought 'always sleeping outside' was a core condition of our journey, and he didn't want to imperil this with an offer of comfort. Our hesitant English etiquette, we realise, can sometimes hold us back. We should have learned from the 'dole' in Winchester. If you don't ask, you almost certainly won't get.

Back in the woods, Samhain comes around, All Hallows eve. The night of roaming ghosts feels incredibly calm, as though the spirits have all gone to town in pursuit of old loves and quarrels. Sitting fireside, we sing *George Collins*, and carve spoons in the flickering dark.

Lyndhurst to Brockenhurst

When our food-bags get light, we visit the village of Brockenhurst for song and supplies. After taking two minutes' silence among the Remembrance Day celebrants, we meet a music teacher called Patricia, who invites us to sing at the local primary school. We don't have a huge range of child-friendly songs, so we try *Harvest Song*, about farmers drinking on the job. The kids like it, but uncertainly. *Oats and Beans* goes down better. But it's *Lish Young Buy A Broom* that has the whole class circling the room, pretending they're walking over 'yon white mountain'. Afterward, they mob us for autographs, shouting "Robin Hood! Robin Hood!"

As luck would have it, we've arrived on food-tasting day for local parents. But only one mum has come to test the wares. I hover suggestively: "Listen, if help is needed..." So we play Friar Tuck and get stuck in. The dinner ladies coo with delight after all the sparrow appetites. Organic meatballs, sweet potato curry, fish pie, sponge and custard for pudding, with flapjacks for the road – the kids don't know how good they've got it! Later that week, Patricia throws a dinner party where we meet an ex-Head of the Foreign Office and the director of an international oil company. We try to talk about peak-oil, but the oil man pooh-poohs us and his wife says we carry too much baggage.

Later that night, Ed and I talk with Patricia about how we sometimes spark into friction, and how to best fix this? She replies that this antagonism might be a symptom of the energy pushing us forward. "It could be your saving grace," she suggests, "are you sure you need to fix it?" Not for the first time, we realise how little we know what we're doing.

Back among the trees, one morning as we collect water, we find a deer, shaking and shuddering in the stream. He's a roebuck, short horned and in his prime. He entirely ignores our slow approach, we're invisible through his obvious pain. When we return later that afternoon, the deer lies dead in the water. We're uncertain what to do. Here is meat, as fresh as possible, delivered to our leafy door. But it died by unknown causes. Fearing poison or disease, we drag him from the water and bury him under bracken. That night, I've never heard such howls as the deer sing around us. Wailing metallic screams haunt the wood, lamenting the loss of their strong beautiful youth. I once heard a man tell me that animals can't mourn. Now I know he was only talking about his own inexperience. In Brockenhurst a few days later, a man in the pub tells us that this deer was probably a road traffic victim. After being hit by a car, deer have a huge adrenaline surge and try to outrun their injuries. When they reach exhaustion, they seek water, where they die of bruising gone terminal.

A few days later in the wood, Ed's toothache returns and he needs clove oil. So I volunteer to hit town in search of medicine. On my way I pass Brockenhurst church, whose yew is the oldest tree in the New Forest. I make sure to tap it with my staff from Kingley Vale. Elsewhere in this graveyard lie the bones of Brusher Mills, a postcard-glorified local snake-catcher. Brusher was itinerant and homeless, and his many efforts to settle in a self-built woodland home were thwarted by forest wardens. Brusher wasn't a Gypsy, who were the main wandering folk of the Forest, and by all accounts he had terrible relations with the local Gypsies. Also, Brusher Mills killed thousands of adders to sell as questionable folk-medicine. He's a very mixed figure. I suppose we all are. I sing *George Collins* by his grave.

Returning to our forest hideout with Ed's medicine, I turn a corner to find myself among a herd of deer. I slow down my breathing, and try to sink into my heart. They watch me calmly, unperturbed. After some minutes I start singing long slow notes. The deer seem curious but not scared. I resolve to try *Claudy Banks*, when I suddenly remember that I've got venison sausages in my bag. As quick as the thought arrives, the deer all leap and flee.

After two weeks in the New Forest, we realise someone has found our camp. Small piles of twigs and coals, messages in some brushwood patteran, are being left whenever we venture away. It's a subtle but effective way to shift us on. We dismantle our shacks and clean away all trace of our occupation, then walk for Brockenhurst once more. My aunt used to live here, and before we leave I'm curious to see who now inhabits her old house. We knock, and the new owners have two small boys who recognize us from the primary school. We're fed and watered, and even given a digital camera. Back in the village, Ed chats with the newsagent while I photograph the latest OS map. Zooming in after we can see all details in perfect clarity. It's surely the cheapest and lightest way to keep up-to-date mapping!

We sing one final time in Brockenhurst, until a man wearing a red hunting jacket and top-hat, riding solo on a tandem, stops to make a breathless request: "I'm from Oslo, come sing for my wife, ten minutes, her birthday." We pen rapid rhymes to the tune of *Harvest Song*, then burst past confused waiters to serenade the lunch party. Our lyrical triumph is slightly marred by the stresses of translation, but the birthday lady squeals with delight. Then we leave the New Forest, and walk south toward the sea.

Brockenhurst to Lymington

As we approach Lymington, a man bellows at us from a layby. I wave my staff in vague reply, but he keeps shouting, so we peer more closely and realise it's our hop-farmer friend from Kent. He's here to visit his grandma for her ninety-third birthday, and invites us to join tomorrow's celebration. We sleep under silver birches on the edge of town, and in the morning grab a quick busk in Lymington. Throwing down our hat outside the Masons' temple, I'm croaky, but somehow this is our biggest show to date. Cars stop in the road, passengers leaping out to listen, and shopkeepers leave their tills to stare from doorways. A hundred people surround us. *The Farmer* is our top hit:

For I raise my own ham, my own chicken and lamb,
I shear my own fleece and I wear it.

The song's vision of humble agricultural sustainability seems to appeal powerfully here. An abundant and sustainable farm has been a common human dream ever since the birth of agriculture. Perhaps the people of Lymington think we've brought good news about this dream? Perhaps the song is the good news? As we pack away, an Estate Agent emerges from his glassy office to donate a heavy biscuit tin of his year's collected change. There's over a hundred pounds in this drop alone! Before we can repeat our stunned thanks, he's gone. Then from the still milling crowd, Michael from Lyndhurst steps forward to hand me a book: *A Time of Gifts* by Patrick Leigh Fermor. He says he couldn't let us leave Hampshire without it.

At a Lymington pub, we donate twenty pounds of copper coins to Children in Need. The barmaid asks if we robbed an amusement arcade? Later, we visit our friend's uncle's farm, and enjoy a gentle blast at his grandma's birthday. Over sherry and trifle we're taught by a canny cousin the secret of welly throwing: to fold down the boot's floppy end and create a discus shape, for greater aerodynamic efficiency. When we sing *The Farmer* here, our hosts lean back with deep sighs of self-satisfaction.

Lymington to Bournemouth

Departing next morning, we follow Lymington River toward the coast. On a sandy path between oaks and flowing water, we turn a bow of the river and come face to face with a huge brown animal. For one fearsome moment I'm sure it's a giant lion, until it shuffles away mooing. Reaching the coast, the Isle of Wight shimmers over dark water. It looks close enough to swim to, but paddling proves devastatingly cold. We walk through saltmarshes toward Keyhaven, with crunchy sea purslane everywhere underfoot. Halfway there, our digital camera battery dies, leaving us mapless. So we must follow roads, stamping orange-lit tarmac to Christchurch, before crossing River Stour to find ourselves deep in urban Dorset.

CHAPTER 5

Dorset

Bournemouth

Dorset begins like a great grey moorland. Endless roads and rushing cars make everywhere look and sound devoid of difference. The bitter November wind and rain don't help much. We're grateful to have a friend living here, whose cul-de-sac we find after hours of hunting. He works as a teacher, and we spend the evening helping with his marking.

Horribly early next morning we're back on the streets, searching for somewhere to sing. At least the rain has now stopped. In Bournemouth's enormously wide high street we try for a busk, but our efforts fall entirely flat. We're inaudible and invisible beside blaring Burtons and neon Next. It feels like a soggy duvet has covered everyone, especially us. There are limits, we admit sadly, to what even the old songs can do. Though perhaps something of the city's maritime heritage still echoes, as *Adieu Sweet Lovely Nancy* causes the shoppers to look up briefly.

Here's adieu, sweet lovely Nancy,
Ten thousand times adieu.
I'm a-going round the ocean love,
To seek for something new.

One of our few donors nervously praises my 'thirds and fifths'. I don't know what this means, and cherishing my musical un-education, I don't ask Ed. After our failed singsong we feel rather bleak, until Australian Ruby returns to walk awhile longer. So we cheer up and head for Sandbanks, an enclave boasting England's most expensive property prices. We hope to catch the ferry from here over Poole harbour, but it's stopped for winter repairs. For an hour we seek friendly fishing folk with whom to hitch a boat-ride, but all we get is fierce glares from retired millionaires in pastel casuals. "You do look a bit like tramps?" Ruby suggests with Australian upward inflection. Eventually we accept the thirty mile detour round the bay. Passing all the concrete and glass cuboid palaces, we press occasional buzzers, hoping to sing down an intercom and win tea or a tv deal; but no-one answers. In a dank wood near Upton we settle for the night, Ed and Ruby building a brushwood shelter, while I take a more distant grove and leave them to construct.

Bournemouth to Corfe Castle

At dawn, the woodland's gloom transforms into golden glory. After soaking up sunny blessings, I nip to town and meet a friendly newsagent. I ask him of local cafés, and he clicks on the kettle. An ex-Royal Marine, he nods rapidly when I explain what we're doing, and while we sip tea he talks quietly of Falklands yomps, a few times drifting into heavy silence. When I leave, he hefts my backpack to his chest to help me put it on without strain. "Can't afford an injury in the field" he explains. I'm excited to show Ed my military training. Back in the wood, the others are still rising, so I settle between willow roots to read *A Time of Gifts*. It's the true tale of an eighteen year old who walked from Canterbury to Constantinople in 1933, and the writing seems to herald from an era of richer mental aspirations, of belief in greater communication and increased meaning. The author, Patrick Leigh Fermor, looks at a house and talks of Palladian belfries, parabolas, and quatrefoils. I'm delighted to not understand what's going on half the time.

When we're all breakfasted and ready to leave, I help Ed on with his backpack, and he in turn helps Ruby. Then we begin a long slow day trudging tarmac through icy wind and biting rain. There's not much to tell of the day. When light dims, ever earlier, we stop near Wareham. Today is the anniversary of my dad's death, and with *A Time of Gifts* still in my mind, we visit a small pub to take "thimbles of the frozen north" (Finnish Vodka) while crying "white fire, red cheek, heat us and speed us!" among the surprised locals. But the buzz soon fades, and rain falls ever harder. Our new drinking friends are shocked by our plan to sleep outside in this weather, and their disbelief infects our confidence. We stumble away down puddled pavements, Ed complaining of a massive headache. Hunting for somewhere to sleep, I clamber barbed wire into a derelict house, to find it full of rocks and brambles. Ed tries a church, but it's modern and porchless. Ruby eventually spots a flat-floored patch of trees where we can string our tarps. We finally sit without heavy rain sloshing over us, before crashing into sleep.

I rise in sunshine, and straightaway rig a line to steam-dry my damp kit. When Ed wakes an hour later, he groggily does the same, but the instant his sleeping bag is offered to the sun, heavy rain returns. Ed looks softly crestfallen, so I make cinnamon porridge with butter, his favourite. Then we drag ourselves on through another cold wet day. We have no real plan where we're going, but we both feel certain something good awaits, a place we'll recognise on reaching. It feels like a pilgrimage recalled from a dream, to a destination urgent yet only half-remembered. I'm not sure how much fun this vague journey is for Ruby, but Australians are tenacious and she doesn't complain. Under serious downpour, we don't explore Corfe castle's cannon-shattered ruins. Instead we shelter in a pub, and sing for players in a cribbage tournament. The landlord's seven year old son tells me that he's a 'super boy king', but local boys aren't nice, so we sing him *Diggers Song* as a lesson in steadfastness:

> *Your houses they pull down,*
> *To fright poor men in town,*

But the gentry must come down,
And the poor shall wear the crown,
Stand up now, diggers all!

After a donated supper of leftover sandwiches, we're offered the pub's tin-shed for shelter: "It's got a brand new concrete floor, you'll be alright here," the landlord promises proudly, so in we squeeze with mugs of tea to see us safe. Long after midnight we're wakened by huge metallic crashes, as heavy hail turns the tin roof into a deafening drumskin. Under the boom of echoing unrhythm, I lie wide-eyed for hours. Wherever we're looking for, this isn't it.

Corfe Castle to Worth Matravers

In the clear morning, Ruby takes a bus back to Brighton. Ed and I choose our route forward by spinning my yew staff high in the air. It lands pointing south, so we clamber over tightly coiled Purbeck hills, through salty fields sliced by stone walls. Eventually, with cold noses, wet backs and dry throats, we arrive in Worth Matravers. Finding the church porch reassuringly open, we head straight to the pub. The Square and Compass' garden is a melee of pumpkins the size of coracles, among stone-carved monsters and vast spiralling fossils. We enter the pub through a front door whose lintel droops with parsley. "It's a death 'erb," a grinning man advises in thick Dorset burr, as I pluck and chew a leaf. Inside, the Square and Compass has two rooms and six tables. The ceilings are low, the beams lower, and all drinks are served from one small hatch. There's no food save pasties, meat or veg. The landlord, with his foot-long goatee and perma-beret, greets us with a grace so breezily gentle it almost conceals his depths of kindness. We begin to relax. Have we arrived?

Tonight the pub is saying goodbye to a local lady who leaves for New Zealand in the morning. So late that night we adapt *Farewell Nancy* to sing her off, and the parting lass weeps.

> *Fare you well, dear lovely Sarah,*
> *For you must now leave us.*
> *Far off to New Zealand you soon must away.*
> *But let your long absence be no trouble to us,*
> *For you will return in a year and a day.*

Next morning we get stuck into local matters. The landlord's family has owned this pub for a hundred years, so we volunteer to help make centenary cider. For two chilly days we diligently cut cores and rot from many thousands of freezing apples. Our hands are sweet and bloody, but too cold to feel the wounds. "It's a wise man who knows the poor bits don't spoil it," the landlord shouts over the press, "but my cider's glad for you two fools!" Our reward is a wooden railway carriage in which to stay as long as we're here. So for the next fortnight we become resident singers in this tiny Dorset pub. Each day we wander the fossil-rich coast, while every evening we answer the calls for song. Purbeck is famous for its limestone quarries, started by the Romans, from whose stone St Paul's Cathedral is made. We explore vast caverns sliced from the cliff. Silent and warm, we consider sleeping in one, but fear the night-time slap of falling slabs. Outside, climbers grapple cliffs under an azure sky, while on great rocking boulders we sing into rich sea-winds. We're now fully certain that this is the place we sought.

Here in Worth we learn a song called *Drink Old England Dry*, a celebration of the national ale habit. But in truth, our regular beer-drinking sits heavily, and after the pub's generous lashings of cask Ringwood ale, most mornings we wake feeling groggy. Ed reads in the small book that cleavers (goose-grass/sticky-weed) can offer a cleansing morning tonic, so we gather armfuls to steep in water. The resulting silver hedgewater heals our hangovers almost as swiftly as song.

One stormy night, Ed and I walk the cliff-path through harsh blasting rain to St Aldhelm's chapel. This tiny stone micro-church stands at the very edge of England, on the balancing point between land, sea and sky. Arriving, Ed circles the squat grey chapel clockwise and I follow. I circle it twice more and Ed follows. Side by side at the threshold, I tap the door with my staff and Ed turns the latch. The heavy door catches the wind and almost slams. We fight to close it, and when the latch clicks, the violence of wind and waves fades. Lighting a beeswax candle reveals a small grey salty room with an altar in the centre. Singing *The Leaves of Life* unlocks a sense of welcome, and we unpack our bed-rolls. Lying wrapped up and warm, through the thick stone walls only the finest sea-winds whistle and dance with the candlelit dark. This is surely the very best hotel imaginable.

In grey morning light, we leave coins in the wall-safe before stepping back into the wave-crashing world. Back in the village, early dog walkers smile and wave. The people here all seem remarkably happy, though they do share one common complaint: that so many village houses are bought as holiday homes. These captive dwellings sit empty throughout most of the year, which 'ain't none too friendly'. It also inflates house-prices, so folk born here, working traditional quarrying jobs, can only afford to live in caravans. "But we've got a damn good pub!" they laugh, raising glasses.

We meet many good people in Worth. A Romany man called Kit, who lives in a hi-tech van making bespoke mirror frames, tells us that he initially spread the word that we were to be trusted. It wasn't because we'd walked here - "though that's something...", but because we didn't swear - "and that makes a bloody change!" Kit takes us for a walk to teach us tricks, like never looking at animals we approach, as 'all living creatures can feel eyes on them'.

We also meet an elderly local man called Cyril, who teaches us two songs. The first is about a English song-thrush taken to Australia, and the 'mockling throng' of listeners who gather to hear it. For some reason, I fail completely to write this song down. The second song is about a girl getting married, who boasts of her petticoat being dyed green and her shoes getting mended. And one day, she'll inherit the family bed! This song, called 'Lasses from Banyan', I manage to jot down. Cyril cries as he sings, as old men shameless might. After song, he invites us for food. Walking to Cyril's bungalow, we politely call him 'sir' until he points out a shattered concrete pad hidden in the nettles: "See that lads? I helped build that. It were a four minute warnin' system for Russian mizzels. Four minutes?" he cackles, "hardly enough time for good shag, is it?" After this we talk more freely. At his bungalow, Cyril disappears into the kitchen to emerge with plates of white bread, margarine and corned beef. We'd normally avoid such food, believing it unhealthy, but Cyril presents the plates with such sincerity and delight that the meal is transformed into a deeply nourishing feast. It's surely a trick Jesus knew. After we eat, Cyril talks of liberating concentration camps in World War Two. He offers little detail, nor do we chase it, his rolling tears telling plenty.

That evening, back in the pub, we're waxing our boots and drying our sink-washed socks by the pub's fire, when a man in a long leather jacket slides along the bench toward us. He says he's called Smooth and he wants to record us singing, pulling from his pocket some sheets of paper: "Just a basic contract to keep things fair, since we'll be using my laptop and microphone." Though Ed and I are green in such things, we're not born yesterday. Here is the ghost of career future, come early to haunt us. Without reading them, we slide the papers back with a promise to think it over.

Smooth scowls and slinks away like an angry panther, and we don't see him again.

Next day, we walk the Priests Way to Swanage. This town is Poole's poor cousin, but even on a gusty November afternoon the people here are curious and engaging. At first it's young lads on push-bikes, who welcome us by fighting each other. Then teenage girls arrive to demand 'What? Why? How?' with folded arms. When the older lads turn up, we sing *Diggers Song* and they do half-mocking dances before throwing coins. Later we meet a lady who saw us sing in Winchester. She warns us it's unsafe to sleep outside. When we ask how she knows, she admits to reading it in the Sun. After a moment's almost sincere silence, she bursts into laughter, and we join in.

Back in Worth, we rise one morning from our train carriage and smell something new in the air. The wind is blowing west and it's time to move on. So we pack up and make our farewells. As we climb the stone stile away, the landlord whispers urgently: "We're all made of limestone and seashells." Singing this great truth to the gulls wheeling above, we walk toward Cornwall.

Worth Matravers to Dorchester

West along the Purbeck hills, after the great bay of Kimmeridge we're diverted north by an Army shooting range. Up heath and down lane, we slowly regain our wayward momentum. At Chaldon Herring, recognising the name, we check our notebook to find a jotted invitation. Knocking at the scrawled address, we're welcomed for supper. After food, Barry says he's arranged for us to sleep in a nearby barn: "I've called the farmer, so you won't get turfed out" he grins. But the barn's roof is holey, and sometime after midnight, rain falls and puddles rise. By two am we're almost afloat, and depart to escape the flood. Half-asleep under the dark deluge, we find a bus-stop, built so recently we can smell the wood-preserving chemicals. But its roof is sound and there's two benches, so we stretch out dry and grateful. As a jeep makes pub deliveries at four am, we sluggishly discuss whether alcohol and tobacco are still smuggled in Britain. "Casks of rum afloat on grey brine," Ed mumbles from his huddle.

When the sun rises, we move with surprising steam. North, we make our way to the Five Marys barrows, where more heroic ancestors were buried - though here they've been mostly dug up for treasure. Then we follow the snaking hills westward, until mid-morning our power abruptly ebbs. When a hailstorm arrives, we surrender to it, lying down on the damp hillside to let it beat our backs. This is a bad plan. The fierce winds make us shiver, and the ground's chill creeps eagerly into our bones. We rise and stumble to the valley below, which we follow west to Owermoigne. Seeking sanctuary at a shack called 'Artists' World', the shopkeeper brews us instant soup. Ed buys a sketchbook and some water colours. "It's just that there's all this space in my bag now," he replies to my invisibly-raised eyebrows. As we sip soup and watch the weather blast against thin windows, I ask the shopkeeper about four strange domes in the car-park, cobwebby fibreglass demi-spheres. "They're free-domes," he explains, "someone's plan for affordable housing that never took off. Pop in if you fancy a kip, ignore the security warnings." A handwritten sign pinned to the door asserts that 'this domes ullarmed'. Inside we find a large round room, with carpets, a desk and disconnected telephone. We gratefully unpack our beds and snatch forty winks.

Waking hours later, the day is already dark, and our art-shop friend has shut up shop and gone home. We consider staying the night, but the orange glow of nearby street lights is discouraging, so we march hot-footed through rushing Broadmayne until footpaths offer a softer path to West Knighton. It's always such deep relief, the transition back to earth underfoot. The song of tarmac is so powerfully sung, it can be easy to forget that everywhere is earth below.

When we see the winking lanterns of an inn, we steer to the door and enter to huddle by a radiator. After our long stay in the moneyless luxury of Worth Matravers, we're now poor again, so we order bread and cheese. It's a menu choice that can mean almost anything, but thankfully here it's a winning bargain, with a half a kilo of cheddar and heavy wedges of bread. We eat and regain strength. On the other side of the pub, a ladies darts team are limbering up. We recognise the opportunity. A newly learned song called *Sovay*, about a woman who disguises herself as a highway robber to test her lover's devotion, could make a great offering. Or it may be entirely offensive. Either way, tonight we lack the energy to try.

When we leave the pub, I wait in the car-park while Ed fills our water bottles. As I huddle in my jacket from the blasting wind, an upstairs window clicks opens. "Where you going?" shouts a concerned lady. "To the woods," I call back, trying to sound happy about it. The window shuts, and a minute later the landlord steps out: "There's seventy mile an hour winds tonight, oak spears'll be dropping. Stay here, it'll be safer." We gratefully string tarps from a picnic table in the pub's back garden, till Mick reappears with a frown: "No tents? Come on, you'd better have the laundry room." So among the hum of parfum and electrics, by the big boxes of non-bio we sleep. In the morning, Mick invites us for machine coffee at the bar, where he shares his laments for modern Britain: "This country's forgotten its past," he cries, "our heritage and community's been sold." We offer him a song, but he says he's got things to do.

We walk for Dorchester, an ancient Wessex market town just two miles north west. This is Thomas Hardy country, so we're confident that the minstrel tradition will be well-remembered. Sure enough, we arrive to find the high street occupied by an amplified guitarist at the top and a violinist in the middle. So we take the bottom of the street, and soon smiling crowds gather. *Spenser the Rover* is Dorchester's favourite, possibly because this town sits at the foot of a ridgeway, an ancient wayfarers' super highway, so the townsfolk all live in the shadow of journey's lure. We ask donors to recommend local songs, and one old fellow tells us about *Cold Haily Windy Night*, which we jot down eagerly.

Taking tea at a café, when the owner asks what we're doing we offer him song. But he looks panicked, as though two men singing for him might break some crucial taboo. So he calls the two waitresses over to transfer the gift: "Sally, Jo, these two guys want to sing you a song". He leans back, looking much more at ease. "Crack on then lads!" We blast out *Harvest Song*, and it looks like all three enjoy it.

Leaving the café, we notice three men previously drinking on a bench have now taken over our busking spot, to blast out accapella Aerosmith songs with a baseball cap thrown down. We wave, and one of the singers jogs over, can in hand: "We never knew you could make money just by singing, no guitars or nothing. Here, take some, it's your trick." He offers us a handful of change. Appreciating this guild solidarity, I pluck fifty pence from the offered hoard, as Ed winks: "The town's all yours."

Dorchester to Abbotsbury

Walking into the night, Dorchester behind us shimmers like a Tokyo dream. In the darkness ahead stands Maiden Castle, once Europe's largest hill-fort. I really want to visit here, but instincts say not now. So we keep to the high-hedged lane, plodding slowly west. The moonlight is slender, and the air tastes of earth and metal. Suddenly we hear an angry roar, as out from the dark a shirtless man runs between us, to instantly disappear into the night beyond. We're too surprised to be shocked. I'm not sure he even noticed us.

An hour up the road, following a tip from town we visit a village pub. Stashing our backpacks outside, we try to be low-key, but before very long the landlord demands song. *John Barleycorn*, the high hymn of beer, goes down a storm. On its merit, the landlord brings us plates of leftover food and offers the pub's skittle alley for sleep.

Rising chilly among the skittles next morning, we're bundled with plump packed lunches by the landlord's smiling wife. As we leave the village, I spot a car-battery peeping from the roadside brook, and scoop it out with a gardener's borrowed hoe. The gardener thanks us on behalf of local tadpoles. Uphill, we walk through fields scattered with tumps and barrows, the small hills of long dead heroes. At the peak of Black Down stands the most modern memorial, a great granite obelisk built for Vice Admiral Hardy, kisser of dying Nelson at Trafalgar. This monument's eight corners point in the cardinal directions, and being visible a hundred kilometres away, it's a famed landmark for shipping. A short way on, we pass the Valley of Stones, a deposit of countless scattered grey sarsen rocks. Was this also once a great memorial, destroyed long before memory?

Then comes Abbotsbury, a tiny ex-abbey village with more than a hint of Glastonbury. Only one wall of the once mighty abbey still stands – the refectory. Is where people eat together the holiest locality? Christianity's highest ritual is, after all, eating supper with friends. Perhaps obeying a similar impulse, on our way to visit the chapel on the hill, we are waylaid by a café offering 'bottomless coffee'. We get our kicks, but thrill turns to throb as afternoon passes into night. With aching heads, we follow the setting sun to St Catherine's chapel, and crash on her gravel floor.

Abbotsbury to Bridport

Early pink promise glimmers through the arched stone windows of our borrowed church hotel. After cold oats, *Leaves of Life* and a handful of coins for the wall-safe, we step into soft but soon strengthening rain. The coastal path below the hill is probably beautiful in fine weather, but wind and rain whip at us, keeping our heads down. Some miles west we reach Burton Bradstock, surely a 1930s detective's name. The village's stylish café smells good, but it booms with damp families, so we stay out in the rain. The path onward is perilous with rowdy bulls and puddle-floods, but eventually we reach River Asker. I drop a feather from my hat into the flowing waters, and then we're in Bridport.

When I ask a passer-by for a decent pub, they laugh and keep walking. So we try the first open door, where soon we're singing for the bar staff, before with a whoosh of steam the kitchen emerges to listen too. After, we're told of an open-mic session up the road, so we head along to find rowdy cowboy rock and psychedelic sitar jams. When it's our turn, we ask the sound engineer to switch off the mics so we can step beyond the electronic veil and blast hard farming classics into the crowd. The songs feel like wild creatures released in their native forests, and the drunken crowd dance like frenzied fools. Pints of thanks line up on the bar. Realising our peril, we soon try to leave, but get cajoled into a birthday pub-crawl, with the promise of carpeted sleep afterward. Two pubs later, we're blurry and wobbling, when the birthday girl gets in a screaming fight with her boyfriend, and we abandon our hope for comfort. Thankfully, a man called Jason takes us in hand: "I'm homeless," he explains, "but I've got just the spot, there's plenty of room for three." Around the corner in a car-park, Jason proudly points out a tin-roofed lean-to. He's lived in his tent here for the last six months. "I've got a job, but it's not enough to pay for a flat. So this is how life has to be right now." Ed and I scamper into bivys, and lie with drifting drizzle cooling our overheated brows. "Is Bridport always like this?" I ask Jason as he zips up his tent. "Oh yes," he sighs, "it's a town of constant joy."

When we wake, our host has already departed for his garden centre job. He's kindly left us two tins labelled 'breakfast', but we can't face this orange melange, so leave them for Jason's return. At the confluence of rivers Brit and Asker, we sit to recover from last night. We realise, yet again, that good times can become too good. As Shakespeare said: "If all the year were playing holidays, to sport would be as tedious as to work. But when they seldom come, they wished-for come". We may need to increase the seldomness of our celebrations. Singing to the conjoining rivers calms our bellies and soothes our skulls, especially the long slow harmonies of *Claudy Banks*. Rising to check our pockets, we find most of our funds have been claimed by the ale-houses of Bridport. But I do find a scrap of paper with lyrics to a song called *She Moves Through The Fair*, given by some merrymaker last night.

In town, we fall to song outside the oldest butchers' business in Britain, run by the same family for five hundred years. Though we're far from our sparkling best, we soon make friends and coin. *Sovay*, with its sudden explosive conclusion, works well here:

> *For if you'd have given me that ring, she said,*
> *I'd have pulled the trigger,*
> *I'd have pulled the trigger and shot you dead!*

We sing until the butcher emerges to wordlessly place hot sandwiches in our hands. We instantly stop singing to eat, which may well be the point. It's certainly a good way to ask. After food, we shift to sing by the post office. But within a few sailors' love songs, we're emptied of power, and retreat to a health food shop. "Oh dear, how long have you been in Bridport?" the kind ladies ask as we stumble in. "Just one night," I explain, and their frowns grow. They load us with vegetables and honey, and Ed buys Ricola lozenges, which he swears by. Then on a scrap of cardboard the shopkeepers write directions to 'recovery'. We accept the quest with hazy thanks.

Bridport to Pilsdon

We leave Bridport under Allington hill, and walk north until dusk fades blue. Spotting an ivy-wrapped sign, we follow its arrow and peer about, unsure if this is our destination. Suddenly a bell clangs, and a voice shouts: "Wayfurrers!" The gate swings wide and a couple rush out, peeling the bags from our backs and bustling us into the steamed-up kitchen. We're asked if we'll take tea or coffee, and whether we're vegetarian, before we've even had a chance to say hello. This is Pilsdon Manor, a refuge for people finding life a bit much, a harbour between the 'real' world and rougher seas. People on parole, out of care, unemployed and homeless...and over-celebrated wandering singers. We're given beds in a dormitory, a washing machine and showers. We eat, wash and sleep.

Next day, we attend the seven am church service in Pildson's tiny chapel. The pews are all straw-bales, it's ultra low-key but feels right in the heart. After breakfast, we're allotted our work detail – muck spreading. Determined to outdo expectations, for the next nine hours we shovel donkey manure, jogging with the wheelbarrow between loads. "It doesn't have to be finished today," the other workers say, sucking roll-ups and looking puzzled. But we work as hard as fools, spreading muck till blisters blossom wide. Our reward is to stay a second night, despite the rules. Passing wayfarers usually get one night only at Pilsdon. In thanks, after supper we sing - though we realise most of our songs feature alcohol or broken relationships, so we choose carefully. *Fiddlers Green* proves reliable. Afterward, we talk with the other residents till late. We're introduced to the Welsh triads, the ancient grouping of everything into threes. Apparently, 'genius' requires: 'an eye that can see nature, a heart that can feel nature, and a boldness that dare follow nature'. We also learn about Welsh perpetual choirs, where songs were sung in decades of unceasing harmony. And we're introduced to Robert Graves' poetry:

Love without hope, as when the young bird-catcher
Swept off his tall hat to the Squire's own daughter.
So let the imprisoned larks escape and fly,
Singing about her head, as she rode by.

We sleep rich with imaginary gold. In the morning, our vigour restored, we wave goodbye and return to the lanes, singing *When I die I'll live again* to the sleeping hedgerows.

Pildson to Lyme Regis

Despite recommendations, we don't climb Pilsdon Pen, the great hill behind the manor. Instead we take lower paths toward Whitchurch Canicorum. We've heard that the church here holds one of just two English shrines to survive the Reformation, when Henry VIII and Thomas Cromwell destroyed England's pilgrimage infrastructure. Only Westminster Abbey and Whitchurch Canicorum endured these purges. Westminster is the shrine of Edward the Confessor, the father of England's post-Norman national myth. But what's so special about this small Dorset village?

The saint buried here is called Wita (or Vita, Vit or Whit). Above the church door a carving depicts her as a smiling pregnant woman holding a flaming torch. It's a powerful and surely ancient image, though I'm not sure where I recognise it from. Perhaps a dream? Some people say Wita was a local girl killed by the Danes in the tenth century, but others say the truth is far older. The reliquary – where Wita is buried – offers three holes in a stone chamber below the coffin, to let pilgrims get close to her remains. Letters and candles are scattered about, so people still come here seeking blessings. After singing *Leaves of Life*, we sit in silence. We don't know what else to do. Should we put our hands together and pray? Dance like no-one's watching, sing like no-one's listening, but what of prayer? Pray like no-one's heeding? Our tentative spiritual experiments end abruptly when a gang of chatting flower-arrangers arrive, and from saint Wita's bed we wander on.

Westward is Monkton Wyld, a community of successful hippy life-coaches. I've got a good feeling about this place, and get so lost in daydreams of spicy feasts and firelit revelry that a bus almost knocks me over. We finally reach the promised place, and stroll up the driveway, ignoring a sign that says 'We're Closed'. Monkton Wyld manor is old and massive, and we're materially impressed. Hippies have done well here. Now they surely need wandering song! The main door offers no handles, knockers or bells, so we skirt about looking for people. Peering through a stone framed window, we see three longhairs watching a screen. I think it's CCTV, but Ed reckons they're playing Mario Kart. Seeing us, a woman gestures toward the main door. We return and wait. The door creaks open a few inches, and a skinny chap squeezes out with one foot still in the doorway. He bows at an awkward angle and says 'Namaste", both hands together in a gesture of prayer. "Hullo," we reply, and wait in grinning silence, our breath misting the dusk. He goes for it: "Monkton Wyld is closed for the winter, so we can't take guests. But I have a brochure you can read if you like?" "We've walked a long way to find you," Ed explains, and the doorkeeper winces. I ask if we might sleep in the gardens? "Er, sorry...no. But the brochure has all our courses, do look through it." He bows 'Namaste' again and slams the door behind him. We retreat to the nearby church lych-gate to read about the courses available. 'The Ecology of Money', a day of lectures including lunch, for only one hundred and eighty pounds. "Such a warm welcome..." says Susan from Ludlow.

Following footpaths through Hole Common to Dragon's Hill, long after dark we arrive on the gusty coast of Lyme Regis. Rain hisses over grey waves, with clouds of purple jagged promise not far behind. We seek shelter, but though the beach-huts look tempting, surely such obvious nooks are regularly checked? Then inspiration strikes, and we scurry under the blades of a beached catamaran. Wrapped tight with marine tarpaulin, it offers a roofed wing each, hidden and dry. It's probably the most expensive tent we'll ever borrow. Sure enough, at eleven o clock a police car cruises along the seafront, torches shining all round the beach huts. But nobody looks under the boats.

In the first light of dawn, we rise to avoid earnest yachtsmen. After a few chilly hours of seaside contemplation, we step onto the hilly high-street for song, taking our spot beside a Masonic bench. I imagine Masons as grey-suited shamen, mappers of unseen urban grids. I'm sure they don't just plonk their benches down any old where, so we borrow this hotspot. It seems to work, for despite the blasting sea-winds and ever-screaming gulls, the old songs are heard and welcomed here. *Adieu Sweet Lovely Nancy* summons a great haul of coins and kind words.

> *But when the wars are over,*
> *There'll be peace on every shore.*
> *We'll return to our wives and families,*
> *And the girls that we adore.*

We also win another new song, or at least a title

and a hummed melody: *All things are quite silent* is a shore shanty about press gangs dragging a young man away from his lover for a forced life at sea. There seems to be an endless spring of these coastal songs, echoes of lost love claimed by the hungry sea. We jot this corker down to learn later.

Our hat well-padded, we take tea and plot our path. Next along the coast is Sidmouth, home to a famous folk festival. We're excited to sing there. But reaching Sidmouth without roads seems to require following a very odd-looking path from Lyme Regis. According to the map, the route passes right through the cliffs. As we peer confused at the map, an old man leans over to say: "It's the Undercliff you lads want. I just hope you're ready for it!" We're not sure what he means. It's only a few miles - how hard can it be?

We leave the café and descend a flight of steps. Like a door closing, Lyme Regis disappears behind us, and we enter the lost world of Devon.

CHAPTER 6

Devon

Lyme Regis to Sidmouth

The Undercliff was born from landslides behind the sea-facing cliff. Ancient ground, never ploughed or tamed, was rudely awoken from Jurassic dreams by the ripping away of its deep chalk blanket. Abruptly exposed to sun, wind and rain, this land is now understandably resentful of surface monkeys' feet. It never got the memo about humanity claiming mastery of all Earth. Here we're just more tiny animals on an ever-changing planet. Facing the Undercliff's jungled chalk passage, my first instinct is to try another path. Once we start walking this path the only way out is at the far end. To begin requires commitment to finish, a relatively rare condition for south English walking. But there's no alternative except narrow busy roads.

We step in. The fresh chalk has been hungrily colonised by ash and maple trees, who fight to close off the tenuous human trackway. Ed and I walk far apart, to avoid the flick-back of whipping boughs. More than once, my hat is pulled from my head by grasping thorns. Underfoot, the way is never flat, but always rocky and rooty with corners and climbs. No single step is simple, it's like a slow perpetual assault course. Within a mile, my strength fades. Last night's sleep under a beached boat in a sea-storm was thrilling, but not especially restorative. Today, to keep my legs moving in careful co-ordination, lifting and treading with sufficient precision to avoid a painful stumble, requires fuller focus than I feel able to give. I lean into my yew staff ever more, like an oar urgently propelling a leaky vessel. I constantly wonder if I'll make it out, and look for spots to collapse in rest, but everywhere is sharp with rocks and brambles. The only way is onward.

After increasingly blurry hours, at last the green underworld spits us out, and we stumble sweat-drenched onto a golf-course in clifftop Devon. We've only walked five miles, but it cost more than I had. We wild nap by the incongruously human-friendly fairway, drinking up sea-winds until refreshment becomes freezing. Rising to cross River Axe, I drop in a pinch of Undercliff chalk caught in my boots' lace-hooks. Under whipping rain, we pass through Seaton with our heads down, crossing the coastal road only to drive our bodies through pathbursting seafront rosemary. Aphrodite wore this herb when she rose from the sea, and we haggardly feel similar need to re-emerge in beauty.

At the village of Beer, we follow prompts. In the welcome warmth of a pub we try to stay low-key, until a smart elderly couple spot our soggy sign and request song. But the barmaid quickly cuts in, saying the pub has no entertainment license. Our new friends are amazed: "Hang on Debbie, do you mean I've paid one hundred and twenty pounds for tickets to new year's eve, and we can't even sing Auld Lang's Syne?" Debbie has no answer, so to smooth waters we pop outside and sing *Adieu Sweet Lovely Nancy* through an open window. It's a loophole. Back in the pub, we talk about protesting this absurd law. How can it ever be illegal to sing? We decide the most effective protest would be to cease talking altogether, and instead just sing. So we try it, ordering our second pint with improvised melody. But the whole pub turns to stare like we've broken some ancient taboo. Sheepish, we return to monotone mumblings. When we're told that Beer's other pub might offer food for song, we wander over, and find the Anchor abuzz with a care-workers' Christmas party. *Three Drunken Maidens* works best here. After feasting on donated leftovers, we escape the high-life to a concrete shelter on the headland. It's like a brutal secular twentieth century St Aldhelm's chapel, utility without wholesomeness, but it keeps the rain from our faces as we sleep.

Sunrise stains the clinking sailboats pink, as we follow Beer brook down the winding high street and climb toward Sidmouth. But a mile up and down later, I fade again. I think my hands are shaking. Is it too much beer and rough sleep? Am I getting enough food, water, vitamins? Whatever the cause, the chalk peaks ahead, like stormy seas set in stone, threaten to drown me. So I opt for calmer inland paths from Branscombe. Ed remains coastal to grit his teeth and slog, and we plan to meet in Sidmouth.

It's deeply relaxing to walk alone, to simply stop when I'm tired or curious. I sing at a donkey sanctuary to braying retirees, and in a church to a stained glass pilgrim. Then comes Sidmouth. I've high hopes for singing here. After a few hours wandering the town, Ed arrives looking grey. I feed him tea and lardy cake, and soon he's ready to sing. We find our spot in the pedestrian town centre, and song soon flows merrily. But midway through, competition arrives. The Rotary club, with their tinsel-wrapped trailer and sound-system, are blasting out Christmas carols with a motely swarm of money collectors shaking buckets in festive counter-rhythm. Though heavily out-gunned, we hold our corner. As long as we keep singing, they can't simply roll over us. Sure enough, they stare in mild disdain but limit their patrol to the centre of town. Steadily fills our hat of supper. A lady in a sharp suit teaches us the first verse of an Irish song called *The Parting Glass*, which we eagerly copy down. But perhaps we look like we feel, as one donor drops bic razors in our hat, while another makes us promise not to spend her fifty pence on drugs.

When we pack away, a friendly forager called Pat steps forward to invite us home for supper. A break from pubs is just what we need, so we keenly take directions. Leaving Sidmouth, we're soon lost on Bulverton Hill, and arrive hours later at Pat's house to find him sat on the doorstep. "Perfect timing," he grins. As we thump our backpacks down in the hallway, Pat's wife Sarah is shocked: "These are far too heavy – are you trying to be the hippy SAS?" We pull out a few less necessary items - mini candle lanterns, old maps, some books and spare catapult rubbers, which Pat agrees to give to a charity shop. When Sarah offers to wash our clothes, we're too tired to pretend to argue. I'm now tingling with full-body pins and needles. Whatever power has carried me this far has nearly gone. Seeing me wobble, Sarah brews skullcap tea, ideal for restoring nervous calm. Her medicine helps tremendously. As we revive, Pat tells stories of returning political post to Conservative HQ in a black sack with a Pierre-Joseph Proudhon quote stuck on, which led to the whole building being evacuated:

He who lays his hand on me is a usurper and tyrant, and I name him my enemy.

"Nineteenth century anarchism still makes the fat cats cower!" Pat roars in triumph. For supper we eat gingered sea-bass with grape-juice, and after song, deep relaxation thuds in, with sleep its crowning joy.

Sidmouth to Exeter

Waking late, our hosts feed us granola and bananas, before giving us a loaf of bread and our dry clean clothes. I feel twice as alive as yesterday. Pat and Sarah accompany us to a bridge over River

Otter, where we fling the waters a quartz pebble, before waving goodbye and walking west. Rainbows pierce the slate sky, and we constantly dive under pines to hide from sudden rainfall. In a wood near Hawkerland, a dog walker says with amazement that he heard us sing in Hastings three months ago, and thought we were drama students in costumes.

A mile later, hopping a barbed-wire fence, I slip and rip my trousers. While I sew myself up, Ed brews rosehip tea. Reading the small book he tells me that during the Second World War (and probably forever before) British folk picked as many rosehips as they could, to replace the lemons and limes lost to U-Boats. Rosehips offer more vitamin C, weight-for-weight, than any citrus fruit, a truth we can taste in the tea's twang.

Walking on, we find ourselves in a nook of strongly-held peace. No cars are seen or heard. No litter lies roadside. The hedges are healthy and the trees stand proud. Before long, this golden path leads to Woodbury Salterton. Everyone grins as we enter the pub. We learn that all the barstaff are from New Zealand, and clearing litter from local hedges is just part of their culture. As we take tea, a blind man at the bar turns to announce with calm certainty: "No life – no death – one mind." An ex-Metropolitan policeman turned Buddhist, he explains the difference between cats and dogs: "When old people die in a flat, we'd find their dog lying dead at their feet from starvation. But their cat would be alive and prowling, having eaten half their owner's face." In exchange, we sing *Claudy Banks,* and the blind ex-copper weeps.

We cross the Countess Wear bridge and backtrack along River Exe, before spending two days at my cousin Molly's house in Exminster. Then we hit Exeter, which is furious and loud. Taxis rankle for custom, shops blare carols, everyone is last-minute panic-buying. It's either Christmas or the end of the world. Looking for somewhere quiet to sing, we settle by the cathedral. Though fewer folk roam here, they seem glad for song. *Three Drunken Maidens* summons the most grins and coins.

> *There was a woodcock and a pheasant,*
> *A partridge and a hare,*
> *And every sort of dainty, no scarcity was there.*

After song, we pop into the cathedral, but there's a carol concert starting soon, so we only get a few minutes to stare in wonder at the stone vaulted ceiling. When we leave, we avoid pubs, guessing they'll be as hectic as the high-street. Instead we take an early night in Exeter castle's dry moat, the only place in the city we can hear birdsong.

Rising early, we pop back to town for a morning busk, as this is our last urban venue for some time. Singing *Drink old England dry* wins us nods and coins from three tough-looking chaps with shaved heads. "I think we just won the Nazi pound'" Ed mutters, so we chase them away with sailors' love songs. As morning rolls on, song keeps flowing, and soon the day grows dark again. And just when all we want is to slump on sofas, into the cold rainy dusk we walk out of Exeter.

Exeter to Moretonhampstead

We ford the great metal river of the A303, then walk till the road-scream fades. A smiling dog-walker asks if we know where we're sleeping tonight? "Not a clue sir," we reply. He sighs with deep satisfaction: "That's the dream, lads, that's the dream."

Spotting a village pub, we pop in to warm up. We're keen to avoid another evening of raucous song, but tonight even basic welcome evades us. The pub is entirely unfriendly. The bartender eventually explains that a backpacker recently got so offensively drunk here that now no-one likes backpackers anymore. We do our best to undo the bad pattern, but a few quiet hours later, we're tolerated but still not trusted. So we don't ask about local shelter, and instead make polite farewells before stepping into the frozen dark. A hundred metres down the lane, we stop. It's late, we're tired, and we must answer the 'where' question of sleep. And while we respect the pub's right to be moody, their back garden is dark and flat, with thick privet hedges for concealment. It's the best choice all round. So we sneak back down the road, torchless and silent, and tiptoe to the bottom of the pub garden, to tuck into bivys and steal forty winks.

The night is starbright, and the air bites my nose. Long before the sky dreams of dawn, we rise with frosty beards. Up and down the icy roads, we slide the frozen corners to Doddiscombeleigh. We call good morning to an elderly couple, scraping ice from their car windscreen. "I hope you didn't sleep out last night?" the woman asks worriedly. We admit we did, and briefly explain our journey. Breaking into great smiles, the pair invite us in for tea and toast. In their cosy kitchen, we talk of Hillaire Belloc, ley-lines and organic farming. It's a meeting of strangely instant kinship, this couple feeling like lost grandparents. I can't tell if they're joking when they suggest we stay for the winter to help them with the house and land? But we have miles to tread.

In Doddiscombeleigh church we see a five hundred year old stained glass image of St Christopher, once England's most pictured saint. His popularity was based on the tradition that seeing Christopher guaranteed all-day protection from violent death. Stepping back into the chilly world beyond the church, I wonder if Christopher's protection includes the violence of winter weather? We meet many types of cold on the way to Dartmoor, from creeping hollows, small flashes, subtle glimmers, and great assaults of chill. Hat, scarf and gloves (hsg) are constantly readjusted. Thankfully, the internal furnaces of walking are powerful engines. By the time we cross River Teign, the air is sun-warmed and we're flowing well. I drop into the waters a wilted leaf from my hat. At Mortonhampstead church, we meet a tree-surgeon cutting down churchyard elms. "They've all got the Dutch," he shouts between chainsaw blasts. He explains how a tiny beetle carries an even smaller spore, which causes Dutch elm disease, the great killer of English elms. This curse arrived via the mass-importation of timber, though elm itself was an import to Britain, brought by the Romans who used it to train grape-vines and as leaf-hay for their animals. Apparently elm was once renowned as famine food, its seeds being almost half protein. Some of the lopped churchyard boughs look straight and strong, and we discuss exchanging staffs. But my Kingley Vale yew is too good to release, and Ed's persisting with his original chestnut.

Mortonhampstead village centre offers only one venue for song, below the villager clock between the roads. It's a slow trade, but the songs work their magic, especially *Cold Haily Windy Night.* Busking in our full woollen garb, the pounds of chilly sympathy fill our hat. We stop when we're shivering too much to sing. As we pack away, a passing gang of neon youth invite us to a trance party in Ashburton, promising easy hitchhiking. But we're far too near Dartmoor to go jumping in cars. We wish them joy, then hit the pub for warmth. We've been talking about hot chocolate for the last hour. But as soon as we step inside, the landlord cries: "Ale for the minstrels", and we must play our part. We take packets of peanuts for calorific heat, and fireside armchairs for comfort. As we get warm, we meet a couple called Cosmo and Susie, who invite us to their comfy cottage. Ed and Cosmo jam on Dartmoor oak congas, while Susie and I make scones and our long-awaited hot chocolate. Banging his drum late into the night, Cosmo shares a triple-test for decision-making: "Is it good for me? Is it good for humanity? Is it good for the environment? If the answer's yes to all three, then it's good for the Universe and you've got to do it!" Examining our journey in these terms, Ed and I happily agree that we're on the right track.

Moretonhampstead to Totnes

In the warmer morning, we walk south in search of a community called Steward Wood. Ed met one of its dwellers at a festival last year, and ever since he's talked of this place as a vision of rural Utopia. Seeing silver smoke rising from a wooded hillside, we climb the path until a man steps from the trees in challenge: "You two lost?" We explain Ed's friend and vision, and the gatekeeper grins: "Main lodge is up the path." The track opens to a hillside hamlet housing six happy families. Laughing children jump and sing, chatting adults dig and build, and snoozing dogs dream in sunny corners. Ed's festival friend Lucas tours us round the low-impact dwellings, wood-fired hot water system, and communal kitchen gardens. "It's wonderful here," Lucas explains, "but our planning permission is temporary, so it's hard to fully invest, knowing we could be turfed out any moment." At least this place has been permitted to begin. The families here share a joyfully sustainable lifestyle, and it's hard to see the benefit of compelling them into separate brick houses. Encouraging low-impact communal living alongside the 'modern norm' seems deeply sensible, considering the UK's pressing environmental and housing needs.

We chop parsnips for this evening's Winter Solstice feast, and lull a crying baby to sleep with *Oats and Beans*. Come supper time, everyone takes their place round the Yule fire, lit from last year's ash log. Small children pass the plates with blessings: "I love you, and you and you..." they call to friends, parents and roast potatoes. After food, the children head for bed, keen for the Solstice Fairy to visit, leaving the grown-ups fireside to talk, laugh and sing.

Late after breakfast, we walk south. Dartmoor around us feels empty. Heavily industrialized a few hundred years ago, thickly wooded a long time before that, twenty-first century Dartmoor in winter seems to be mostly cloud. We daren't venture too far from the narrow track, as the mist sings sweetly of total disappearance. Darkness falls around half past three, and we camp a few yards from the path, by a stream that I'm sure is flowing uphill.

Next day, we visit Ashburton for breakfast, then continue south toward Totnes. Arriving at sunset, we're welcomed to 'New Troy' by a laughing Rasta whose crystal pipe plumes up the hilly high-street. Though we're very glad to have reached this famous town, it's already dark and cold and almost everyone's gone home. So we phone a couple met in Exeter, who respond with all the enthusiasm we could hope for: "Travellers on a winter's night – you might be Wodan in disguise!". Phil & Vicky are inventors of a boardgame called Buddha Wheel, which we play till after midnight, when I gain dice-rolled enlightenment and Ed gets a little miffed.

In the morning we hit Totnes high street. The town is gently abuzz with festive anticipation, excited families parading past the gleaming shop-windows of promise. We set up to sing. Though it's Christmas Eve, we ignore traditional carols, as we imagine Tesco will be playing them in the chemical aisle. It's a banger of a busk, people stopping in amazement to hear the songs' ancient secrets freely given. *Adieu Sweet Lovely Nancy* again summons the jolliest grins from the wandering townsfolk. Between numbers, a bright tall lady with two young daughters approaches, and after the usual questions, she asks of our plans for tomorrow? We admit to not having thought that far ahead. "Perhaps you'd like to spend the day with my family and friends? There'll be music, games and food. How does that sound?" No sideways glance is needed to know our grins are mutual. Arrangements and directions given, Rebecca and her daughters depart, leaving us merry with the joys of Christmas future.

That night, exuberant with Totnesterone, we join a gang of long-hairs and get kicked out our first pub. Fault lines, heavy though invisible, separate the local hippies from their stauncher neighbours. Tonight we're happy to have our side chosen, as plenty more inns' doors beckon. We walk from pub to house to alley, singing and meeting everyone between. Hours later, throbbing harmonies among the bustling chaos of the town's final closing pub, we're invited to stay at a caravan community a mile out of town. We follow the small crowd home, singing as we walk.

Come Christmas morning, the caravan dwellers gather in the frosty sunlight. Ed and I duck out when an early bottle begins to circle. Back in town, by River Dart the harmonies of *Claudy Banks* offer uncannily rapid neurone-cleansing joy, our headaches literally melting. It feels mildly miraculous. Transformed, we head for Christmas lunch. At Rebecca's family home we're welcomed like long-lost cousins. There's food, games and music galore, and we even find a Toblerone wrapped for us beneath the tree. After food, Rebecca shares songs that kept her family alive in World War Two ghettoes, when music was the only commodity the Nazis couldn't steal. She sings a carol called *Maria Durch Ein Dornwald Ging*, which she translates as: 'Mary walks through a leafless thorn-wood, Jesus under her heart, and the woodland blossoms'. This sounds like very advanced pilgrimage, to actually change the natural world through a journey on foot. But I suppose it's not mythical, for if many more people walked instead of driving cars, pilgrimage really could change the world.

It's a Christmas without TV or arguments. We stay for three days, gardening and cooking, and reading from the house library. Suzuki, Hesse, Nietzsche and Rumi all offer guidance for the journey ahead. On my birthday, Ed and I invade Totnes castle with new friends, climbing over the walls to drink rum in the empty fortress. We wonder why the 'occupy' movements are so busy capturing car-parks when these ancient centres are so easy to take? The night is spent envisioning great reconquests of British power-spots, with high bright pennant flags and deep bronze cauldrons feeding all. Then we slope back over the dark walls and return to our borrowed beds.

Totnes to Newton Abbot

Early next morning, Ed visits a Sufi master who has a nasty cold. Afterward, we sing at the Red Wizard café, and sip our reward of hot chocolate in the winter sunshine. As we drink, a man steps up with a diamond grin, saying he saw us sing in Exeter. He invites us to his mansion in Newton Abbot. Walking there takes all day, but it's worth it. Daracombe is a two hundred year old manor in which Micky and his gang live on some security/squatting arrangement. One day the developers will come, but that's not today. For now, with its flagstone corridors, labyrinthine cellars, overgrown gardens and huge range-heated kitchen, this is a dream home for eight good people and their friends. We help the house prepare for its New Year's Eve party, volunteering to manage the bar. We agree to remain sober, as we're holding other peoples' money. Wrapped in masks, horns and feathers, we soon sell all their cider, then dance wildly as the rippling roar of midnight rolls from the east. After, I retire to sleep under an ancient tulip tree.

We stay at Daracombe with our new friends for a while longer. One evening, the whole house ventures to a local medieval-themed pub night, everyone dressing as knights and maidens. I carelessly let myself be persuaded to put a pudding bowl on my head for an 'authentic' Richard the Lionheart haircut. But I've gone too far, and people in the pub wince at such stark stylelessness. Thankfully, I have a hat.

Before leaving Daracombe, we meet a local taekwondo champion who teaches us a basic kata of sword strokes. We spend the evening chopping, hewing and slashing, imagining dark futures where such martial dances might be needed. Then we walk north, to keep a promise.

Newton Abbot to Yelverton

Two months ago in Chichester, a lady asked us to pray for her grandson Milo at Buckfast Abbey. Though we're still not sure what prayer really means, toward the famed stone sanctuary we walk. The sky is already dark when we reach Buckfastleigh, a Benedictine monastery restored from ruins in the nineteenth century. We arrive in perfect time for Evensong. The great church is dark and warm, with no-one in the public pews except us. All the action is at the distant altar. We bow our heads and silently focus our best hopes for young Milo of the many operations. I hope he's not scared. Perhaps when he's better, he could go for a very long walk? I try to imagine as many good outcomes for Milo as I can, sailing and climbing and loving and thriving. And then I wake to a black-robed monk clearing his throat. The service is long over and they're locking up. I grin, certain that sleeping visitors are nothing new in a monastery, but the monk isn't impressed. We're ushered curtly into the dark rain, as the heavy door slams and bolts behind us.

Taking shelter in the first pub we see, a lady suggests we camp in a local ruined church, promising that it's terrifically haunted. The barkeeper chimes in, saying there's a broken tomb in which the devil will bite your hand, for the villain from *The Hound of the Baskervilles* is buried here. This sounds like the worst sleep-spot imaginable. Instead, we find hillside woods with great swaying pines, where sleep feels like coming home.

Waking late in fresh resinous breezes, we move on and soon get heartily lost, scrambling through farms and derelict cottages. We eventually find ourselves at the edge of River Dart, on the border of Dartmoor. Slowly we cross the stepping stones. But I'm so busy thinking significant thoughts that I don't pay attention to my body's thirst. So rather than greeting the river and filtering water, we step dry, brisk and blind into Dartmoor.

A few miles onto the moor, the day fades and we

settle among a copse of young birches. The sky is hard to read, it's cold and dry with occasional gusts of wind, much like us. After supper, we realise our water bottles are low, each of us having thought the other carried extra. I'm too tired to walk back to the river, and persuade myself it can wait till tomorrow. We camp a way apart. When I check Ed's spot, I see he's stretched his tarp ultra-tight using shop-bought metal pegs. I missed this upgrade cycle, and am still whittling pegs from twigs each night. I'm not sure why – I read it in a bushcraft guide and just carried on doing it. But on Dartmoor there's no decent wood, only flimsy saplings, meaning my tarp is looser than I'd like. To compensate, I camp on the wind-protected side of the wood. Two hours after sunset, the temperature plummets, giving us deep backbone shivers despite all our woollen layers. It's six in the evening, so we retire to sleeping bags.

When I wake some hours later, the wind has changed, and I'm now fully exposed to the hammering gusts. As I debate tiredly about repositioning my camp, the wind is suddenly joined by heavy rain, and I find myself in a winter storm on Dartmoor. The young leafless trees offer no protection whatsoever. Shocked by the abrupt onslaught, I huddle into my sleeping bag, laying low and hoping for the best. But my twig-pegs keep ripping from the soft ground, making my tarp flap loose and useless, and opening my bed to the storm. I push the muddy twigs back into the soggy earth, but just as quickly they pull out again. I'm busy with this back and forth, when I realise that rain has unexpectedly pooled beneath my bivy. Shifting my body in alarm, I lean wrongly and dark icy water flows into the depths of my sleeping bag. This is a disaster. Into the violent world I must now rise, shivering and stumbling, to grasp after my windblown kit. The storm crashes insanely, the wind screams and the rain claws at my eyes. I shout back into it but can barely hear my voice. I consider looking for Ed's shelter, but what help can he offer? All I can think to do is bundle my wet gear into the foot of my bivy bag, then get in, cinch up the hood, sit back against a tree and try to breathe. So that's what I do. As the storm smashes into my back, tiny lights flash and bounce around the wood like dancing folk with lanterns.

Eventually I must win a slumped doze, for I open my eyes to fresh blue skies. I stumble soggily over to find Ed. His pegs held fine, and he's reading Buddhist texts under his taut tarp. "You look like you've been in the bath for a month," he yawns. As I squeeze the water from my sodden sleeping bag, I realise that I should certainly have drunk from the boundary river. Not doing so created an internal dry spot that Dartmoor naturally re-balanced. Also, perhaps we should be checking weather-reports? Hindsight aside, my sleep kit is soaked, and my backpack is almost too heavy to carry. Also, I'm shaking with fatigue. So we retreat over River Dart to the nearest village, where I phone Mick, who laughs and invites us back to Daracombe to dry out.

Before crossing Dartmoor again, I also buy new

metal pegs from the army surplus. Checking the weather report, we walk onto a Dartmoor shiny and still. I filter water from River Dart, which tastes cold and wild, and we sing *Claudy Banks* as offering. Then we cross the moor, following stone alleyways, running light-footed over bogs, and wild napping on craggy mounds. At nightfall, we camp sensibly by a dry stone wall, sheltered from wind. The weather holds bright, and by sunset the next day we reach Sheeps Tor on Dartmoor's western edge. We're grateful to have been granted safe passage. We sing at the 'Piskies House' on the hilltop, and down at St Leonard's church, which has a Green Man above its porch doorway, making *John Barleycorn* the most appropriate offering. In the church we learn of local brothers who somehow became Rajahs of Sarawak. Then we camp by Burrator reservoir in smashing rain.

At Yelverton we visit a man called Humphrey, whose name we were given in Totnes. He invites us into his smoky caravan and talks of the Holy Grail Society, a gang of German mystics that Humphrey rates highly. Another storm passes overhead, exploding against the caravan's plastic windows. I feel like it's looking for us. The next evening, Humphrey takes us to a local pub's 'Sing, Say or Pay' session, where everyone must give a song, story or poem, or buy a round. There's no sitting out in the corner, and nobody mentions licensing. One of the folk we meet here teaches me how to flip a coin and control whether it lands heads or tails, which feels like life-changing technology. My teacher mentions that he has no birth certificate, passport or bank account. I'm mildly sceptical, but how could he prove it? In contrast, Ed and I feel very list-visible. Humphrey sarcastically announces that 'if you've done nothing wrong, you've got nothing to hide'. I'd like to find a really good rebuttal to this. Perhaps: 'If you're not a radical activist, why would you think you deserve privacy?'

Yelverton to Gunnislake

When we leave Humphrey's caravan, he loads us with Holy Grail pamphlets. Later today, Ed's brother Ginger is visiting in his campervan, and Ed wants to spend some time with him, so we decide to walk separately awhile. We divide song funds and shared kit, then diverge. As I walk down the lane alone, I'm struck by a sudden doubt that we'll ever meet again. But that's just fear talking, and after a few miles at my own pace, singing as I walk, I relax in trust that the journey will guide me perfectly.

Toward Tavistock I walk Edwardless. Perhaps this creates a vacuum, for on the town's edge a lady steps alongside me to talk without cease of her life, her son's girlfriend, her car problems and her sister's birthday. All the way into town I nod and listen in silence. When we finally arrive in the centre, I turn to say cheerio, and she stares as though shocked to see me.

Tavistock doesn't hold me long, it's too big and grand and empty. I fill my food bag, take a cup of tea, and walk toward Calstock. I've been told this village has no through road, so people only go there if they really want to be there. Down lanes and tracks, I soon meet the ancient edge of Cornwall at Gunnislake. A mighty stone bridge runs high over roaring River Tamar. There's no climbing down to drink, and anyway, Ed has the filter. But at this great border of my westward striving, I'm keen to offer an appropriate gift. I don't want to offend another boundary river. Some internal instinct immediately suggests my yew staff from Kingley Vale, but my covetous mind resists fiercely. Instead, I fling in a shell I've carried from the Dorset coast. As the shell tumbles toward the Tamar, after four and half months journey, I step into Cornwall.

CHAPTER 7

East Cornwall

Calstock

I cross the bridge into Cornwall. I don't think Ed
and I were racing, but I'm glad to get here first.
South toward Calstock, I'm singing *The Gardener*
when a lady with bright blue eyes leans over her
gate: "That's lovely, you *will* be welcomed in
Calstock." At the edge of the village, I find the
church reassuringly open-porched. With sleep
secure, I hit the local pub. It offers a bookshelf, so I
take Macbeth with my pint of Tribute. The
barman asks where I've walked from, and when I
explain, he sports me pie and chips. That evening,
I get into long conversations with a lad whose
father died last year. He thinks he's becoming
Christian and wants to talk about it. We discuss
the difference between 'sacred' and 'holy'. 'Sacred'
is from the Latin *sacre*, meaning set-apart, distant,
unobtainable, while 'holy' is from the Old English
halig, meaning complete, whole, healthy. Sacred is
the impossibly distant star, while holy is the jug of
fresh drinking water. Sacred is the sailor's longing
for home, while holy is his lover's embrace when

his ship finally returns. These two terms are often used interchangeably, but I think their difference matters. Perhaps the dynamic tension between longing and fulfilment, going away and coming home, leaving on pilgrimage and returning with a blessing, is like a spiritual gravity, an as-yet-unmapped force that helps explain the restless striving of humanity? So Sean and I talk, resolving little. When the pub closes, I'm invited to stay at Sean's family home. Since his father died, no-one has stayed over, and though I explain my church porch option, this seems an important milestone for him. I shiver outside while Sean clears it with his mum.

After morning thanks and farewells, I make my way to River Tamar. By the flowing waters, I check my pockets, and realise I face a repeat of the journey's start, having ten pounds in my wallet that certainly won't last. I now know how to make money, but this time I'm solo. Is it possible to busk money singing alone? I can knock out a rocking harmony, but Ed's the one with the sweet voice. I debate internally and get nowhere, so instead I sing through every song in the songbook, harmonising with the river roaring past my feet. An eight year old footballer calls me 'the good singer', which helps tremendously. After song, I notice a bicycle rusting under the river's surface, so pluck it out. Then a promenading gentleman called Hugh invites me for tea, on the way showing me how to pick up a duck. You let it bite your finger, then clamp its bill shut with your thumb. It's now unable to escape, so you can tuck the duck under your arm where it can't flap or poo on you. And you have a duck! Over tea, Hugh tells me how important it is not to envy people who are better than me, but to use their example as a gift of inspiration by which to improve myself. I instantly think of Ed's singing voice. Yet I can only sing my best with the voice I've got. When I depart, my host pats me on the shoulder with sorrowful eyes: "By Christ lad, so long as I live, I hope never to have a haircut like yours."

My hat pulled low, that evening I visit a community choir in the village hall. They're learning a Cornish song called *Ryb an Avon*, about a girl who loves a sailor so her parents lock her in Bedlam. In the end, the sailor either rescues her or joins her in the asylum. It's a corker, so I copy it down to sing with Ed. Or by myself. We'll see.

But oh, my cruel parents, they have been too unkind.
They drove and banished me, and tortured my mind!
But though I'm ruined for his sake, contented will I be.
I love my love because I know my love loves me.

In the pub afterward, I meet a pair of boaters who invite me to sleep on their 1930's yacht, called The Poodle. Anchored on the Tamar, we row out at dusk. I'm given a tiny guest cabin, just big enough to squeeze my backpack in. But my walking staff blocks all access, so I leave it in the rowing boat moored alongside.

Sunshine and condensation drip in my eyes as I slowly wake. On all sides, River Tamar grunts, rolls and slaps the hull of this wooden boat. I rise to deck and stretch in the sparkling light, before noticing that another boater has borrowed our rowing boat. With my arms stretched high, I watch as the rower reaches down to pick up my yew staff, and with a waterman's disregard for a paddleless pole, he flings it in the river. With a splash, River Tamar claims its chosen gift. I briefly consider diving after it, but the quick dark waters have already carried it far from sight. Farewell yew staff. Hello again Cornwall.

Calstock to Fowey

I clamber out of Calstock through the woods of Cotehele. It doesn't feel right to walk staffless, so when I find a hazel stand, I cut a new one, red and brown and fine. After wandering the woods all day, at nightfall I camp in a tiny stone chapel overlooking River Tamar, built five hundred years ago by a local landowner to celebrate his outwitting a band of soldiers who pursued him. From this rocky outcrop he flung his hat into the river, which made the soldiers believe he'd drowned. It must have been a well-loved and distinctive hat. River Tamar seems to like fine gifts.

I move on early next morning, but disaster! The songbook falls out my pocket to land in my morning cat-hole. It's unrescuably smeared. I want to bury it, but it holds the only copy of all our gathered songs. So instead I seal the spoiled book in two clear zip-lock bags, then buy a replacement at St Dominick post office. In weak sunshine I sit by the church and copy out all our tiny songs, turning pages through the double plastic bags. Hours later, I'm cold-fingered and stiff-necked, but the songs are saved.

From Pillaton toward Quethiock, I walk through fields of budding daffodils edged with nodding snowdrops. Solo walking is a simple joy, chat becomes internal and I rest when I feel like it. But solo singing still scares me. I'm convinced it won't work. Yet the trees are bare of fruit and the fungi have shrivelled to slime, so if I'm to eat, I soon must sing.

After Quethiock, rain has turned footpaths into lakes of silt, which I negotiate while being mildly harassed by farm dogs. When darkness falls, I take soup at Menheniot's pub. At closing time, I'm unsure where to go. There are no woods nearby, it's all hills and cow fields, and the church porch is locked. I feel the cold grow deeper around me, the village shimmering with midnight frost. I decide to sleep in the church lych gate, right in the centre of the village. It's surrounded by houses, but no-one's roaming in this frozen darkness, so I dive into my sleeping bag and drift to slumber. When I wake, I hear schoolchildren queuing at the bus-stop ten metres away. Quickly and invisibly I dress and pack away, to suddenly step past the baffled queue. "Where'd he come from?" an incredulous voice asks.

Some hills and valleys later, the village of Duloe arrives, and I help an elderly couple pick litter from the drowsy hedgerows. They tell me of Duloe stone circle, the smallest in Cornwall, so I take breakfast there. After food, my fears of moneylessness and solo-singing rise like fireworks, and I must walk on to quieten my mind. In Pelynt two hours later, sheltering from sudden rain in the village hall porch, a couple approach bearing umbrellas and concern. Do I intend to sleep here? I grin and assure them not. They smile back and wish me good luck. I admire their polite direct interaction with a potential problem. They could have been afraid, confused and angry. Communication is always the best way. Though a cup of tea would have been nice too. In Pelynt church porch I eat bread and apple, washed down with holy-ish tap water. Reading the church history booklet, I learn of the local Trelawny family, a name associated with pirates, madmen and politicians. But the most famous Trelawny is a song. Written in the nineteenth century, *Trelawny* is the definitive Cornish communal singalong for sporting and drinking events.

And shall Trelawny live?
And shall Trelawny die?
Here's twenty-thousand Cornishmen
Shall know the reason why!

The hero of the song is sometimes thought to be Sir Johnathan Trelawny, Bishop of Bristol who in 1688 opposed Catholicism in England. Or perhaps Sir John Trelawny, a Cornish Royalist imprisoned by the English Parliament in 1628. However, the true hero of the song is no individual, but a shared

Cornish pride and identity. It can be easy to forget that like Wales, Cornwall since the Saxon invasion remained a sovereign nation of the ancient British people, independent from the invaders' newly-formed 'England'. Though the Cornish were driven to the corner of Britain, the threat of these native giants rising in rebellion to cast out the invaders has long been a dark fear of London royals, who still remember that the Cornish were here first.

Leaving Pelynt, I stamp through sunlit woods toward Llansallos, with a stranger's scrawled address as my hoped-for destination. Waving at every passing car on the long lane into the village, each one waves back. Finding the written house, I knock but no-one's home. Llansallos church is locked and sad, having been burned out by confused youngsters a few years back. That wouldn't happen with more overnight pilgrims! On the edge of the village I spot an unused pigsty, which will do in a pinch. Then I sit by the sea and sing. Some hours later, Tim arrives home. He's wonderfully unsurprised to find someone he's never met, yet who knows his name, knocking on the door. Over supper he strongly recommends a project called 'Plants for a Future', calling it a 'true Cornish miracle'. I sleep by the glowing woodburner.

In fresh morning light I walk for Fowey. This coast is shockingly beautiful, lichen rainbows decking blue-green boulders. I'd like to linger on Pencarrow Head and Lantic Beach, but I'm driven forward by the weight of the last few coins in my pocket. I'm hungry and fearful among the intense Cornish beauty. It's a powerful tension, and I find myself smiling with it. I've just enough money to pay the ferryman to cross the river, and then I'm entirely moneyless. Now I really must sing for my supper.

While I settle in Fowey's stone harbour square, my internal doubts repeat like an enemy's dark mantra. I don't try to argue, but when the square is empty and nobody's here to listen, I simply fling down my hat and begin to sing. I launch with *Ryb an Avon*, which has haunted me since I first heard it:

> *Should I become a swallow, I'd ascend up in the air,*
> *And if I lost my labour and I should not find him there,*
> *I quickly would become a fish,*
> *And search the flowing sea.*
> *I love my love because I know my love loves me.*

As the song echoes round the stone quayside, I relax into its flow. When a ferryful of listeners arrive, I'm mid-song and unable to stop, even for embarrassment. And suddenly that's that, I'm busking solo. People smile, drop coins and offer kind words. An elderly lady beckons me to her car to offer thanks and a note. A strong-bearded man hands me a small Cornish pasty made of local tin and copper. "It takes balls doing that lad..." he nods in gruff appreciation. My best contribution to the harbour-sound is *She Moves Through the Fair*, the song of a doomed love affair with an unholy end of incomplete longing:

The people were saying, no two were e'er wed,
But one has a sorrow that never was said.
She went away from me, with her goods and her gear.
And that was the last that I saw of my dear.

A burly chap in motorbike leathers freewheels over on his Raleigh racer to listen very closely: "If I could sing just one song," Mark laments, "it would be that one." I offer to teach him it, but he replies with the classic 'I can't sing'. I explain that a few hours ago I couldn't either, but he doesn't understand me. Mark asks where I'm staying, and invites me to kip in his flat. Above an oily garage, up a ladder through a hatch, it's one room with open-plan bed, kitchen, bath and toilet. While we drink tea, I'm told about the Fowey tradition of twelve year olds swimming over the estuary. "If you live by the water, you've got to know how to swim," Mark says. "Anyroad, we send a boat so no-one gets drownded." He cooks us beans on toast, then recommends a pub. Though his drinking days are over, Mark says I can come back anytime, so off I roam.

In the pub I meet a young lady and sing for her:

And then she went homeward, with one star awake,
As the swan in the evening moves over the lake.

A neighbouring table of rugby players cheer my good efforts, but sure to the song, she leaves soon after. Then I sit at the bar with a Christian and a pagan, who debate whether God exists inside rocks. No conclusion reached, I return quietly to Mark's garage to sleep.

Next day in town, I smash my busking cash on food supplies and a fry up. Once more reaching poverty, the way is paved for dramatic rescue. I sing by the harbour again, this time far less nervously, and all the wealth I need swiftly returns.

Fowey to Middle Penpol

Rich with song, I cross back over River Fowey in search for 'Plants for a Future' (PFAF). At a red box I phone Ed, and though he's many miles away, he pledges to meet this afternoon. Under serious-looking but rainless clouds, I eventually reach Middle Penpol and 'The Field' of PFAF. One of its owners, Jasmine, tours me round this stunning project, which aims to show the many thousands of edible plants that can grow in England. It began in 1986 when Jasmine and friends bought a potato field. The week they got the land, the valley flooded and the topsoil was washed away, so they had a soilless field, whipped by wind, which had intensively grown potatoes for as long as anyone could remember. But once hedges grew, plants settled in increasing droves, and today PFAF is a living encyclopaedia of edible plants and trees, the true Eden of Kernow. Yet planning permission is their blight. The owners can't stay on the land for more than four weeks a year, even in caravans, which means they must rent houses elsewhere, and take other jobs to pay their rent, rather than wholly dedicate themselves to their great work. Appalled, I cry for instant rebellion, but Jasmine talks me down: "You're not allowed to live on your land anymore, didn't you know?" I admit I'd heard rumours, but never really believed them.

Later that afternoon Ed arrives, red-faced and limping, having walked fifteen miles since our phone call. We volunteer at PFAF for a few days, with non-permission to sleep in a shed. It's the perfect place to reconnect. We meet and taste many edible plants - pink purslane, tree mallow, daffodil garlic, Polish sorrel, and every kind of hawthorn. One of our jobs is to strip plant-pot skeletons from Eucalyptus trees now growing seventy foot high. The plastic wrappers have half-grown into the bark they once housed. I wonder if protective structures from my childhood, long since outgrown, similarly encase my adult life?

Middle Penpol to Lostwithiel

On the last day of January, we walk north from PFAF. Approaching Lerryn village over stepping stones, I turn mid-river to challenge Ed in Little John fashion. But as he readies his staff to meet me, I realise that whoever won this game would be bound to the loser's consequences. How long river-soaked boots need to dry I've no wish to learn! So I retreat onto dry land, giving the river a tap of thanks for its insight. At Lerryn post office we entrust Royal Mail with some kilos of baggage – books, stones, that sort of thing. The postmistress is startled when she learns how long we've been on foot: "You must be the slowest walkers in Britain!" It's our favourite compliment yet.

We approach Lostwithiel along the wooded edge of River Fowey. Entering town, a sign advertises a 'folk jam' tonight at the Earl of Chatham pub. As we talk about what this could mean, a heavily perfumed man passes and laughs: "The Earl of Crapham, hah! You'd be better off at the Talbot on the main road, it's got banging club classics tonight." As he swaggers off, Ed and I agree that the journey's prompts are getting easier to follow.

It's a few hours until the folk jam starts, so we explore Lostwithiel. There are many good venues for singing, but no people about. Until a young woman jogs past us, her hair bobbed in short dreadlocks. Ed and I both inhale at once. She passes without turning, but further ahead the railway crossing slowly lowers to block her way. She jogs on the spot while we catch up. Her name is Rachel, and talking with her is as good as looking at her. She's lived in Lostwithiel all her life, and when we invite her to the folk jam she laughs, saying: "I should be inviting you." Then the railway barriers rise and Rachel jogs on. Both struck by the same feather, Ed and I are still afloat when we return to the Earl of Chatham. As we step through the door, a man at the bar turns to loudly announce: "You're from Canterbury, and you walked here." "That's right," we smile. "And that," the man declares to his pals, slapping the bar to make his point, "is what I mean by fate and coincidence." He peers back to us: "By the way, I'm a nutter." Another old boy in a tattered green jumper pipes up: "And you're a pair of hillbillies!" "Takes one to know one!" Ed replies with childish aplomb, and the commenter squeals in delight. We seem to have arrived right on time.

Over pints of Betty Stoggs, the nutter tells us his intelligence came from a friend in Lerryn post office. He introduces himself as Tom, skipper of the Queen's yacht Brittania until he got manically depressed and realised he was the Angel Gabriel. So Tom entered an asylum, where time stood still and he learned about eternity. He matter-of-factly explains about the battle between good and evil: "Two recordings always run, taping all the good we think, do and say, as well as all the bad. Good always wins, of course, but evil's punishment is to forget that it always loses, so it endlessly keeps trying." He tells us how he climbed a wall to escape the asylum, but got run over by a truck. "I was let out when I started behaving," he whispers, "but don't tell them: I'm still Gabriel". Tom asks if we'll sing at his funeral, and the publican berates his dark foresight.

The hillbilly is a brass worker called Jack, who says we can see his work on top of Lostwithiel church. When the old weathervane broke, steeplejacks quoted the vicar thousands of pounds to fix it. "Said they needed cranes, insurance and all that. The vicar was flustered, couldn't afford none of that. So I undercut them by a half-mile!" he exclaims joyfully, "Weren't nothing to it, just made a new weathercock and sent the boy up a ladder to fix it on."

Tom invites us home for supper and a place to

sleep, and with two hours before the folk jam begins, we follow happily. At his house, Tom points out the washing machine and shower, saying we need both. Afterward, we take pie and mash with single malts. Then Tom hands us a house key to come back later, and Jack shouts goodbye, singing as he wriggles down the street: "Oh I'm the king of the hillbillies!"

Back at the folk jam, serious musicians tune their instruments before launching into complex jigs and reels. We sing along with *Pleasant and Delightful*, though they say we've got the tune wrong. When Rachel arrives, Ed and I both burn with instant attraction. But we're not quite conscious of being competitors, so it doesn't knock us down yet. We sing, play and talk. Rachel and I draw single-line portraits of each other without looking at the paper or lifting the pencil, simply staring into each other's eyes. My portrait makes her look like a wobbly minotaur, but her brown and green eyes blast my heart dangerously open. At quarter to one, only we three remain in the pub, and the landlord orders us out. "But don't you take advantage of Tom's hospitality!" he warns. "The old share their wealth, the young their dreams!" Ed solemnly announces, and the landlord shakes his bar-towel at us. All holding hands, we skip down the hill to River Fowey. Sat on the ancient bridge's bowed back, Ed and I sing *Farewell Nancy* and Rachel sings *The Trees Grow High*, about a girl who doesn't trust her father's choice for her marriage partner. Then we walk Rachel home, and slip quietly back to Tom's.

The smell of frying breakfast wakes me. When I emerge in newly-clean clothes, Tom places Foucault's *Madness and Civilization* in my hand. I stychomant it (open it randomly) and read aloud the first word I see: 'Unreason'. Tom nods in happy confirmation, pulling down a book by Stephen Fry dedicated to Tom with the words: 'To one of two unreasoning men'. "Unreason prevails," Tom nods knowingly, "now there's fate and co-incidence for you."

We bid Tom fond farewells and walk for Rachel, who's now at work weaving rush chairs. It's a skill she learned from her parents, each chair taking sixteen hours to complete. As we sip tea in the front parlour, it finally dawns on me that Ed and I are here as rival suitors. Rachel's mum seems to know exactly what's going on. She feeds us a half-moon clotted-cream cake and interviews us about our families. After tea, Rachel gets back to chairmaking, while we visit Lostwithiel library, Ed researching Celtic knotwork while I read Kurt Vonnegut's *Slaughterhouse Five*. When the library closes, we return to say goodbye to Rachel, both hoping to stay forever or a night. She opens her high window to call farewell, then we walk away. Parting is sweet torment, a beautiful sorrow. But I think we'll get over it.

> *Especially he looked on the fair women there,*
> *And desired them, and loved them;*
> *But lightly, as befalleth young men.*
> (William Morris)

Lostwithiel to Bodmin

On the edge of Lostwithiel I spot a house whose name we were given at the folk jam. I knock, the door opens, and Janet insists we stay, for it's Imbolc, first of February, and the fire is lit. We watch moonrise with Janet's family, and eat honeyed butter pancakes to the light of beeswax candles. After Janet records us singing on her four-track, we sleep on sheepskins by the fire.

> *Brigit, excellent woman, a flame, golden, delightful.*
> *May she, the sun-dazzling,*
> *Guide us to the eternal kingdom.*
> (Broccán Clóen)

In the morning, someone knocks to collect a futon. Ed and I carry it outside to find a donkey and cart stood on the cobbled hill. Their owner Jim is a musician of Romany Gypsy descent, and he invites us to tea. Every year, Jim travels from Cornwall to Scotland in a wagon pulled by horse and donkey. The journey there and back takes six months, during which Jim busks with Breton pipes to raise money for his family. This seems an admirably sustainable life-cycle, the best of all worlds. At Jim's house, we meet his wife and their two small girls. The children are learning fiddle and tin whistle, and blast out table-shaking reels. When Jim joins in with his pipes, the whole house thumps with joy. After, Jim tells us how he used to run Lostwithiel's music shop in a distinctively Cornish manner: "I'd leave the shop open all day without being there, it didn't need staff at all.

People browsed and bought things, and nothing ever got stolen." Later, he casually suggests we might borrow his donkey and cart to learn about travelling with animals. We're hugely keen. Dominingo the donkey could carry our bags on his small firewood cart. But we're warned that a donkey can't climb stiles, so we'd have to stick to roads and lanes. Also, Dom doesn't like woods or water, for ancestral fear of tigers and hippos. And there are certain plants he can't safely graze, like ragwort, bracken, horsetail, ivy, hemlock and yew. Jim suggests we think it over, and if we still want to try, to return to his house on Sunday before sunset for a trial run.

Excited as children before Christmas, on Saturday morning Ed and I walk for Bodmin to raise funds for our donkey adventure. Past Restormel Castle and Lanhydrock House, we follow leafless avenues of ash and birch into Bodmin high street. Arriving, we're assailed by shadowy blasting winds. We shiver and sing, but after an hour we've won barely seventeen pounds, our lowest haul to date. We suppose that not having crossed Bodmin Moor, we haven't yet unlocked our welcome here. But it's money for food, so we remain grateful. As we sit on a bench eating bread and cheese, a young girl asks if we're poor, offering to buy us chocolate. But her friend pulls her away, saying poor people aren't welcome in Bodmin. A few minutes later, a gothic teenager steps forward to ask if she can have my hat? I say no, because I really like this hat. But after my yew staff's fate, I fear for my hat's future, and pull it down low as we walk out of town.

Bodmin to Lostwithiel

From Bodmin we backtrack to Lanhydrock house, a huge Victorian mansion, in whose exotic rambling gardens we find a secluded corner to camp under rhododendrons. Morning rises bright and warm, so we stash our bags under leaf mounds to visit the manor house. This is National Trust property, and weekend visitors browse like sleepy bees in the early February sunshine. No uniformed officials are visible to say no, so we set to song. *The Farmer* is our big winner here. Perhaps today the dream of self-sufficiency feels most viable in the setting of a vast manorial estate? England's last hunter-gatherers, they say, are the Royal Family. We sing by the manor's locked entrance, re-directing confused visitors toward the proper access, thus doubling our service. As the day darkens, we pack away our hat and sign, cut rosemary from the vast bushes to make hair-washing tonic, then repair to our garden hideout. Our bags are undisturbed. "Wouldn't it be fun to find everything gone?" Ed asks, and of course I agree.

That evening, small animals scramble beyond our bubble of firelight. I try telling them we're not harmful, but they don't believe me. For supper, we cook quinoa with miso and raisins, wild thyme, chili, garlic and overripe brie. It's a culinary triumph. That night, Ed sleeps little. His new inflatable mat, bought in Tavistock, loses pressure in the night's deep cold, leaving his shoulders touching the heat-sapping ground. My old foam mat, despite having been mauled by a feral cat, remains an insulative delight. But there's no way to share it.

Morning frost sheens our bivys as we shiver and pack. Ice is better than coffee for getting going, though it's tough on the fingers. We cover all trace of our camp, then head for Lostwithiel and our appointment with a donkey. Beyond the trees, the open fields are blue with frost. We realise just how much warmth woodland offers, from wind-blocking, root heat, and mouse biomass. Last night would have been grim in the open. This is one of the benefits of tarps over tents, that tarps need trees to work best, making sleep spots harder to find, but usually better.

Reaching Restormel Castle, our blood is warm with movement. This fortress was a Norman status symbol, boasting Cornwall's largest deer-park. Alas no more. Built to overlord River Fowey, lucrative tin-mining made the castle rich, but also silted up the river, making it inaccessible and poor again. It's an encapsulating micro-tale of colonial capitalism. Today the ruined castle is closed for visitors, but we invade through a hedge-hole to discover the broken bones of an incredible home, featuring huge fireplaces and kitchens, great feasting halls and epic libraries. The porter's lodge would make a decent sleep-spot even now. We retreat as patrolling builders arrive, and return to Lostwithiel with summer on our skin, spring in the air and winter on the ground. Outside the co-op we sing for the busy shoppers. *Ryb an Avon* is our big hit here. The song asks a powerful question: is love madness? Do its sufferers belong in Bedlam, even if they sing sweet songs? And could we ever have such songs without love's unreason?

After, we rest among snowdrops by River Fowey, until a passing lady invites us to meet her husband, apparently a big man in the Sixties Norfolk folk scene. Over tea, Graham warns us how chasing cash can smash even the best musicians. It's an important warning, though we're too busy eating and listening to share any songs. It's hard to sing with a mouthful of cake.

The hour now approaches sunset, but today has been so generous, we feel that even time can flex a little. In an organic shop I try to buy a new satchel, as my current side-bag is bedraggled beyond my skill to repair. But funds are inadequate, so the shop-keeper ducks out the back to bring us perishable foods past date. Glutted with kindness, we mosey to Jim's house as the sun inches toward the horizon. In golden light, we greet the family with well-fed smiles. But Jim turns angrily: "It's late, you fools, a donkey doesn't walk in the dark. If you can't turn up on time, how can I trust you with my donkey?" Humility kicks in, we apologize profusely, and he relents a little: "If you get right on it, there might still be time..." We do as Jim says, practicing and demonstrating techniques taught. Thankfully, he's soon excited again, and under Jim's watchful guidance we take turns to harness Dom and attach the cart. There's a whole language of swingle-trees, collars and pins to learn.

Jim helps us guide the donkey and cart to a hilltop half a mile away, where we tether Dom with water and grazing. Satisfied, Jim waves goodbye until tomorrow morning. As the sun disappears, we're left on the side of the road with a donkey. Passing cars slow to stare, one stopping dead at the sight of me cooking supper on the fire, Ed sewing his socks, and Domingo crunching grass. "F-ing hell!" the driver shouts before speeding away. We're uncomfortable being so exposed, but Dom doesn't bat an eyelid, so we follow his lead. Sleeping in the open, I hope it doesn't freeze tonight. Happily, rainclouds blanket the earth and we're snug.

Lostwithiel to St Austell

Dom grazes a perfect crop-circle overnight, so I rise and knock out the pin to refresh his dining plate. After breakfast, as we harness Dom we notice his ears start wriggling. Fifteen minutes later, Jim arrives. He's glad to hear we had no problems. Our first test passed, we're invited back to Jim's for tea and toast, after which we spend the day delivering wood with Dom for further practice. All goes well, though halfway through the day, Dominingo tests his place in the pack by walking as slowly as he can. Jim advises us to pluck a twig from the hedge and wave it about. If this fails, we're to whack the twig on the wooden cart, which is guaranteed to get Dom moving. Back at his house that evening, Jim marks on our map a few reliably donkey-friendly verges in the local area. It's no good looking for camp as darkness falls, we need to know where we're going. He also lends us a small nylon tent which we eye distastefully, but it's not on our backs so why not?

Next morning, our donkey journey begins. Over the hills we walk, trot and roll with backs unbagged, and in our hand a donkey on a string. Within two hours a stranger offers us his field for the night, but we're enjoying the clip-clop of movement too much to stop. After several more pleasant hours among the Cornish lanes, filling the mostly empty cart with hedgerow firewood, we reach a clifftop carpark recommended by Jim. Dominingo seems happy with his grass verge. But as we gaze out to sea after supper, the sky brews purple danger. So we tether Dom behind an ash tree for maximum shelter, then set up Jim's tent with our bivys inside, before retiring to ride out the storm.

Amid the night's great onslaught of rain, the tent leaks only mildly. More disturbing are the sudden blasts of wind that flatten the tent-poles to whack my nose as I doze. But what really wakes me up is a sudden silence in the heart of the storm, an unnerving total absence of wind and rain. The calm is far more fearsome than the fury. I stick my head out the tent to see the outline of an unperturbed Dominingo happily crunching grass. Ducking back inside, I zip up as the wind and rain hammer down once more.

In calm morning sunshine we watch Dominingo's fur steaming dry, and string up a line for our own damp kit. Dom has left another great circle of grazed grass, so Ed shifts him for fresh fodder while I make porridge. Then we walk into Fowey to sing at the harbour. Having felt so welcomed here, I want the town to enjoy our full show. Everyone waves as we pass, from bus, car and garden. Dom replies with occasional manure. But at the harbour, he won't go near the water. Donkeys are evolved from desert creatures, and carry genetic imperatives we cannot dissuade even with our best twig-waving. So we park Dom far from the water's edge, and throw down our hat. Before we can sing a verse, curious hordes gather to pat Dom's damp fur. Jim told us he can nip pushy strangers, but our warnings won't keep them away. Thankfully Dom is calm after the ferocity of last night's storm. When we sing, *Adieu Sweet Lovely Nancy* is Dominingo's and the town's favourite.

> *There's a heavy storm arising,*
> *See how it gathers round.*
> *While we poor souls on the ocean wide*
> *Are fighting for the crown.*

I wonder whether a long journey on foot is somehow akin to a sea-voyage, in terms of the commitment and distance from home? Perhaps that's why we've met such welcome as bearers of these sea-songs of separation and longed-for return? Whatever the mechanics of it, Fowey accepts our offering, and thanks us with a heavy hat. The greengrocer tops it off with a juicy bunch of carrots, which Dom, Ed and I crunch happily as we roll out of town. Until a silver Skoda pulls up and a moustachioed man calls from his window: "Say lads, have you lost something?" We look round, as though the missing item might be floating behind us. The driver holds up Ed's shoulder bag, which carries his tools, passport and money. It was left hanging in a tree at last night's car-park camp. "How did you find us?" Ed asks amazed. "Oh, I knew you'd be round here somewhere," the man grins, waves and drives away.

We leave Fowey toward Golant, climbing the hill as hail hisses down. I drape a jumper over Dom's head to protect his eyes from the stinging ice, and he looks grateful. Twenty minutes later, the sun is shining again. Then it rains heavily, before settling into clouds. Each day in Cornwall is a many-seasoned event. We keep seeing footpath signs, promising green escape from the road, but Dom can't climb stiles, so we stay on tarmac, following Jim's map-markings toward Tywardreath. At one point Dominingo slows down, again testing his pack position, but this time twig-waving proves motivational. Walking without backpacks makes it much easier to talk, and among other things Ed and I discuss how men in India hold hands in friendship. We give it a try, but it's clammy, and when a car approaches we both let go.

At our destination we meet Laura, with a ten month old baby at her breast. She offers us her paddock to wait out the rain, so we tether Dom and pitch the tent. We're invited inside to cook supper, after which we write a testimonial for Laura's polytunnel planning permission. Then she switches on the TV, and we both reel from the power of the flickering sham-box. It's been months since we've seen a screen, so our defences are low, and before long we're sucked in completely. As the body stops moving, the mind blinkers out all duller concerns, and the presenter's over-enthused chat becomes a complete reality, as full as the wind and sky. We finally break away in horror, and retreat to write bad poetry in the tent.

All night, rain falls with ever steadier power, and by morning it rattles down full throttle. Everywhere is waterlogged, and Domingo won't tolerate the puddles. He looks soggy, so we house him in Laura's barn among the goats and horses, loading him up with oats and hay. We spend the day chopping firewood and digging the disputed polytunnel. Laura promises us her hospitality is good for the rain. On the radio, England has snow and letter-bombs. That evening, Laura tells us about the 'Battle of the Beanfield', when Margaret Thatcher sent riot squads to destroy the Stonehenge travellers' convoy: "Back from breaking the miners' strike, like all armies fresh from victory they needed further use. So our families, whose crime was living in vans not houses, were smashed and dispersed. Pregnant women, children and elderly, were all beaten by armoured men with batons. The cops were zombies, bashing everyone and everything. Our homes were wrecked, and we were left crying and bleeding on the roadside." She tells how a wave of Church outreach followed, with evangelical missionaries bringing food and blankets: "People needed hope for a future, and the

Church took its opportunity." Laura shows photos of her getting baptised a few weeks later. When I ask if she still attends, and she scrunches up her face like I'm crazy.

For two more days it rains. We try walking Dominingo to the local village, whose small square is dominated by a supermarket. We sing outside in the drizzle, until staff emerge to nervously call us "enlightening", but ask us "for corporate regulations' sake" to remove our donkey and cease our songs. We're too damp to muster sufficient agreeableness to resist. Back on Laura's land, we begin to understand that travellers with animals have good reason to wait for spring before setting out.

> *The snow has snowed, the grass has growed,*
> *And it's time that we were on the road.*
> (Vashti Bunyan)

At last we wake to dry clear skies. Waving goodbye to Laura, we return to the path. Dom looks fatter since his rest, but he's happy to move, trotting at a brisk pace. We take turns leading him while the other forages wood and early greens from the hedgerow. Aiming for another of Jim's map-marked verges, we arrive to find it's become a construction site. There's nothing else marked nearby, so we must improvise. We trot slowly up a hill, one of us keeping behind the cart in case Dominingo loses power. People call out from their gardens to offer tea and rest, but no-one has grazing, so we keep going. A mile up the road, a lady chases after us to breathlessly hand over a bag of picnic goods. She refuses all quibbles, and doesn't even want the thermos back. Best of all, she knows of a good hedged field half a mile further on. Immensely grateful, we reach the field to strike camp under a thunder-struck beech, as more rain rolls in.

Next day, Ed and I both wake in bad tempers, which soon grow into petty conflict. It's probably sourced in our unspoken rivalry over Rachel of Lostwithiel, but we lack the wisdom to unpick this. Luckily we're a gang of three, and Dominingo keeps us on track with his total unconcern at human moodiness. As we walk in sullen silence toward St Austell, a passenger in a Nissan yells: "Never eat baked beans!" For the first time today we smile. The road into St Austell is busy behind us, cars queuing to overtake. We realise we're something of a nuisance, an anachronism demanding excessive road-space. "St Hostile," I venture. "St Awful," Ed counters, as a small Honda zooms past. Dominingo treads on oblivious.

Reaching the pedestrian town centre, old songs and donkey-admiration soon fill our hat with coins. *Fiddlers' Green* is song of choice here, lapping gently down the stony lanes. But we're told by one listener that it's not as old as we thought, having been written in the Sixties. I believed it was hundreds of years old. We wonder if the songwriter was actually remembering a forgotten ancient song, rather than writing a 'new' one? Perhaps that's what all songwriters do? Mid-busk, a police officer approaches to pat Dominingo and tell us she's has no complaints about us. A pair of yellow-jacketed site-workers smoking outside a mobile-phone shop shout "Permits" meaningfully, but the policewoman just chuckles. A bunch of lads, swaggering down the high street like argos gangsters, veer fretfully away from Dom. I help a blind man walk up the street, arm in arm, and he calls me 'my love'. It's all good plain Cornish sailing. Thank-you St Austell.

St Austell to Lostwithiel

We leave town via a landscape of huge holes, the ground having been extracted as clay for St Austell's famed porcelain industry. Between two great pits, Ed and I agree to return Dom home, for despite the joys of donkey-life, rain has made things hard and we really don't like the tarmac. But first we'll need somewhere to stay tonight. The sky again promises violence. We consider a football field, but it's too open. Then we spy Luxulyan village hall, which has a large hedged garden. It's perfect. We pop in, subtly as we can with a donkey and cart. Ed cooks a stew of our heavier foods - tinned fish and parsnips – that we won't want to carry without a cart. I sew up a hole in my bag, Ed practises knots, I plot our path, Ed reads, I write. Then we sleep.

In the early morning I wander round the village looking for a tap. Two worried villagers ask how long we're staying? "We're off in an hour," I assure them, and they visibly relax. They're even more glad when I donate seven pounds of silver for the village-hall roof fund. By mid-afternoon, we arrive back at Jim's place in Lostwithiel. The whole family appear to welcome Dom. In thanks for the experience, Ed and I cook roast chicken with nettles and quinoa. As we feast, Jim tells us tomorrow is Valentine's Day, and suggests we serenade Rachel. Seeing us both scowl into our gravy, Jim's wife suggests we go outside right now to fight over her and clear the air. But we don't. Perhaps our unwillingness to honourably fist fight is a tree-protector, donned in early life, still wrapping our adult lives. Jim talks about Gypsy horse fairs: "You're the perfect age to be challenged by every young fella there. Fighting is how a Gypsy lad gets to know strangers. Everyone would want a pop at you two, so I wouldn't recommend it till you're a bit older." After supper I make hot chocolate with melted Bourneville and double cream, while Ed buys an old fiddle from Jim's collection. Then we try planning our next move, but lacking unity, we disagree on every suggested destination. In mild exasperation I open our map to full width, and suddenly spot the tiny village of Perranuthnoe where my aunt lives. Plotting a rough route, it's forty-seven miles away. Back at Pilsdon in Dorset we were told about Victorian race-walking, and the 'centurions' who could walk a hundred miles in twenty-four hours. Perranuthnoe isn't even half that far! So I suggest to Ed that we walk there tomorrow, all forty-seven miles in one go. He flares from glumness to glory. It's just the unreasonable quest we need. Hearing our plan, Jim laughs: "You fools, you'll never walk that far in one day, what are you thinking?" This is exactly the encouragement we need. We sleep in the peace of newfound resolve.

CHAPTER 8

West Cornwall

Lostwithiel to Perranuthnoe

In the earliest blue of dawn, we slip from the house and begin our unreasonable journey to inner Cornwall. As daylight fills the hollows, lesser celandine flowers blaze golden yellow at the hedgerows' feet. These earliest spring flowers were once renowned as a remedy for winter piles, after a long dark season sitting on cold earth floors. Ed says they're also a remedy for the King's Evil, though neither of us know what that is.

We walk steadily all day, stopping and speaking little, simply clunking our staffs and thudding our feet. As night falls, we steam past the Valentines couples into a pub. We could probably make a few bob crooning love songs tonight, but we have greater deeds afoot. When bar-staff ask where we're aiming to reach this evening, they're shocked to hear Perranuthnoe. "You're crazy, that's impossible!" they cry, spurring us greatly. Two pints strengthened, we fall back to the path. The moon coyly lights our way, as the dark Cornish lanes flow beneath our feet. After several hours we meet the tiny village of Frogpool, where coffee is seventy-five pence per cup, a price I find irrationally wonderful. The villagers are amazed we found them. "No-one ever does!" They send us on our way with back-patting sympathy: "You'll never make it!" By now we're grateful for all the encouragement we can get.

At three in the morning, we're stopping half-hourly to apply calendula lotion to chapped skin. After our spell of bagless donkey-travel, backpacks are an unexpectedly heavy burden. Stithians water, Burras and Nancegollan are all a dark blur, less real than the pain in my body. Around thirty-seven miles, I start seeing cobwebbed labyrinths in the corners of my vision. An hour later the hedgerows come alive with little people watching us. At dawn, the ache in my legs, hips and ankles passes from pain to injury, my thoughts become screams, and resting is impossible, muscles shutting down after even a moment's pause. I constantly imagine sleep, but the rhythm of the path drills such sense out of me. Ed's lost in his own labyrinth: "It's not the North Pole," he quietly repeats.

When the sun is fully up, we limp to the coast at Prussia Cove, and turn west for Perranuthnoe. But we stop one mile short. The wind has risen, the path feels dangerous, and I think I'm crying. We've walked forty-six miles. It's a miraculous non-victory. On sharp grass above a crashing cliff, among thousands of wind-hollowed snail-shells, we tuck into our sleeping bags and let go of consciousness. Some hours later, we rise and hobble to my Aunt's back garden. She emerges to find us sprawled on her lawn. "Oh dear," she says, heading in to make tea. De-bagging, washing, donning clean clothes, eating fresh eggs fried in butter and lounging on sofas, is all sweet reward. Sleep, when it hits, is a black rock thrown hard.

Perranuthnoe to Penzance

My aunt is a bohemian potter with cats, and we stay at her sanctuary for a good few days. Swimming on Perran Sands, with the freezing sea booming under granite boulders, surely aids recovery. We explore rock-pools, climb cliffs and sing among palm-trees and primroses, the spring sun flickering through quick grey clouds above. Eased and fully rested, we say goodbye and follow clifftop paths for Marazion, the shore village adjoining the legendary island of St Michael's Mount. Windsurfers leap and gulls shriek, as pilgrims who think they're tourists wander back and forth along the tidal causeway. St Michael's Mount was home to a prehistoric giant, and much later the sighting-place of an Archangel. We'd like to visit, but by the time we've eaten vast delicious pasties from a baker named Philps, the causeway to the island is underwater again. On public weighing scales from the pre-tourism fishing industry, we're pleased to find our backpacks have halved in weight since setting out. At a gift shop next door, we buy a pack of seed balls, wild-flower seeds embedded in clay. These seem a genius way to optimise our buried wild-poos and leave a trail of biodiversity.

A short walk west, Penzance arrives. A serious-looking geologist assures us this is a 'very holy town'. We contact friends of friends and stay in their back-street fishing cottage. After a supper of skip-foraged veg, our host talks of when he joined the 'Moonies', a Korean church that swept Europe and America in the 1970s. His experience culminated in getting married to a stranger at a football stadium mass-wedding. He explains: "Mr. Moon said money was evil, so eight of us lived in a minibus selling Taiwanese goods door-to-door, to send Mr Moon the money to make safe." I ask how he fell for it? "I was lonely, poor and depressed, in a world of meaningless struggle. They offered me community and purpose without judging my past. How could I resist?"

Late at night, our host records us singing *Harvest Song* for his morning phone alarm. It's strange to wake hearing ourselves sing, but perhaps it sets up the day's busk. Penzance skies are gently raining, so we automatically qualify for the pound of weather-sympathy. Our sign now says *Walked from Kent*. We sing all over town, starting early and ending late, meeting everyone in between. The pedestrian high street is our best show yet, in terms of solidity, connection, joy and reward. Old men discuss local folk traditions before donating, and tiny children offer their parent's gold to win our twin bow of thanks. The troubadour tradition is strong here. *Farewell Nancy* is today's greatest hit, a soft cyclone of love, departure and hoped-for return, the classic sailor's lament. The tragically hopeful harmony of this song means I can rarely sing it without crying.

> *But let my long absence be no trouble to you,*
> *For I will return in the spring as you know.*

Between songs, a grey-bearded man with a storm-watcher's eye steps up to share memories. People often tell us of hitchhiking to Swindon in 1972, but this man looks to have delved deeper, so we stop singing to listen:

"There I was lads, living in a commune in Paris with a bunch of travellers from around the world. We had half a Napoleonic fortress, with moat, portcullis and everything. The other half belonged to the French Foreign Legion, a high wall separating us. Every day we'd busk round Paris, as jugglers, mime-artists, statues, singers, dancers, the lot. And we knew where the restaurants threw out food, so every night we'd feast like Kings, Presidents or whatever. I was with a Russian girl, and life was good, really good, you know? Until one day a politician complained about 'swarms of Gypsies in a cultural monument', and the French police raided, a whole squad of Gendarmes. We pulled up the drawbridge, but knew they'd get in eventually. The Gendarmes don't like hippies, and they hate foreigners, so we were in trouble. But just as they were about to break through, the Foreign Legion heard the fuss and marched round from their side of the fort. Now in France it's well known you don't mess with the Gendarmes, but it's unspoken that you never cross the Foreign Legion. So the top Legionnaire says to the top Gendarme, finger in his face: 'This is our land, these are our guests, and you don't ever come here again. Now allez!' And allez they bloody well did!"

As Parisian dreams rise and swirl like oily rainbows in the salty rain, the storyteller laughs to the sky, throws gold in our hat, and winks theatrically: "Keep singing lads!"

Penzance to St Buryan

Departing Penzance, we walk the coast to Newlyn, where a fleet of fishing boats bob in the dock. We seek shelter from heavy rain with new friends, in whose library I read about the Arthurian legends being shamanic initiation traditions. When I excitedly tell Ed we should seek the Questing Beast, he laughs: "What do you think we've been doing all this time?" Further round the Penwith coast we reach Mousehole, pronounced with a z and no h. It's another picture-perfect small stone harbour, with fishing boats bouncing timelessly in the blue-green calm. We sing *Farewell Nancy* at the end of the harbour wall, in memory of the fishermen who never returned to shore. Then we continue around the coast, to sleep on hidden cliffs under wind-bowed hazel trees in a night warm with thunder.

In the morning, we meet my cousin Molly at

Lamorna cove. She's studying film in college and wants to make a documentary about our journey. It sounds like fun, and we agree to meet in a fortnight.

At the top of Lamorna's slender rainforest, a man on a chestnut horse introduces himself as a 'wandering knight of the road'. He has a bronze Buddha dangling round his neck, a kelly kettle strapped to his saddle, and a bundle of ribbon-tied letters of recommendation collected from influential landowners to guarantee safe-passage. He gives us very precise directions to find a man named Hayden, and calls back as he trots away: "I expected to meet you sooner!"

Seeking Hayden, we first meet the Merry Maidens stone circle, which some people say was formed when God punished nine young women and a fiddle-player for dancing on the Sabbath. I check, it's a Wednesday, so Ed jigs on his new fiddle while I sing and circle the stones. Though this legend of punitive creation is almost certainly religious propaganda, it does tell us that music and dance was one way that the stone circle was met and used in the almost-forgotten past. Nearby, we find a roadside stone chamber splattered with bright fresh blood. That's another way to meet the stones. As we snack on navelwort from a wall, we watch a man drive up, wind down his car window, take a photo of the information board, and then drive away. That's another way to meet the stones.

Northward, footpaths look perilous with mud and

cows, while the lanes seem like remnant outlines of ancient Cornish forests, lichen dangling beardlike from entangled tree and stone. Amid this beauty we approach St Buryan, and despite never having met Hayden, we recognise him instantly, his broadleaf smile giving him well away. With few words he walks us home to a table spread with food. "I'm very glad you made it this far," he nods, "thank-you for coming to my house". We explain we had absolutely no choice, and he smiles even wider. Hayden is a carpenter, and shows us around his latest barn, and the living wagon he pulls with a tractor, as he's slightly scared of horses. After lunch the weather turns vicious, all sideways whipping rain. It always looks worse from behind windows, but even so, we're astonished how quickly the sky here can change. A few minutes later, the sun shines sharp again.

That evening, on a wall in Hayden's new barn, Ed paints a mandala while I recall a long-forgotten song:

> *This merry den of play, says I,*
> *That rises up from earth to sky,*
> *Will hear us drink and laugh aright,*
> *Will welcome freedoms of the night.*

We daub our offerings bright on the wall, as both gifts will soon be covered by wooden cladding, to become blessings hidden below the barn's surface. I hope they help.

St Buryan to Chapel Carn Brea

We leave Hayden's home and circle a funeral at St Buryan's church, before striding north along the narrow strip of tarmac that covers the transatlantic cable between the UK and USA. Among primroses and dandelions, we tightrope the backbone of the internet. We eventually step off for fear of breathing bad facebook.

At a stile to a footpath, a farmer smoking in a subaru warns us that his neighbour has a vendetta against walkers, and has spread slurry on every footpath. We consider braving it regardless, but spotting a red-faced man in a tractor, spraying colourless liquids onto the bare hillside, we evade the sub-lethal clouds and follow the road to Chapel Carn Brea, the first and last hill of Britain. Through gorse and over granite, Ed and I climb the hill together. At the top we meet a tiny brown stoat, who watches us briefly before scurrying under boulders. Beyond us is the end of the earth, a Cornish Finisterre. Sunshine dances on diamond seas, the wind is Atlantic-fresh and ours are the first lungs it meets. We drink it deep and sing it onward.

Continuing toward St Just, we spot a house with a beautiful painting of a golden sun in its window, so we knock on the door to offer appreciation. Clare responds with a mighty welcome, sharing shelter, food and tales. After a night of tales, we dig her potato patch and she records us singing in her home studio. She also gives Ed a forked walking stick that's sat in her shed for years, his chestnut having finally given up the ghost. "It's a stang," she explains, "you'll have to work out what it's for." Clare's mother is ninety, the author of many Regency romance novels, but she recently turned blind, so we visit her care-home to offer song. We imagine she might like *Cold Haily Windy Night:*

> *Oh soldier, soldier, stay with me.*
> *Soldier, soldier won't you marry me?*
> *Oh no no no, that never can be,*
> *So fare-bid-ye-well forever.*

From her bed, the blind novelist sniffs in succinct judgement: "What a stupid girl."

Chapel Carn Brea to Boscawen'Un

After the hospice, we cross cloggy fields to reach Boscawen'Un, another stone circle whose roots defy memory. We arrive as rain flaks in, so hide in a tiny gorse hollow by the path. Cramped in our coconutty micro-cave, we start wondering whether rain at holy places might be the gift of cleansing welcome? So we scramble from our shelter to accept the present, but the rain immediately ceases. We turn a corner to find the stone circle steaming in the sun, like a ring of great grey candles just blown out. With rainbows riding the rough clouds above, we circle the stones in ever closer circuits to the centre, singing *Claudy Banks* as we go.

Some hours later, we find the house of a man Ed

met last summer solstice. Roger opens his door laughing: "I had a feeling I'd see visitors today." His wife is visiting her mother, so Roger cracks open the single malt cupboard. With a crystal beaker of Bruichladdich in hand, on his booming sound-system he plays *English Rebel Songs* by Chumbawumba. I thought this band only wrote songs about curry, but from this album we learn *The General*, a World War One marching song that officers tried to ban soldiers from singing. It'll make perfect fodder to combat Army recruiters in town.

> *If you're looking for the Private,*
> *I know where he is,*
> *He's hanging on the old barbed wire.*

That evening, Roger's friends visit and we play Risk. At the stroke of midnight, we all declare global truce, leaving the world divided among tribes, which is surely the only way to win. Then Roger sings *Green Island*, about the many conquests of Ireland, to remind us that despite our hopes for peace, the board remains set for war.

Next day, Ed and I dig Roger's garden and sing to a visiting mothers and toddlers group. In the afternoon, as we prepare to walk on, sudden rain smashes down. Roger laughs at our confused faces: "Stay another night. There's no point wishing it's not raining when it is!" So we settle for another night of single malt and song.

Boscawen'Un to Sancreed

Under bright blue skies, we cross the gorse moors of Carn Euny and walk for Sancreed. This village is surrounded by seven hills, like a tiny Rome, with its famous holy well a short walk from the hamlet. The water dwells in dark stone at the base of a mossy tunnel into the earth. Over the well grows a great warden hawthorn, entirely bedecked with ribbons. Traditionally these 'clouties' were cut from clothes covering an injured body-part, the magical tradition being that as the cloth disintegrates, so the wound will heal. But these modern clouties are all nylon and shall never biodegrade. Are people unwittingly knotting their wounds and wishes into indissoluble bonds? The hawthorn looks half-drowned in this spiritual detritus. It's tough being a modern human. The more we crave connection with Nature, the more clumsy our outreach becomes. I badly want to remove these plastic prayers, but we're just guests here. Below the hawthorn, mossed steps lead down to the well, its surface a black mirror skimmed with rainbow plant oils. We take tiny sips of the cool electric water, then rise again to rest under ferns in the ruined chapel alongside.

An hour later, feeling a bare minute has passed, we return to the village. Sancreed is dedicated to St Credan, who became a swineherd (a pig keeper) after accidentally killing his father. In old British lore, pigs were a gift from Annwn, the Underworld. As we knock at the well-keeper's door, congregations of rooks scream in the high beeches. Inside her cool dark rooms we sing *Claudy Banks*, and the silence that follows is the loudest and longest I've heard. After a supper of garden greens with toasted seeds and sprouted grains, we lie in the garden to watch the blood-red lunar eclipse, which feels like a great emptying. I write a letter to an ex-girlfriend, which I subsequently burn. Then we settle into the house library, Ed taking enlightenment advice while I learn of old English sports. I especially like the sound of 'Ankle Tap', where two people with sticks try to bop each other below the knee. You must keep two hands on your stick, and hit the ground three times to begin and end each bout. Perhaps this will help release our locked-up combativeness? We agree to try tomorrow.

Sancreed to St Just

Departing our hostess next morning, after fresh sips of Sancreed holy water we play ankle tap in the empty streets. I find the trick is to present Ed with false openings, encouraging him to over-commit before counter-striking. We both enjoy mildly bruised shins before tapping three times and walking on for Cape Cornwall. Along the way, the path gets so muddy that we're forced to walk on top of a hedge, where we see a cow licking clean her newborn calf.

The sky, as ever, flickers between squalls and sunshine. In the village of St Just, we sing outside the small shop to no audience whatsoever. But after half an hour, front doors along the street open and smiling folk emerge to plump our hat. At the Star Inn, the barmaid turns the coins to notes with amazement: "I've never known anyone busk St Just, it just doesn't happen here."

We continue to Cape Cornwall, the connoisseur's Lands End. While not so far west as the more famous landmark, it's also not Disneyland. There's no-one else here when we arrive at the great granite tower, remnant chimney of the local tin-mine. We're now as far west as we can go, as deep into Cornwall as the path will take us. Checking the date, we find we've been walking exactly six months. We sing *Claudy Banks*, and the song erupts into howling harmonies as we leap among the granite boulders. It's some kind of arrival. We rest at Cape Cornwall until the sky blossoms, then darkens. I pluck from my bag the crumpled postcard from the Plough Inn near Hastings, which we write with thanks for the beer and beetroot. Then we turn back from the edge of the world, to meet the lichen-stained chapel of St Helen, roofless in nearby fields. Helen, Ed assures me, is a saint's name derived from a far older British Goddess. So we sing for her as well.

Returning to St Just, we remember that Frank the artist, met in Sussex, lives somewhere nearby. Toward our best guess of his home, we pass through the Kenidjack valley, a graveyard of industry whose towers and engine-houses slowly crumble back to bedrock. The land beyond the narrow path is green with fern and gorze, peppered with purple violets and yellow trefoil. The track leads us to St Just church, whose noticeboard announces a forthcoming marriage. Ed and I are busy singing *For he's a jolly good fellow* when we notice a gang of hooded folk on the road, watching us curiously. "Hello Ed, hello Will, long time no see," says Frank, pulling back his hood, "we were just talking about you last month. I said you'd never make it. Walked all the way have you? Great timing! Let's get you to the pub." We stash our backpacks under the churchyard yew and follow Frank and family. "Back again?" the barmaid grins. Watching rugby and guzzling guinness in this tiny stone pub, jokes roar across the tables. At one point Frank is invited outside by an angry man, but it only comes to laughter. Lads in the pub try to steal my hat, but seeing the pudding bowl haircut below, they agree my need is greater. After sport, we sing *John Barleycorn* for the gathered drinkers. Everyone falls silent to listen, before all roaring loudly. It's an indescribably delightful moment. "An artist's life is pretty good," I later comment to Frank. "From where I'm sitting," Frank laughs, "yours don't look so bad either."

Next thing it's morning, and I wake in Frank's spare room with Ed snoring softly by the window. After breakfast we tour Frank's house, with its geothermal heating, organic veg garden and watercress-filtered swimming pool. But best is a new-built fogou, a stone tunnel dug into the hillside. "Teenagers bring their lovers here," Frank points to the wine bottles and candle stubs left behind, "so it's already a community asset."

Returning to the house, we're advised with seriousness that piskies will mislead us unless we wear our clothes inside out, or carry new-baked bread. Piskies are Cornish pixies, and their lore is taken seriously round here. Frank hands us a fresh loaf wrapped in a tea towel for the road. Today he's off to paint the sea for Greenpeace. Thankfully I don't ask how he keeps the paint from running. Ed and I wander away eastward, chatting happily about this beautiful image of success. Artists don't have to starve, or be ugly with greed, a paradox that's good to see made real.

St Just to St Ives

Over the moors we meet the Hooting Cairn, surely named for the song of wind here, which almost drowns us with sheer force of air. Later at Chun Quoit, we crawl through the dolmen's narrow opening to sing long notes to the stones. It definitely feels like a church. Further down the path we meet Men an Tol, the rod and hole stones, which we circle and climb nine times, the standard prescription for fertility. I can't help feeling that important elements are missing from this ritual. Perhaps a spoken or sung element, and a best time of the moon/day/year? Also costume, most probably its total lack. The 'simply walk the track' format feels artificially stark, perhaps reflecting modern life's general spiritual scarcity.

Passing the towered halls of faery kings, or maybe bankrupt mining chimneys, we reach Bodrifty.

Here once stood an Iron Age village, with one roundhouse recently rebuilt. It took volunteers a year of work and two tons of reeds to make. After so much effort, why does nobody live here? The wind answers us with bitter blasts. Either the climate has changed, or there were many more trees in the Iron Age, or the people who lived in Cornwall two thousand years ago were more climate-resilient. Probably all three. Pulling woollen sleeves over goose-pimpled arms, we walk on.

A mile down the path comes Lady Downs, where we've been told of a musician to visit. We find a likely driveway, full of half-restored camper-vans, but nobody's home, so we sit in a hedge to sing and wait. An hour later, a van trundles along the lane and we leap out waving. The driver rolls down his window suspiciously: "Who and what?" We explain, and his doubts dissolves in smiles: "Well, in you come then!" Over tea, Jack explains how energy is stored in, and flows from, the joints of the body. He offers us camping among the willows, which we accept with thanks. But seeing the gathering clouds, he upgrades us to the music room. Jack shows us round his living willow domes, home-made tipi, and new-planted woodland. Water is drawn from a well, the toilet is a wheely-bin compost loo, heat comes from a gas-bottle wood burner, and electricity is twelve volt via a hospital battery. Like Frank the artist, Jack practices advanced eco-living, but at a very different price-point. Long into the night, we sing and play stringed instruments together, until Jack's dog runs away and we all go hunting the hedgerows.

Snow falls silently during the night, and we wake to a world turned white. We make sure to turn our merino baselayers backward, as we've already eaten the fresh bread and it would be fearsomely easy to lose direction among the swirling whiteness. Huddled in all our clothes, we walk for St Ives. The sun is grey and distant, still dreaming of night. We follow a track waymarked by frosted church steeples, until at lunchtime the snow suddenly stops, the sky clears, and sunshine returns king, to melt the snow with ferocious speed.

Arriving in St Ives, we follow the back-lanes of closed gift-shops to Tate Modern, a fortress of art. The tourist season has not yet begun, and locals aren't sure what we're up to, but the songs soon work their strange magic. *Adieu Sweet Lovely Nancy* is again our greatest hit. A man in a large brimmed hat and woollen poncho replies in kind by teaching us a pastoral love song called *Searching for Lambs*, which has an incredibly haunting melody.

> *I'd rather rest on my true love's breast,*
> *Than any other where.*

After song, we consider visiting the art gallery, but St Ives in spring sun is beautiful enough. At a shoreside café we learn that the town was founded by a saint called Ia. From the coast of Ireland, Ia's brothers departed for Cornwall without her, saying she was too young and a girl. In frustration, Ia tapped a floating leaf with her pilgrim staff, which grew into a boat and carried her with great speed to Cornwall, arriving long before her brothers. The holy well she probably caused to flow with her pilgrim staff still flows in St Ives town centre. We sing *Oats and Beans* to the water, before filling our bottles with thanks.

St Ives to Perranuthnoe

At one of the few shops open in St Ives, Ed buys a piece of adventurine crystal on a brass chain. Armed with this new technology, he begins to dowse. With silent intensity, Ed asks a question and holds the stone as still as he can, trying to interpret its movements according to some internal map. To my un-surprise, the pendulum seems to say exactly what Ed wants, though every decision's rotational distinctions take an age to interpret. It seems like an inefficient outsourcing of instinct, but dowsing is certainly well-reputed, and used by the Army and various large landowners. Though no-one wholly agrees on its scientific mechanisms, it works regardless, like gravity did before Newton.

Ed now wants to navigate our day's walking according to the whim of his crystal. He hopes it'll direct us to a man called Hamish Miller, whose reputation as one of Britain's foremost dowsers has reached us through a dozen conversations. I agree to give it a go, and the stone leads us to the Knill monument, a granite tower built as the tomb of John Knill, an eighteenth century customs controller and chief smuggler. Every five years on

St James' day, ten maidens dance round this monument accompanied by a violinist playing *Old Hundredth*. This has happened for two centuries. But today is March and there are no dancing girls. We hide under gorze as fresh snowstorms blow over. When the clouds pass, Ed's pendulum sends us south. Past a vast caravan park, we reach Trencrom hillfort. At the hill's foot is a barn-sized boulder, said to have been flung by the giant of St Michael's Mount. In reply, the Trencrom giant threw a boulder that accidentally killed the other giant's wife. It's like a Cornish Cain and Abel story, but more reasonable – here the ancient murder was a playful accident, not an act of innate cruelty. Among the stones atop the hill, we filter water from a tiny spring. Overlooking Cornwall from coast to coast, the strategic benefits of holding this hilltop are obvious, even without giants. When Ed checks his pendulum for updates, we learn that Hamish Miller is now many miles east. Perhaps he's driving somewhere? Ed starts to talk about following Hamish down the road, until a heavy wall of black cloud drifts from north to south, entirely blocking our eastward view. When it starts to drop a massive curtain of snow, we both agree that Nature's pendulum is greater. Ed puts his dangling crystal away, and we clamber down Trencrom through banks of unbloomed fireweed. Spotting a house at the foot of the hill decked with Green Man statues and bamboo windchimes, we knock just in case, but no-one answers. So as sun sets, we walk south through a farm, round flooded footpaths, across fields, under barbed wire, over a railway, into a stream, down a cycle path, up a wooded track, and along a lane to Perranuthnoe, to once more reach my aunt's house and her famed vegetable lasagne.

Perranuthnoe to Falmouth

Our West Penwith circuit now feels complete. Under skies cornflower blue and cloudless, we walk east to Falmouth. The lanes we met in gritty darkness last month now glow with daffodillies. The north wind still bites, but clouds comfort with warming drizzle. We arrive in Falmouth and knock on doors to meet Pete and Paula, married musicians in a successful folk band. With his waist-long hair and flared trousers, and her complex plaits and Medieval smock, they take us to a dockside pub where students explain reiki to salt-burned fishermen. Pete warns us about their band's success: "Money nearly destroyed us. As soon as we got a little, everyone wanted more. We'd have been better off with none." Back home, Paula plays us a record called *Silly Sisters* by June Tabor and Maddy Prior. It has one of the worst covers I've seen, but the songs are two-part accapella corkers. *Grey Funnel Line* is a modern classic about longing for home while serving with the Royal Navy, and *The Burning of Auchidoun* is a fragment of a Scottish clan warfare dirge. Best of all is *Hal an Tow*, a Cornish song especially for May Day. We tuck these treasures away in the songbook, and fall asleep humming them.

Despite the declared virtues of cashlessness, next

morning Ed and I hit Falmouth high street to sing for gold. We try *Hal an Tow*, but it causes a sombre-suited solicitor to open his window and ask us to move on. We're clearly singing the song too early, as it's barely yet April.

For summer is a-coming in, and winter's gone away.

Shifted down the street, we sing *Sovay* as a grinning policeman approaches. He starts to speak, but I hold up the finger of patience as we follow the song through to its bursting finale, before we turn to greet the copper. He politely bows and clears his throat: "If you're as entertaining elsewhere as you have been here today, you're going to do very well indeed." "Fascist!" Ed whispers when he's out of earshot.

Falmouth has the second deepest natural harbour in Europe, so shore shanties echo well here. *Farewell Nancy*, with words embracing the lovers' seabound hope for return, and harmonies suggesting the dark likelihood of loss, offers a resonant tension that people here remember well. Our hat fills accordingly. After song, we run errands round town, fetching milk for a café owner, buying pasties for a shopworker, and offering directions to American tourists. We spend the afternoon in a student house, lounging on thin carpets with endless mugs of tea. When people burst in with news of an acapella folk group singing in a pub on the other side of town, I'm keen to go, as we haven't yet met any others. But when we get there, the singers turn out to be us.

Next day, we wait on Falmouth's dock for a boat to carry us to Pete and Paula's barge. We were told to be here at eleven sharp, but it's now past midday. We're puzzled by the delay, when up the granite pier walks a woman I recognise. "William?" she says, "It's Jenny, from Bristol. Remember?" Of course I do, we read English Literature together at university. She's now studying Art in Falmouth, and shivering from a recent surf, she scrawls her number in the song book. "Will – you might not believe it, but I've been looking for you for the last two years, ever since you disappeared from uni without trace. All over Europe I've been picking up hitch-hikers, telling my friends they might be Will. You've been the legend of every hitchhiking stranger. One of my friends is in the car right now, annoyed at me for stopping again. But this time it really is you! What are you doing here?" she asks. As I begin to explain, the long-awaited motorboat finally putts over, flinging up a line. "Sorry we're late," the boatfolk shout, "a rope got caught in our propeller, and it took ages to untangle." I'm struck. Surely a rope in a river is the perfect symbol of chaos. Like DNA in blood, or a song in time, it could have appeared anywhere, anytime. But here and now it met the propellor of this small boat, creating the delay that let me re-meet Jenny. It's far too strong a coincidence not to be taken as a deliberate gift from River Fal.

As Jenny returns home to warm up, we climb down the harbour's iron ladder to the waiting boat below. Ed says I'm grinning like an idiot, and he's right. When we disembark at our destination barge, I quietly return the fateful rope to River Fal with thanks. Then we spend the evening playing music on this fabulously rickety craft. "Not long left in the old girl," the owners admit, "the wood's nearly rotten through in places." After music, we sleep in the hold, hoping we won't wake up on the riverbed.

When we rise, I immediately want to find Jenny. "She mentioned roast dinner..." I try, but Ed's right, we've got appointments to keep. Today we're filming with cousin Molly. We spend all day on camera, sound-biting and singing as Molly sets up scene after scene. Boots are filmed stamping through mud, Ed jigs with his violin in a woodland faux-camp, and we play ankle-tap on the beach. It's a strangely unreal true image of our journey so far. Molly says she's spent the last two weeks interviewing people we met along the way. "Were they nice?" I ask uncertainly. "Oh yes, don't worry, you're a hit," she reassures. Finally Molly departs, promising to shout when the edit's ready.

Falmouth to Perranporth

I call Jenny next morning, but she's busy with classes, so Ed and I walk for the north coast. Skirting Redruth, we aim for Perranporth, where St Piran, Cornwall's patron, landed after being thrown in the Irish Sea with a millstone round his neck. Legend says the sea calmed, the millstone floated, and Piran drifted safely to Perranporth, where his miraculous journey ended. Our friend

George now lives at the edge of this village, in a hut overflowing with surf-boards and fishing gear. As George limps through the door, Ed asks worriedly how he's doing? "Not too brightly," he grimaces:

"You know I'm an acupuncturist. So I was looking to rent a clinic in town, and I'd just finished checking out this studio, when I heard a loud repeated banging. I opened the front door, and right next door, the jeweller's shop was being robbed." He stretches in pain. "I'd normally say good luck to jewel thieves, but the noise they were making was just so offensive. They were hitting a plexi-glass window with a sledge-hammer, but plexi-glass is designed to foil hammers, so it only kept wobbling. Two robbers were by the shop window, and another sat in the getaway car, all wearing balaclavas." George is a thick shouldered fellow, the sort to lead a rugby scrum or shield-wall, and we anticipate heroics ahead. "If I could go back in time, I'd have walked the other way. But that's not how life works. So I threw myself in and took down the lookout. As we wrestled on the ground, I felt someone kicking my back. Then the shop-owner came out with a chair, to take on the hammer guy like a lion-tamer. Finally, the police arrived and the robbers sped off." I guess the punch-line: "Those kicks on your back, were they the sledgehammer?" He shifts uncomfortably. "Yeah. People said it was awful watching the hammer crashing down. They thought I'd be dead! Half an hour later, when the adrenaline faded, I suddenly couldn't walk. Doctors at the hospital said the hammer missed my spine by half an inch. They called it a miracle! But there's massive trauma, and I've been on morphine for a month." He laughs bitterly: "After all their efforts, the robbers made a hole in the window the size of an apple, but six feet high, so even with time to stretch their arms through they could never have reached the Rolexes." His eyes grow reflective: "They should have used an axe, you get much more pressure with a sharper tool." The robbers, three lads from Essex, were caught a mile down the road. Local papers feted George's heroics as 'Cornish bravery', even though he's from London.

Talk moves onto us and walking. We sing a couple of songs, and I pull off my hat. George's girlfriend Silka is appalled. "What happened? Do you want a haircut?" I'm amazed. I hadn't considered this option. Sat outside in breezy sunshine, my pudding-bowl finally drifts away.

We later sing in Perranporth, and win as many flung donations from passing cars as from people on foot. After, Jenny drives over, and we swim and play on the windy beach. Flirting is mildly outrageous. She tells me she's returning home to Kent tomorrow for two weeks, and invites me to come along. It's an irresistible invitation. Ed agrees I should follow my heart. So on the first of April, seven months after setting out, I return to Kent with river-met Jenny. It feels like a wholly miraculous end to my journey.

EPILOGUE

Home

Kent to Glastonbury

Eastward along busy roads, England becomes a glassy blur, as seven months journey are unmade in seven hours drive. I sing myself sane as we zoom past everything.

Back in Kent, I spend a beautiful week with Jenny, before seeing my friends and family. Busking solo in my hometown Canterbury tests my newfound courage, but I pull it off. Though at a cost, for I lend my hat to a fellow busker called Taigh, who promptly loses it. Alas the Bodmin goth.

Ed meanwhile walks the north coast of Cornwall and Devon, playing fiddle in caves and chapels, sleeping on river islands, and meeting Satish Kumar, the 'no destination' pilgrim who walked from India to England carrying 'peace tea' for nuclear leaders.

Two weeks later, Jenny returns west and drops me

at Croyde in Devon, where Ed is staying with the man who makes the Honey Monster adverts. We start walking east together, but the path has stronger plans. After busking in Barnstaple, Ed suffers his most terrible toothache yet. Beer and clove oil don't cut it, so Ed phones an emergency dentist. The only available appointment is in Bridgwater tomorrow, an unwalkably distant quest. Ed suggests we hitchhike. Having just driven to Kent, I can't argue. Ed's teeth are now the crystals dowsing our path. So in a few brisk hours we hop half the West Country, in the Volvo of a teacher and the Vauxhall of a fireman. Ed gets his tooth fixed, and we find ourselves two days walk from Glastonbury.

It's now mid-spring, the rain is warm and the wild garlic funky. In sandals and waterproof socks, like Germans of a certain age, we walk the levels into Glastonbury. Here we celebrate Mayday, gathering fallen blossom from the holy thorn on Wearyall hill, dancing the Maypole, wrestling local champions, and singing *Hal an Tow* for the town procession at exactly the right time. We score gigs supporting Martha Tilston and Robin Williamson (of the Incredible String Band). We even support Sir David Frost at the opening of a new pub. "This is the high point of my career," Frost assures us with pink socks and arch-sarcasm. When Jenny visits, I compete in a welly-boot throwing contest, and using the Hampshire farmers' secret technique, I win a bottle of champagne.

The final song of our journey comes at the foot of

Glastonbury high street, where we lean back in throbbing sunshine to sing *Grey Funnel Line*. As harmonies rise like new-released birds, the windows above open wide and gold coins fall sparkling down.

> *O Lord if dreams were only real,*
> *I'd have my hands on that wooden wheel.*
> *And with all my heart, I would turn her round,*
> *And tell the boys that we're homeward bound.*

The wellington boot soars, the champagne pops, the song is given and well-heard. All is joy and glorious culmination.

Glastonbury to Kent

The welly falls to earth, and somewhere in a field in Somerset we spend the next two months decorating a festival, helping it to take beautiful shape, flash with people, then dissolve again. Afterward, we get a lift home to Kent, to celebrate Midsummer and to prepare for our next walk. May the journey never end!

Jenny and I spend six sweet months together, but she's off to Oxford for teacher training, and our lives float apart again. Cousin Molly's film wins an RTS award and gets played on BBC1, after which a Guardian journalist and World Service radio want to talk. Feeling we owe Britain a debt for the songs and blessings, we build a website to share songs, stories and information, and record an album with Ed's brother Ginger, which with devastating originality we name 'Songs'. The Archbishop of Canterbury buys a copy, and it gets airtime on Radio 2.

Things keep getting madder. We get into Rob Macfarlane's book *The Old Ways*, we win a front page article in the Telegraph travel guide, and a twenty-five minute *Ramblings* interview on Radio 4 with Clare Balding. We become a chapter in an EFL textbook, and we even get a photo-shoot with Vogue magazine. At least two make-up artists cry as we sing *The Burning of Auchidoun*. We score a gig at the South Bank Centre in London, where we persuade the sound-engineers to switch off the microphones so we can fill the space with pure echoing harmony. Afterward, we sing with Romanian gentlemen by the South Bank Centre's hot air vents, where we hope the songs might rise.

London

One morning in Kent, we're practicing *The Parting Glass* when a large packet crashes onto the doormat. Inside is a contract offer from Decca Records, offering us tens of thousands of pounds to record six albums. There's even a popular TV personality lined up to be producer. We're in mild shock. Is this precisely what we want, or exactly what we most fear? So we walk to London to meet the label, and after three days singing in motorway tunnels, we finally tramp tarmac to the London offices of Universal Records, Decca's owner. "We should have demanded a limo," I half-joke over the traffic. "They might have sent one," Ed shouts back, "then what?" He's right. We must be careful what we ask for.

Reaching a shiny unmarked gate, the guard confirms our appointment before buzzing us through. All hopefuls must pass his portal. I'm sure his half-grin would tell us everything, if only we could read it. Beyond the gate is a red-brick Victorian warehouse. The windows are sunglasses, so we can't tell what the building is thinking. Inventing professional struts, we try not to look like tourists. Passing more chrome barriers, we sign our real names and a polite young man seats us. Browsing the glossy magazines we see little we like, just more made-up popstars saying cool things about their success. "It could be us" I jest, and a scowl flickers over Ed's face. We try to sing *The Begging Song*, for courage and joy, but here in the pumping heart of the music business, where international distribution networks converge and the culture of continents is sold, it doesn't feel quite right to sing.

After twenty minutes wait, softened up, we're summoned. Thudding through the open-plan rows of trendy computer-tappers, I glance back to see our boots have left an emergency trail of mud. At the indicated door, I knock. It swings open, and a grinning executive peers out: "Ed, Will, so glad you could make it, we're really excited about this contract. Come and take a seat. It's only fame and fortune you know!"

The avuncular exec explains that Decca want to buy the rights to everything we've already done, calling this a "three-sixty deal". He hopes our first album will sound like the Pogues, but the producer mentions Robson and Jerome. This producer is a BBC TV celebrity, and hot property with what the exec calls 'the passive massive', the people who buy CDs in Asda. The producer eagerly discusses songs like *Blow the Wind Southerly, Waly Waly* and *Greensleeves,* which to us are the sugary dregs of Victorian choral folksong. These forced melodies of schools, factories and workhouses, heavily regimented and over-flogged, lack the raw fire of their wilder cousins. But the producer insists it's vital his mother-in-law enjoys our album. We've no idea who his mother in law is, or what she's got to do with our dreams, songs or journeys. But we recognise the red flag of total control loss. Though we want to share the good old songs more widely, to let them flourish and flow through the land and people, this record deal will be a forced amplification we cannot hope to shape or direct. We'll become contracted servants for a vast corporate enterprise to present however they deem profitable. They'll probably end up dressing us. This gang is bigger, sharper, and more experienced than we can imagine, and they can only be trusted to pursue their own interests. So how can we possibly claim the right to sell them these songs, or this dream of wandering freedom?

The answer is clear. We say thank you and farewell, and walk home singing.

And all I've done for want of wit,
To memory now I can't recall.
So fill to me the parting glass,
Good night, and joy be with you all.

Acknowledgments

Great thanks are owed to everyone who supported this journey.

Gratitude begins at home, with my mother's constant support, despite the unlikelihood of our quest. Also thanks to my father, who didn't live to see my embracing his two favourite pastimes. Thanks to my sister Laura, for her patience and love. Also thanks to Ed's family, Reine and Martin, who housed me before and after the walk, and treated me as another son. Ginger too, for the long loan of his wayward brother, and for all his contributions to this and other journeys.

Further thanks to Derek, Caroline, Pete and Kate, Molly and Sam, Thomas, Arnie and Lisa, Liz, Chris P, Thaphne, Marion and Jamie, Danika, Justin, Genevieve, Ayla and Susi, Rose, Olivia, Ellie, Carrie, Rawley, Rupert G, Kate, Gail, Charly and Lee, Risha, Steph, Alaric, Rob McF, Merlin and Cosmo, and Sam.

For their welcome during this journey, my thanks to: The Berrys, Matt F, Flo, Des, Emma and Jacob, Hugh, The Flying Marrows, Gillian, Jim, Jesse and Hannah, Tom, Malcolm and Pat, Bryan, the Copper family, Joe, Polly, Tim, Mika, Lynton, Chrissy and Leni, Loupos and Julia, Carly and Denesa, Ryan, Rhianne, Andy, Ruth, John, Little Ben, Norah and Tony, Sarah, John, Gary, Cate and Liam, Claire and Davy, Jim and Charly, Trig,

Andrew and Jenny, Susannah and Angus, Cynthia, Pal and Bryan, Phil and Jane, Alan, Bob, Cranleigh Paddock, Sir John, Mal and Denise, Jack and Harry, Colin and Charlie, Tom B, Bryan and Pauline, Petr, Richard and Natalie, Jeff, Mark and Jenny, Charlie and Cath, Janet, Robin, Nobby, Kevin, Nuni, George, Kim and Anne, Gary, Ozzy, John, Jerry, Carl and Deborah, Nick, Margaret and Roy, Rob and Zee, Liam, Space and Amy, Bella and Dave, Dan, Richard, Bryony, Steve and Emily, Ruth, Bobbie and Charlie, Fergus, Lot, Conrad, Maeve, Rashad, Lewis and Dominique, Liam and Hayley, Lynn and James, Gordon, Laura, Cee, Danny, Billa and Simon, Jenny, Sam and Val, Dominick, Jasper and Pip, Ellie and Steve, Polk, Addy, Phil, Ruth, Rod and Sally, Lawrence, Kim and Martin, Michael and Kim, Iain and Mary, Helen, Malcolm, Chris and Lynn, Hugh, Jane and Hugo, Frank and Caroline, Clare, Graham, Lydia and Chris, Jarvis and Tiffany, Richard and Marje, Lucinda, Taigh and Lex, Zid, Anthony, Nathan, Dan and Sophie.

For help with the writing the book, I owe gratitude to Suresh, Penny, Felicity, Toby, Daniel and Saskia.

And of course, thanks to everyone who dropped a coin in the hat and/or taught us a song.

I hope to see you on the path. Walk well.